The Institutions of the Enlarged European Union

STUDIES IN EU REFORM AND ENLARGEMENT

Series Editors: Thomas Christiansen, *Senior Lecturer, European Institute of Public Administration, Maastricht, The Netherlands*, Anne Faber, *formerly of University of Cologne, Germany*, Gunilla Herolf, *Stockholm International Peace Research Institute, Sweden* and Wolfgang Wessels, *Jean Monnet Professor, Universitaet zu Koeln, Germany*

This exciting new series provides original contributions to one of the key debates about the European Union: the relationship between the twin processes of 'widening' (EU enlargement) and 'deepening' (EU reform). Arising largely from a European-wide research network (EU-CONSENT), the books published in this series will deal with the important issues emerging from these twin challenges facing the European Union at a crucial period in its history. Individual books will focus either on the broader questions of European governance that are raised by the widening/deepening debate, or will look in more detail at specific institutional or sectoral areas. Containing cutting-edge research with a multi-disciplinary approach, the books in this series will be of great interest to scholars of European Studies, politics, economics, law and contemporary history.

The Institutions of the Enlarged European Union

Continuity and Change

Edited by

Edward Best

Professor, European Institute of Public Administration, Maastricht, The Netherlands

Thomas Christiansen

Professor, Maastricht University and Associate Professor, European Institute of Public Administration, Maastricht, The Netherlands

Pierpaolo Settembri

Official, General Secretariat of the Council of the European Union

STUDIES IN EU REFORM AND ENLARGEMENT

Edward Elgar

Cheltenham, UK • Northampton, MA, USA

Published by
Edward Elgar Publishing Limited
The Lypiatts
15 Lansdown Road
Cheltenham
Glos GL50 2JA
UK

Edward Elgar Publishing, Inc.
William Pratt House
9 Dewey Court
Northampton
Massachusetts 01060
USA

Paperback edition 2010

A catalogue record for this book
is available from the British Library

Library of Congress Control Number: 2008932903

ISBN 978 1 84720 345 8 (cased)
ISBN 978 1 84980 033 4 (paperback)

Printed and bound in Great Britain by
Marston Book Services Limited, Didcot

Contents

Contributors

Manuela Alfé was a Researcher at the European Institute of Public Administration, Maastricht, The Netherlands and is now an Official at the European Commission.

Edward Best is Professor at the European Institute of Public Administration, Maastricht, The Netherlands.

Milena Bigatto is a Ph.D. Candidate at the University of Siena, Italy.

Andrea Birdsall is a Teaching Fellow at the School of Social and Political Studies, University of Edinburgh, UK.

Thomas Christiansen is Professor at Maastricht University and Associate Professor at the European Institute of Public Administration, Maastricht, The Netherlands.

Brendan Donnelly is Director of the Federal Trust, London, UK.

Kenneth Dyson is Professor of European Studies, Cardiff University, UK.

Caroline Naômé is a Legal Secretary at the European Court of Justice, Luxembourg.

Nieves Pérez-Solórzano Borragán is a Senior Lecturer at the Department of Politics, University of Bristol, UK.

John Peterson is Professor of Politics at the School of Social and Political Studies, University of Edinburgh, UK.

Simona Piattoni is Associate Professor at the Department of Political Science at the University of Trento, Italy.

Sonia Piedrafita was a Researcher at the European Institute of Public Administration, Maastricht, The Netherlands.

Pierpaolo Settembri is an Official at the General Secretariat of the Council of the European Union.

Stijn Smismans is Professor at the School of Law, Cardiff University, UK.

Wolfgang Wessels is Professor of Political Science at the University of Cologne, Germany.

Abbreviations

AER	Assembly of European Regions
AFET	Foreign Affairs Committee (EP)
ALDE	Alliance of Liberals and Democrats for Europe (EP group)
ANEC	European Association for the Coordination of Consumer Representation in Standardisation
AT	Austria
BE	Belgium
BEPGs	Broad Economic Policy Guidelines
BG	Bulgaria
CAP	Common Agricultural Policy
CCIC	Consultative Commission on Industrial Change
CEBS	Committee of European Banking Supervisors
CECED	European Committee of Domestic Equipment Manufacturers
CEE	Central and Eastern European
CEMR	Council of European Municipalities and Regions
CFI	Court of First Instance
CFSP	Common Foreign and Security Policy
CoR	Committee of the Regions
Coreper	Committee of Permanent Representatives
CY	Cyprus
CZ	Czech Republic
DE	Germany
DG	Directorate-General
DK	Denmark
EC	European Communities
ECB	European Central Bank
ECJ	European Court of Justice
ECO	economic and monetary union and economic and social cohesion
ECOFIN	Council of Economic and Finance Ministers
ECSC	European Coal and Steel Community
EE	Estonia
EEC	European Economic Community

EESC	European Economic and Social Committee
EL	Ellas (Greece)
EMCO	Employment Committee
EMU	Economic and Monetary Union
ENVI	Environment Committee (EP)
EP	European Parliament
EPC	European Political Cooperation
EPP	European People's Party and European Democrats (EP group)
ERM	Exchange Rate Mechanism
ES	Spain
ESCB	European System of Central Banks
ETUC	European Trade Union Confederation
EU	European Union
FI	Finland
FR	France
GAERC	General Affairs and External Relations Council
GUE/NLG	Confederal Group of the European United Left – Nordic Green Left (EP group)
HU	Hungary
IE	Ireland
IEA	International Energy Agency
IGC	Intergovernmental Conference
INT	the single market, production and consumption
IT	Italy
ITS	Identity, Traditions, Sovereignty (EP group)
JAP	joint assessment papers
JCCs	Joint Consultative Committees
JHA	Justice and Home Affairs
JIM	joint inclusion memorandum
LT	Lithuania
LU	Luxemburg
LV	Latvia
MEP	Member of the European Parliament
MS	member state(s)
MT	Malta
NAT	agriculture, rural development and the environment
NATO	North Atlantic Treaty Organization
NCB	national central bank
NGO	non-governmental organization
NL	Netherlands
NMS	new member states

OECD	Organisation for Economic Co-operation and Development
OMC	open method of coordination
OSCE	Organization for Security and Co-operation in Europe
PERF	Pan-European Regulatory Forum
PL	Poland
PSE (PES)	Party of European Socialists (EP group)
PT	Portugal
QMV	qualified majority voting
REX	external relations
RO	Romania
ROPs	Regional Operational Programmes
SCA	Special Committee on Agriculture
SDO	sustainable development observatory
SE	Sweden
SI	Slovenia
SK	Slovakia
SMEs	Small and medium-sized enterprises
SMO	single market observatory
SOC	employment, social affairs and citizenship
SRP	standard rules of procedure
TEC	Treaty establishing the European Community
TEN	transport, energy, infrastructure and the information society
TENs	Trans-European Networks
TEU	Treaty on European Union
UEN	Union for Europe of the Nations (EP group)
UK	United Kingdom
UN	United Nations
UNICE	Confederation of European Business
V/EFA	Group of the Greens and European Free Alliance (EP group)

Preface

This volume brings together the results of research conducted by a number of scholars in the context of EU-CONSENT – a 'Network of Excellence' funded under the European Union's 6th Framework Programme for Research and Development. EU-CONSENT brings together researchers from some 50 institutions from across Europe to share their research output on the question of 'Wider Europe, Deeper Integration?' The activities of the network, which is led by Wolfgang Wessels at the University of Cologne, are organized around a number of different 'work packages' focusing on theoretical questions, sectoral studies and institutional dimensions of the relationship between EU reform and enlargement. This present volume publishes the research output of those who have been working together in 'Work Package IV', which addresses the evolution of the EU's institutional system in the context of enlargement. This work package, which is coordinated at the European Institute of Public Administration (EIPA) in Maastricht, is made up of four teams which are, respectively, looking at the role of national governments in Council and comitology (led by Edward Best and Thomas Christiansen), the European Commission (John Peterson), the European Parliament (Brendan Donnelly) and the bodies representing sub-state authorities and organized civil society at European level (Simona Piattoni). Each team has examined the way in which the enlargement process and the arrival of the representatives from the new member states has, or has not, changed the institutional mechanisms in those spheres. This book is the first joint effort by those active in this work package, and the editors are grateful to the contributions and the active support from the team leaders and their co-authors in making this publication possible. In addition to the contributions from scholars in the different teams in Work Package IV, we also commissioned additional chapters on two key bodies that would otherwise not have been covered – the European Court of Justice, and the European Central Bank – and we are glad to have found leading experts in their field to contribute the chapters on these institutions.

The budget of EU-CONSENT, as a 'Network of Excellence', does not pay for additional research time, but only funds meetings bringing together scholars who are already working on these issues in order to allow them to share their results and collaborate in the presentation and publication of completed research. Given these limitations, we have been impressed by the dedication of the contributors to this book to produce original work and to respond to the common framework and set of questions that we developed in order to provide a systematic account of the interaction between institutional dynamics and the process of enlargement. Drafts of the chapters published here were presented at a number of different workshops and conference panels, and we are grateful for all the useful feedback and comments received from participants on these occasions. Our special thanks go to several colleagues at EIPA: Sonia Piedrafita and Araceli Barragán for their help in managing the work package and organizing the workshops; Sarada Das and Johanna Oettel for the research assistance they kindly provided for several of the chapters; and Moritz Reinsch for his help in putting together the final manuscript. At Edward Elgar, Alex O'Connell has been an incredibly friendly, efficient and supportive editor, and Suzanne Mursell has been equally helpful during the production process.

Just like EU enlargement itself, this book has been a long time in preparation, and we are grateful that our contributors responded so constructively to our suggestions for revisions, while remaining patient during periods of silence from the editors. We are glad that this volume is now being published – as the first text in the newly launched EU-CONSENT book series – at a time when both institutional reform and EU enlargement remain important issues for debate, and we hope that our readers will find this useful in furthering our understanding of these processes.

The Editors
Maastricht and Brussels, December 2007

1. Introduction

Edward Best, Pierpaolo Settembri and Thomas Christiansen

The 'big bang' enlargement of the European Union (EU) in 2004, with two further member states joining in 2007, had been long anticipated and there had been many concerns about the possible impact that this would have on the EU. At least three intergovernmental conferences had been convened to prepare the Union for it, resulting in the Amsterdam Treaty, the Nice Treaty and the abortive Constitutional Treaty. And yet, when the new members joined on 1 May 2004, there was still a sense that the institutional structure of the EU was ill equipped to deal with the much larger numbers of players and the more diverse range of interests.

As the months and years after May 2004 passed, the big debate about the possible impact of enlargement was overshadowed by the larger 'constitutional crisis' of the Union after the non-ratification of the Constitutional Treaty, and the debates about renegotiation of the treaty and a refocusing of the Union on achieving 'results'. However, enlargement was not just a moment in time, but a process that brought in a permanently increased membership of the Union, and thus the question of what impact this may have (had) on the EU remains. It is against this background that, in the context of a collaborative research network, the contributors to this volume set themselves the task to investigate empirically and systematically the precise nature of any changes related to the enlargement process that can be observed in the key institutions and institutional mechanisms of the EU.

When we initially discussed the idea for this book in 2006, the first publications on the institutional impact of the 2004 enlargement of the EU were beginning to circulate (Dehousse et al. 2006; Hagemann and De Clerck-Sachsse 2007; Hix and Noury 2006; Kurpas and Schönlau 2006; Sedelmeier and Young 2006). Regardless of their methodology and focus, there were two common denominators: they all came to the overall conclusion that, *prima facie*, decision-making with 25 member states could be safely described as 'business as usual'; and they all warned, prudently, that it was too soon to tell about wider and longer-term implications.

We were both relieved and intrigued by these preliminary findings. While we could only agree that the predicted deadlock seemed to have been avoided, we wondered about appropriate indicators and the adequate time reference for measuring continuity and change in a complex institutional system such as the EU. Moreover, as most of these works were preoccupied with the consequences of enlargement within a single institution, we started considering whether and to what extent institutional change can be charted in isolation.

At the same time, we realized that the direction of this debate could have significant implications for the future development of the EU. Did the EU really need a new constitutional settlement or would its institutions be able to cope within existing rules? Would the EU be prepared to welcome new member states or had its 'integration capacity' already reached its limits? None of these questions could be seriously answered without assessing what has happened to the EU since May 2004. Official answers on this point have been quite elusive. The European Commission, for example, found a delicate balance in submitting that in the two years after enlargement the '[i]nstitutions have continued to function and to take decisions' but stressing that it would watch to check that the EU's 'institutions and decision-making processes remain effective and accountable' in the future (CEC 2006). The European Parliament even established an explicit link between the notion of 'integration capacity' and the constitutional debate, arguing that, with the accession of Romania and Bulgaria in 2007, the Treaty of Nice had reached its limits and that the proper functioning of the EU in the future would be conditional on a number of further institutional reforms (EP 2006).

The present work thus has a dual mission: first, to expand earlier academic contributions with regard to a time frame which allows more solid conclusions and an approach that charts change beyond and across individual EU institutions; second, to complement rushed ex post assessment performed by the EU institutions themselves, in a way that its findings can be meaningfully used in a debate on the future membership and institutional settlement of the EU. In doing so, it is also intended to contribute to thinking about the significance of enlargement and institutional change for the broader issue of EU governance.

There has previously been very little literature on the impact of enlargement on EU institutions, although a great deal has of course been written about enlargement. Nugent (2004) has, exceptionally, addressed enlargement in general terms and from multiple perspectives. Others have tended to focus on one of four aspects: the process itself of enlargement, whether in overview (Preston 1997; Sjursen 2002; Kaiser and Elvert 2004; Verdun 2005) or on particular rounds (see, for example, Franck 1987; Nicholson and East 1987; Luif 1995; Falkner 2000; Cremona 2003; Ekiert and Zielonka 2003; Higashino 2004; Inglis 2004; Schimmelfennig 2005); the position of the enlarged EU in the international scene (Cemrek 2004; Brummer and Fröhlich 2005; Helly and Petiteville 2005); the impact of EU membership on acceding countries (see, for example, Lewis 2003; Grabbe 2003; Guillén and Palier 2004; Hughes 2004; Neuwahl 2004; Sadurski 2004; Wörz 2005); or the *anticipated* consequences of enlargement on the EU system of governance – whether at a general level (notably Grabbe 2004), or focusing more on institutions, policies[1] or politics (Mair *et al.* 2003; Brou and Ruta 2004) – often including suggested reforms. The discussion about possible future impacts of enlargement on the institutions, moreover, concentrated very heavily on the voting system in the Council of Ministers.[2]

Much less has been done in the past to look back and to assess the actual institutional impact of previous enlargements. In the case of countries that joined the EU after an authoritarian or totalitarian experience (both in the Mediterranean and in the Eastern enlargements), attention has rather been given to the reverse process, namely the impact of EU membership on their domestic systems. For the other enlargements, some institutional consequences for the EU have been detected. Westlake (1994), for example, connects the institution of the question time in the European Parliament to the influence of the British tradition. Others note that the Nordic enlargement has brought into the EU the concern for transparency and parliamentary control as well as the Ombudsman and an update of fundamental rights (Raunio and Tiilikainen 2003). Apart from the very recent studies mentioned at the beginning, therefore, there is little work done on ex post analyses to control empirically the solidity of predictions made. Enlargement is attributed many possible consequences before it takes place, but its actual institutional effects have been somewhat neglected.

The present volume offers individual evaluations of the evolution in the context of enlargement of the EU's main institutional actors (European Council, Council of Ministers, European Commission, European Parliament, European Court of Justice, European Central Bank, European Economic and Social Committee, Committee of the Regions), as well as an assessment of trends in the rules and practices governing the interaction between these EU public bodies, as well as between them and national and private actors (legislative output, implementing committees, non-legislative approaches). We thus use the term 'institutions' to refer both to organizational actors united in pursuit of a common goal (North 1990) and to the 'relatively stable collection of practices and rules defining appropriate behaviour for specific groups of actors in specific situations' (March and Olsen 1998).

These evaluations have been carried out within a loose general analytical framework. This framework explicitly aims to avoid any normative assumptions about the nature of institutional change – for example, that continued deepening is in itself desirable and/or inevitable in the longer run in most spheres – or about ideal forms of formal institutionalization in the EU setting. It draws on different elements of institutionalist analysis, and aims to go beyond any opposition of change and stability by borrowing a simple general model drawn from theories of complex systems.

The starting point is the concept of stability of the system. It is almost universally accepted that the European Union constitutes an emerging political system of some sort (Hix 2005). Yet it is clearly not a simple system in which there is overall hierarchical control, but a complex system in which the function of control is distributed among multiple actors. A complex system needs constantly to adapt in order to maintain a 'fit' with its environment (although this works in two directions as a sort of co-evolution), and there is more than one possible state of stability.

This seems to offer an appropriate way of conceptualizing the impact of enlargement on the EU, when there are a) divergent preferences and b) multiple solutions to the challenge of maintaining stability and 'fit'. In the EU, there is disagreement as to the preferred nature of the system, even if there is also a general consensus as to the need to prevent its disintegration. The environment in which the EU operates is also clearly changing (end of the Cold War, globalization, enlargements, etc.) and presenting pressures for adaptation – but without easy consensus as to what should be done.

It also reflects the multiple ways in which this process of adaptation may take place. There is an obvious issue of the level at which change takes place. Conceptualizing change is all the more complicated in a multi-level system, such as the EU, whose components can be seen as complex organizations or systems in their own right. It is therefore essential to take into account also the 'vertical' interaction between different levels as well as 'horizontal' interaction between the different actors and sub-systems. The treaty provisions constitute a set of general higher-level constraints, yet a multitude of specialized policy networks and sub-systems has emerged at different levels and centring on different organizations (a 'boxes within boxes architecture' typical of a complex system). Organizational adaptation within one of the European institutions, for example, cannot be treated in isolation from higher-level processes of change in the rules governing the respective roles of the institutions and the forms of integration between them.

Other issues concern causality and intentionality. In the EU context, institutional changes in fact result only to a limited extent from either constitutional consensus or from technical agreements as to 'necessary' modifications to the system (Olsen 2002). Even where technical arguments and consensus-building was possible and has been attempted, the realities are of negotiation based on immediate interests, heavily shaped by the nature of the existing system. The gradual increase in the powers of the European Parliament, for example, has not obeyed some grand design. It has come about as the result of institutional tactics by the Parliament (Kreppel 2003; Héritier 2007; Moury 2007) and as part of broader sets of treaty reforms which do not represent genuine 'constitutional' settlements so much as package deals between the particular interests and pressures of the historical moment. The increase in powers has taken place 'without prior reflection, simply pulled along by the strongest current. . . . the authors of the various revisions of the treaties acted on the basis of successive additions without wondering what long-term effect the changes made to the treaties might have' (Jacqué 2004: 387).

Beyond this, the challenge of identifying the precise role of enlargement in the multi-faceted and multi-level process of institutional change in the EU is facing a number of obstacles. First, it may be impossible to identify factors affecting the evolution of EU policies which are specifically and uniquely caused by enlargement. There have been broader changes in the international political and policy environment. There have also been other endogenous changes building up over the years, more or less perceptibly, which may be caught up in – and catalysed by – the specific elements introduced by enlargement.

Second, enlargement has not been a single event, but a process including long periods of preparation on both sides. The incoming member states have been obliged to adopt the 'acquis' and to prove that they have consolidated the necessary administrative capacities, and their representatives participated for some time as observers in the institutions, permitting a certain degree of preparatory socialization. On the EU side, there was prolonged discussion about how to prepare for enlargement, most notably about decision-making rules and organizational practices, and considerable investment in new capacities to deal with the new demands.

Third, the most appropriate perspective is not so much that of *the* Union adapting to newcomers as that of *a* (new) Union learning to manage its (new) self. There are some obvious objective elements which make the Union new and which are specifically a result of enlargement. For example, there are more people around the table and more languages to deal with; and there is a wider range and depth of underlying diversities. These contribute to the accumulating pressures for change. Yet the more important shift in the long term may concern the balance of perceptions and interests affecting the way in which the Union responds to questions regarding the nature of the integration process and the most appropriate way of responding to internal and external pressures. In other words, enlargement may contribute to changes both in the nature of the challenge and in evaluations of possible responses.

Based on these concerns we arrive at a number of key questions to which the contributions of this book respond. The first question concerns the very nature of change: what is it that actually is expected to change? The answer might range from the mindset and actions of individual actors to the direction and nature of the whole political system. In order to organize this complexity, we propose that change may occur at different *levels* within and beyond the institutions and, more specifically, we distinguish between two *loci* where change could happen: change can be either intra- or inter-organizational. The first concerns changes within the organizations: obvious examples include changes in the composition, working methods and rules of procedure of the EU institutions (which are better understood as 'organizations' in this context). The second concerns changes in the interactions between these organizations. A useful example is the pattern of interaction among EU institutions in the generation of EU norms. Others include the network of national parliaments, the network of national and EU courts, etc.

A second set of questions concerns the degree of formalization that institutional change takes. In this respect, institutional change can be conceptualized as occurring along a continuum ranging from changes in the (informal) patterns of behaviour and practice within and among the institutions (e.g. in the management of schedules) at one end to much more far-reaching and formal changes at the highest level (i.e. treaty changes) at the other end.

Changes, obviously, also vary in their *intensity*. Compared to the point of departure, change can be placed along a continuum that ranges from no or minor changes to transformative change. This means that one would seek to determine the intensity of change rather than only its degree of formality: a change can be significant even without having visibility in formal terms. For example, a substantial alteration in the practice of codecision can be seen as having a transformative effect even if such a change is not formally codified.

To the above dimensions a temporal distinction can be added, separating cases according to the timing of any change. In particular, changes might occur before their possible cause (e.g. intended institutional reforms that were agreed *in preparation for* the arrival of new member states) or afterwards (e.g. changes in the inter-institutional dynamics of the EU *as a consequence of* the arrival of the new member states). Among the latter, one could further distinguish between short- and long-term changes.

It is against this background that the contributors to this book have studied the key institutions of the European Union. Starting with an analysis of the European Council, Wolfgang Wessels reports that enlargement has not blocked the activities of this body at the political apex of the EU institutional system. Major decisions continue to be adopted relatively smoothly, and the overall quantity (and substance) of output has not changed significantly: even in a Union of 27, it continues to insert vital national issues into the EU arena, without altering its internal dynamics. In the light of the ongoing constitutional debate, the future European Council may undergo some organizational changes: as a notable example, the Lisbon Treaty would provide it with a full-time president, an innovation partly motivated by the recent enlargement. Nevertheless, if one takes on board lessons from the past, as well as initial experiences following the latest round of accessions, no major changes in the substantive role of the European Council are to be expected in a Union of 27 based on the Lisbon Treaty.

Similar conclusions are reached by Edward Best and Pierpaolo Settembri when looking at the Council of Ministers after enlargement. The Council seems to have successfully assimilated the new members into its decision-making dynamics, and has adapted its internal working methods to the new conditions. There is no major change in the time required or the degree of political contestation. Yet beyond obvious differences such as the number of languages or the number of people round the table, or the need to deal with new substantive issues which have been specifically imported together with the newer countries, it is not easy to pin down the specific role of enlargement as an explanatory factor for change. There are very rarely coalitions of 'new' versus 'old' member states, and acceding countries usually join existing issue-based coalitions in which larger member states continue to play the leading role. Nevertheless, they find that the enlarged Council has become more 'bureaucratized': ministers, for example, become more and more 'excluded' from the decision-making process, to the benefit of diplomats.

As for the Commission, John Peterson and Andrea Birdsall approach it as a uniquely 'politicized bureaucracy'. In line with the other contributions, the main argument of their chapter is that the role of the Commission has not been fundamentally altered by enlargement. Enlargement has only reinforced the impact of other secular changes that are not exclusively or specifically linked to enlargement. They include the emergence of a younger and more flexible Commission, which has become more presidential and can no longer rely on its traditional monopoly right to initiate formal legislation to influence EU policy debates. The most important difference might lie in the strategy pursued by the enlarged Commission to introduce less legislation in order to dedicate more attention to key proposals ('do less but better'). Moreover, on the basis of a round of interviews with Commission officials they submit that, in the view of most interlocutors, enlargement has brought new blood, energy, enthusiasm and youth to the Commission, whereas only the third most frequent answer suggests that the Commission has become less cosy and that enlargement has brought more diverse perspectives to it. In short, they conclude that enlargement was only one amongst multiple rationales being used to try to reinvent the Commission.

The chapter by Brendan Donnelly and Milena Bigatto looks into the changes brought by enlargement to the European Parliament from a number of perspectives. In general, it finds that the specific impact on the EP has been limited, because of both the modest number of parliamentarians involved and their dispersal among and behaviour within the political groups. In more specific terms, other than on institutional questions, where the role of the European Parliament is in any case restricted, MEPs from the newest member states of the Union have followed the example of their predecessors and voted in a manner more easily explicable by their political rather than their national affiliations. To a limited extent, the prevalence of certain political views within the Parliament has been reinforced by the influx of new members (as in the Council and the Commission) and some marginal political views have become slightly less marginal. Prospectively, enlargement has crystallized differing views about the Union's future, which are likely to bear on the development and future role of the Parliament. The process of ratification of the Lisbon Treaty and the capacity or otherwise of the Parliament to take advantage of the new possibilities given to it by the treaty, particularly in the election of the President of the Commission, will provide important clues about the future likely evolution of the enlarged European Parliament.

Like the Commission, the European Court of Justice (ECJ), analysed by Caroline Naômé, also took the 2004 enlargement as an opportunity to address with some determination pre-existing problems, particularly with respect to the reduction of the backlog before new cases came from the new member states. On all accounts, the integration of the new judges has been smooth: they immediately received cases to prepare as rapporteurs, had an equal right of decision in the general meeting, sat in the cases coming before the ECJ for a hearing and participated in deliberations when they were members of the composition in charge of the case. Some changes in working methods did occur because of enlargement, but most of them are interlinked with changes aiming at improving the overall efficiency of the Court. The near future will bring an increase in the number of cases, with the arrival of more cases connected to the new member states. But it will also, possibly, bring the adoption of measures extending the jurisdiction of the Court. The Court has taken advantage of enlargement to prepare itself for the increasing role it is ready to play.

In his study of the European Central Bank (ECB), Kenneth Dyson argues that its *sui generis* institutional character has narrowly circumscribed the direction, scope, intensity and timing of institutional change consequent on enlargement (confining formal treaty change to voting modalities agreed prior to EU enlargement). Its uniqueness – particularly its 'extreme' independence, missionary role and technocratic character – coupled with the context of temporal uncertainty about Euro Area enlargement has conditioned the ECB strategy towards institutional change. This strategy combines a tough, disciplined approach to Euro Area enlargement with a model of reform that internalizes differentiation in voting rules and keeps more fundamental intra- and inter-institutional reforms off the EU agenda. In sum, enlargement itself has not proved to be a catalyst for transformative institutional change. A future crisis may prompt radical reforms, but its nature, timing and effects cannot be predicted. Moreover, it is unclear whether it will derive from new member states or from older member states, or whether it will involve contagion from an extra-EU crisis.

According to Nieves Pérez-Solórzano Borragán and Stijn Smismans, enlargement did not alter the functioning and role of the European Economic and Social Committee (EESC). Formally, hardly any legal provisions have been changed to adapt it to enlargement, except for increasing the number of its members. Neither did enlargement substantially change its representative nature nor its internal dynamics of decision-making. The increase in members and working languages has applied additional pressure to solve well-known weaknesses such as the loosely structured debate in the plenary, the timely delivery of documents or the development of expertise. Decision-making is still very consensual at least in its outcome. However, enlargement has been influencing policy priorities within the EESC for quite some time. While the EESC has limited control over its own agenda, enlargement has contributed to the EESC being proactive in some specific policy fields.

Simona Piattoni argues that the Committee of the Regions (CoR) experienced some changes because of enlargement, but not of such magnitude as to fundamentally alter its functioning. In addition to the changes that took place directly at the institutional level, as a consequence of the increase in members, other changes took place because the evolving environment prompted adaptation in inter-institutional dynamics. Enlargement, together with other developments, has led other institutions – particularly the Commission – to seek allies among actors who may be considered legitimate channels of communication with European citizens. The CoR has seized this opportunity and offered its assistance by making cross-border cooperation and dialogue with the enlargement countries one of its primary commitments. Its current stature is the result of the direct impact of enlargement as well as the reflection of its new role within a Union in which inter-institutional relations have changed, also because of enlargement.

While the above chapters deal with individual institutions and mainly address the pressure for change that these institutions have faced before and after enlargement, the framework that we developed above also seeks to identify changes in the inter-institutional relations of multi-level governance in the European Union. Some of the previous chapters address such concerns in passing, for example with respect to the relations between the EP and national political parties (Donnelly and Bigatto), or relations between the CoR and regional and local authorities (Piattoni). However, in order to provide a more systematic engagement with the impact of enlargement on the relations between the institutions at the European level, and between them and actors within the member states, the following chapters specifically deal with these issues.

The institutional triangle of Commission, Parliament and Council at the heart of the EU's legislative process is examined by Edward Best and Pierpaolo Settembri in Chapter 10. In evaluating the EU's production of legislation before and after enlargement, the authors suggest that the Union has proven to be a flexible system, showing an extraordinary capacity of adapting to a new environment with increased membership and, arguably, increased political diversity. After enlargement, the system delivers a comparable amount of acts; on average, it does so faster and without greater political contestation. A closer look at what the EU produces and the way it operates, however, shows that the enlarged Union is somewhat different from EU15. For example, legislation is shaped by an increased variety of interests and its nature is altered: diversity is contributing to significantly longer acts. In addition, the decision-making process enjoys less political input in the key institutions. The main driver behind these changes is the codecision procedure: all the trends detected in the enlarged Union are magnified when Council and Parliament are required to act together.

Whereas Chapter 10 deals with the relations between institutions at the European level, Chapter 11, by Manuela Alfé, Thomas Christiansen and Sonia Piedrafita, deals with the relations between the European and the national levels of administration in the context of implementation of EU legislation – the system of implementing committees that has come to be called 'comitology'. The authors report that the arrival of the new member states has made little difference to the way in which decisions are taken or the ability to achieve outcomes. Generally speaking, enlargement has not affected the quality and quantity of implementing measures emerging from the committees. The increased formalization of procedures, the limitations imposed on debates, the minimization of the time before putting a measure to vote and the stronger discipline in meetings contributed to guarantee the level of delivery after enlargement. Through selected interviews, the authors find that the increased number of actors, the changing influence capacity of the member states and the tendency to short-term coalitions have strengthened the role of the Commission. In general, the larger countries have lost some of their traditional power to broker agreements, whereas enlargement has made it easier for small countries to build up a coalition and influence the process. In this scenario, the reinforcement of the Commission's co-ordination role and determination to achieve its goals has been amply justified in order to provide the process with some sense of direction and common purpose and to ensure its effectiveness. The comitology system could experience further changes in the near future, as the Lisbon Treaty contains significant provisions concerning the delegation of powers to the Commission.

Edward Best, in a chapter on non-legislative approaches, analyses forms of policy coordination and alternative methods of regulation that involve both public and private actors. He suggests that the adoption of such non-legislative approaches in the 1990s was not caused by enlargement but rather that such new approaches were emerging as a result of the evolving policy context and the nature of the substantive issues. Nevertheless, the increase in underlying diversity within the Union as a result of enlargement is reported as a relevant factor in this overall process of change, and enlargement did bring about some changes in the balance of forces within the Union regarding the design of specific forms of cooperation. At the same time, it is inappropriate to talk of a specific impact of enlargement on the development and perspectives of the open method of coordination (OMC). The new member states were introduced gradually into the process in advance of accession, while OMC is in part conceived precisely as a means to manage diversity with flexibility. Enlargement has not been a factor in the proliferation of new forms of public–private interaction. It could, however, have an impact on the further evolution of such methods as a result of its impact on the credibility of legislative alternatives, the effectiveness of private commitments or the provision of necessary framework conditions.

We conclude the volume with a number of conclusions that cut across the individual chapters. While the dominant impression across the board of EU institutional politics is that enlargement has not fundamentally changed matters, a number of dynamics have been identified that are examined in more detail: first, the nature of both formal and informal arrangements has been affected by enlargement, with greater formalization of official meetings and procedures, but at the same time an increase in the use of informal channels to prepare and 'pre-cook' decision-making; second, enlargement has reinforced a trend of more and more decisions taken in administrative spheres rather than in the political fora of the EU; third, we can observe a growing trend towards a 'presidentialization' of the EU system, with those chairing meetings and heading institutions assuming greater power and influence; and, fourth, we see a pattern of enlargement turning out to be the catalyst in the search for greater efficiency.

These conclusions emphasize that EU enlargement did not cause these developments; nor is it alone responsible for maintaining them. But while these are long-term trends of European governance, it is evident from the contributions to the present volume that the impact of enlargement has been to interact with these dynamics, reinforcing trends that pre-existed. If we look at these observations from a normative perspective, the institutional impact of EU enlargement is mixed. It is evident that the EU has managed to protect the administrative efficiency of the system rather well, but it is also clear that the EU's democratic accountability is further challenged by the greater resort to informal arrangements that are being used in order to make the Union work post-enlargement. The ratification and implementation of the Lisbon Treaty may do something to change that, but in anticipation of that the conclusion here is that the process of enlargement, while not having in itself fundamentally changed matters, has interacted with existing developments and reinforced some of the problems that had already been present in the institutional politics of the EU.

NOTES

1. To take only a few examples, *Environmental Politics* (2004) on the environment; Ackrill (2003) and Daugbjerg and Swinbank (2004) on agriculture; Monar *et al*. (2003) on Justice and Home Affairs; or Storbeck (2003) on the fight against international crime.
2. By way of examples from the huge academic output in this respect, Raunio and Wiberg 1998; Steunenberg 2001; Plechanovová 2003; Hosli and Machover 2004.

REFERENCES

Ackrill, R.W. (2003), 'EU Enlargement: The CAP and the Cost of Direct Payments: A Note', *Journal of Agricultural Economics*, **54** (1), 73–8.

Brou, D. and Ruta, M. (2004), 'A Positive Explanation of EU Enlargement', *EUI Working Paper*, ECO No. 2004 / 30.

Brummer, E. and Fröhlich, S. (2005), *The Strategic Implications of European Union Enlargement*, Washington, DC: Johns Hopkins University.

Cemrek, M. (2004), 'The Impact of EU Enlargement on the US: The New Transatlantic Relations', *Insight Turkey*, **6** (3), 89–95.

Commission of the European Committees (CEC) (2006), *Enlargement Strategy and Main Challenges 2006*, COM(2006) 649 final.

Cremona, M. (2003), *The Enlargement of the European Union*, Oxford: Oxford University Press.

Daugbjerg, C. and Swinbank, A. (2004), 'The CAP and EU Enlargement: Prospects for an Alternative Strategy to Avoid the Lock-in of CAP Support', *Journal of Common Market Studies*, **42** (1), 99–119.

Dehousse, R., Deloche-Gaudez, F. and Duhamel, O. (2006), *Élargissement: Comment l'Europe s'adapte*, Paris: Presses de Sciences Po.

Ekiert, G. and Zielonka, J. (2003), 'The Next Great Transformation: The EU Eastward Enlargement', *EEPS: East European Politics and Societies*, **17** (1), 7–124.

Environmental Politics (2004), 'EU Enlargement and the Environment: Institutional Change and Environmental Policy in Central and Eastern Europe', Special Issue, **13** (1).

European Parliament (EP) (2006), *Report on the Institutional Aspects of the European Union's Capacity to Integrate New Member States*, 2006/2226(INI) – A6-0393/2006, 16 November.

Falkner, G. (2000), 'How Pervasive are Euro-politics? Effects of EU Membership on a New Member State', *Journal of Common Market Studies*, **38** (2), 223–50.

Franck, C. (1987), 'New Ambitions: From the Hague to Paris summits (1969–1972)', in R. Pryce (ed.), *The Dynamics of European Union*, London: Croom Helm, pp. 130–48.

Grabbe, H. (2003), 'Europeanization Goes East: Power and Uncertainty in the EU Accession Process', in K. Featherstone and C. Radaelli (eds.), *The Politics of Europeanization*, Oxford: Oxford University Press, pp. 303–30.

Grabbe, H. (2004), 'How Enlargement Will Change the EU's Political Dynamics and its Foreign Policies', *Slovak Foreign Policy Affairs*, **5** (1), 63–74.

Guillén, A.M. and Palier, B. (2004), 'EU Enlargement, Europeanization and Social Policy', *Journal of European Social Policy*, **14** (3), 203–9.

Hagemann, S. and De Clerck-Sachsse, J. (2007), *Old Rules, New Game: Decision-making in the Council of Ministers after the 2004 Enlargement*, CEPS Special Report, March.

Helly, D. and Petiteville, F. (2005), *L'Union européenne, acteur international*, Paris: l'Harmattan.

Héritier, A. (2007), *Explaining Institutional Change in Europe*, Oxford: Oxford University Press.

Higashino, A. (2004), 'For the Sake of "Peace and Security"? The Role of Security in the European Union Enlargement Eastwards', *Cooperation and Conflict*, **39** (4), 347–68.

Hix, S. (2005), *The Political System of the European Union*, 2nd edition, London: Palgrave.

Hix, S. and Noury, A. (2006), 'After Enlargement: Voting Behaviour in the Sixth European Parliament', Paper presented at the Federal Trust conference on 'The European Parliament and the European Political Space', 30 March, London.

Hosli, M.O. and Machover, M. (2004), 'The Nice Treaty and Voting Rules in the Council', *Journal of Common Market Studies*, **42** (3), 497–521.

Hughes, K. (2004), 'The Political Dynamics of Turkish Accession to the EU: A European Success Story or the EU's Most Contested Enlargement', *Report*, **9**, Swedish Institute for European Policy Studies.

Inglis, K. (2004), 'The Union's Fifth Accession Treaty: New Means to Make Enlargement Possible', *Common Market Law Review*, **41** (4), 937–73.

Jacqué, J.-P. (2004), 'The Principle of Institutional Balance', *Common Market Law Review*, **41** (2), 383–91.

Kaiser, W. and Elvert, J. (2004), *European Union Enlargement: A Comparative History*, London: Routledge.

Kreppel, A. (2003), 'Necessary but not Sufficient: Understanding the Impact of Treaty Reform on the Internal Development of the European Parliament', *Journal of European Public Policy*, **10** (6), 884–911.

Kurpas, S. and Schönlau, J. (2006), 'Deadlock Avoided, but Sense of Mission Lost? The Enlarged EU and its Uncertain Constitution', *CEPS Policy Briefs*.

Lewis, P.G. (2003), 'The Impact of the Enlargement of the European Union on Central European Party Systems', *SEI Working Paper*, 71.

Luif, P. (1995), *On the Road to Brussels: The Political Dimension of Austria's, Finland's and Sweden's Accession to the European Union*, Vienna: Braumüller.

Mair, P., Bozóki, A. and Karácsony, G. (2003), 'Political Parties and the European Enlargement', *Central European Political Science Review*, **4** (13), 5–136.

March, J.G. and Olsen, J.P. (1998), 'The Institutional Dynamics of International Political Orders' *International Organization*, **52** (4), 943–69.

Monar, J., Bort, E. and Grasso, G. (2003), 'The Impact of Enlargement on JHA [Justice and Home Affairs]', *International Spectator*, **38** (1), 33–80.

Moury, C. (2007), 'Explaining the European Parliament's Right to Appoint and Invest the Commission', *West European Politics*, **30** (2), 367–91.

Neuwahl, N. (2004), *European Union Enlargement: Law and Socio-economic Changes*, Montreal: Thémis.

Nicholson, F. and East, R. (1987), *From the Six to the Twelve: The Enlargement of the European Communities*, London: Longman.

North, D.C. (1990), *Institutions, Institutional Change, and Economic Performance*, New York: Cambridge University Press.

Nugent, N. (2004), *European Union Enlargement*, Basingstoke: Palgrave Macmillan.

Olsen, J. (2002), 'Reforming European Institutions of Governance', *Journal of Common Market Studies*, **40** (4), 581–602.

Plechanovová, B. (2003), 'The Treaty of Nice and the Distribution of Votes in the Council: Voting Power Consequences for the EU after the Oncoming Enlargement', *EIOP*, **6**.

Preston, C. (1997), *Enlargement and Integration in the European Union*, London: Routledge.

Raunio, T. and Tiilikainen, T. (2003), *Finland in the European Union*, London: Frank Cass.

Raunio, T. and Wiberg, M. (1998), 'Winners and Losers in the Council: Voting Power Consequences of EU Enlargements', *Journal of Common Market Studies*, **36** (4), 549–62.

Sadurski, W. (2004), 'Accession's Democracy Dividend: The Impact of the EU Enlargement upon Democracy in the New Member States of Central and Eastern Europe', *European Law Journal*, **10** (4), 371–401.

Schimmelfennig, F. (2005), 'The Process of Enlargement', in J. Richardson (ed.), *European Union: Power and Policy-Making*, 3rd edition, London: Routledge, pp. 207–24.

Sedelmeier, U. and Young, A. (2006), 'Editorial: Crisis, What Crisis? Continuity and Normality in the European Union in 2005', *Journal of Common Market Studies*, **44** special issue, 1–5.

Sjursen, H. (2002), 'Why Expand? The Question of Legitimacy and Justification of the EU's Enlargement Policy', *Journal of Common Market Studies*, **40** (3), 491–514.

Steunenberg, B. (2001), 'Enlargement and Institutional Reform in the European Union: Separate or Connected Issues?', *Constitutional Political Economy*, **12** (4), 351–70.

Storbeck, J. (2003), 'The European Union and Enlargement: Challenge and Opportunity for Europol in the Fight against International Crime', *European Foreign Affairs Review*, **8** (3), 283–8.

Verdun, A. (2005), 'The Challenges of European Union: Where Are We Today, How Did We Get There, and What Lies Ahead?' in A. Verdun and O. Croci (eds), *The European Union in the Wake of Eastern Enlargement: Institutional and Policy-making Challenges*, Manchester: Manchester University Press, pp. 9–22.

Westlake, M. (1994), *A Modern Guide to the European Parliament*, London: Pinter.

Wörz, J. (2005), 'The First Year of EU Enlargement: Trade Performance from the Austrian Perspective', *Monthly Report – The Vienna Institute*, **7**, 4–11.

2. The European Council: a bigger club, a similar role?

Wolfgang Wessels

It seems not inappropriate to start any assessment of the institutional impact of enlargement at the top, by looking at the European Council, the body bringing together the heads of state or government of the member states with the President of the European Commission at the political apex of the European Union. No other body has shaped the fundamental developments of the European construction as profoundly as this institutionalized summitry (cf. de Schoutheete 2006, p. 57; Hayes-Renshaw and Wallace 2006, p. 173).

Not an organ of the European Community, this elite 'club' has its legal basis in the Treaty on European Union. According to the treaty formulation, 'the European Council shall provide the European Union with the necessary impetus for its development and shall define the general political guidelines thereof' (Art. 4 TEU). This general and ambiguous description, however, fails to fully recognize the body's political relevance in constructing and running the EU system. It has been called a 'provisional government' ('gouvernement provisoire') (Monnet 1976, p. 598), a 'joint decision centre' (Tindemans 1975), 'constitutional architect' (Wessels 2005b, p. 55), a 'system of collective leadership' (Ludlow 2005, p. 3) and the 'high guardian' ('haute tutelle') (Louis and Ronse 2005, p. 57). It has also been described as not an 'institution', but a 'locus of power' (de Schoutheete 2006, p. 45). The formulations of its role in the Constitutional Treaty and the subsequent Lisbon Treaty have underlined in several ways the rise in importance of the European Council.

This chapter looks at the evolution of the European Council in the context of enlargement in terms of its five main roles, and in the perspective of two alternative theoretical approaches.

METHODOLOGY AND ANALYTICAL FRAMEWORK

For the purposes of the present analysis, we identify five main roles (cf. de Schoutheete 2006; Wessels 2007) in terms of which we can assess the possible impact of enlargement. These are:

- 'agenda setter', as in the adoption of major new steps such as the Tampere Programme, the Lisbon Strategy or, more recently, the Energy Policy for Europe;
- 'highest decision-maker', as in the case of top-level institutional appointments, or issues such as the Financial Perspectives;
- 'coordinator' in the Union, in the sense of laying down the fundamental goals and guidelines for national policies in these areas;
- 'global actor', in terms of defining the principles and guidelines for the role of the EU in the international system; and
- 'constitutional architect', especially for treaty revisions (deepening) and accessions (widening).

Academic observers face significant methodological difficulties, however. Research on the European Council, in contrast to the EC institutions per se, can rely on time series of officially produced data to only a limited degree. Work must all too often be based on anecdotal evidence even though, as the 'club of the bosses' tries to keep out other participants, including high civil servants, this is not an easy task.

Nevertheless, this chapter is primarily based on the formal output of the sessions of the European Council. The topics which are the subject of the 'Presidency conclusions' and the 'Declarations of the European Council' are taken as indicators for the scope, intensity and – to a lesser degree – impact of the summits. Given the fact that most of the points on the agenda are well prepared by the EU machinery before the sessions, these lists do not necessarily indicate the real priorities and the factual debates among the participants. Nevertheless, these formulations from the 'top' can be regarded as having a life of their own, with major impacts on the polity, policies and politics of the EU.

Moreover, the role of the European Council may be addressed from two perspectives, reflecting alternative sets of theoretical expectations (cf. Wessels and Schäfer 2007): on the one hand, (neo-) realism and intergovernmentalism; and, on the other hand, a logic of 'fusion' between national and European levels of government.

REALIST–INTERGOVERNMENTALIST APPROACHES

From the perspective of realism or neo-realism (cf. Morgenthau [1948] 2005; Waltz 1979) and intergovernmentalism (cf. Hoffmann 1966; Moravcsik 1998), the fundamental assumption is simple. Since sovereign states dominate the world – also in the EU context – the heads of state or government are the 'real actors' (Scharpf 1997) in European integration. As 'masters of the treaties' (Federal Constitutional Court 1993), they are the 'principals' (cf. Moravcsik 1993; Pollack 2003, 2005; Kassim and Menon 2003), with ultimate authority based on their national democratic legitimacy.

In this intergovernmentalist perspective, enlargement may be expected to lead to contradictory pressures: a rise in the importance of this body, together with a decline in its institutional power to deal with new political challenges. The increase in membership of the Union, and the concomitant expansion of national interests and preferences which have to be addressed, is likely to increase demands for collective leadership. It would also be expected to generate a higher degree of blockage in the lower levels of the EU institutional architecture, meaning that the 'reserve' function of the European Council as decision-maker of last resort would be extended. In addition, in this perspective, the new member states are expected to stress more than older ones the notion of 'sovereignty', with the result that increased importance would be given to the European Council as the major arena for protecting one's vital national interest. Finally, the cleavage between smaller and larger countries may become more important, prompting the larger members to turn into a 'directoire' (cf. Hill 2006) and the smaller to behave as 'nuisance' powers.

The 'expectation–capability gap' (cf. Hill 1993), or the gap between demand and supply, would thus increase. The result would be a greater inefficiency of this body. This intra-organizational weakening would then – in an inter-institutional spill-over – also affect the EU system as a whole: it would lead to an overall decrease in the productivity of the EU institutional system. The predicted result is a reduced output of the European Council in terms of Presidency Conclusions, a reduced scope of its agenda, and more ambiguous declarations – although it may well be the case that such an impact may not occur immediately. It could be that the governments of the new member states need some time to find the courage to raise their voice, in which case the four years we can observe so far may not be enough to judge.

THE EUROPEAN COUNCIL AS ACTOR AND INDICATOR OF FUSION

In contrast to such an intergovernmentalist viewpoint, the European Council over the last three decades can be seen as both actor and indicator of a fundamental logic of evolution of the EU system which may be characterized as a 'fusion process' (Wessels 2005a). The integration process is thus perceived as an effort of 'rescuing the nation state' (Milward 2005).

The European Council constitutes a natural place for member states to deal with a common dilemma facing them: how to deal with the issue of where (and at which level) to tackle major global and transnational challenges. Given growing interdependencies and increasing trends towards globalization, they realize that the nation state is not the optimal problem-solving area for vital issues for which they are made accountable at home by their voters. The EU, with the European Council in a pivotal position, thus becomes a substitute for the losses of national sovereignty. By acting together, this group of national actors can reinforce its powers also vis-à-vis other national actors (such as national parliaments and regions).

This school of thought also expects that the latest round of accession will lead to an increase in the activities of the European Council. If anything, however, the increase in the number of members in this perspective would be expected to facilitate agreement. A broader agenda means greater scope for negotiation, while pure national self-interest may be expected to lead to a dynamic spill-over in terms of the scope of agenda points, as well as some initiatives into new areas.

HAVE THE EUROPEAN COUNCIL'S MAIN ROLES BEEN AFFECTED BY ENLARGEMENT? LOOK AT THE EVIDENCE

Agenda-Setting and Steering Functions

In the last 30 years, the European Council has developed from a 'debating club' to a provider of strategic guidelines. Undeniably, this development has had lasting effects on shaping several central policy fields in the European Union. The European Council has repeatedly opened new activity areas for the Union. From the early explanations of summit conferences to environmental policy (cf. Paris summit 1972) via the Tampere Programme 'towards a Union of freedom, security and justice' (European Council, October 1999) to the 'strategy for growth and employment' (Lisbon Strategy, European Council, March 2000) and to the fight against terrorism (European Council, June 2004), the European Council has set ground-breaking provisions, usually on the basis of proposals by the Commission or the General Affairs Council. These formalize norms which, in their original sense, were legally non-binding but were subsequently integrated into treaty articles. Therefore, the European Council can be attributed pre-constitutional effects. In retrospect 'a path' (for the term see Pierson 2000, pp. 251–3) or rather 'corridors' can be observed, which have been formed in several steps in and through the European Council. In many cases, the members of the European Council have pursued regular follow-ups and thus ensured that they kept a say in the implementation.

The accession of ten new member states in 2004 has not basically changed this pattern: this agenda-setting function has continued. A listing of the 'conclusions of the Presidency of the European Council' and the 'declarations of the European Council' (Figure 2.1) provides an overview of subjects dealt with. We observe a high degree of continuity with regard to the issues on the agenda. In the first year of its existence, 1975, the European Council dealt with budgetary and institutional issues, energy and terrorism, the economic and social situation of the Community, relations with the People's Republic of China and the UN, all of which are still high on the agenda (cf. Wessels 1980, pp. 140–67). The items on the agenda have not changed to a significant degree. A clear change cannot be discovered in the aggregate data in the overall lists. Some items are recurrent, owing to the programmed schedules like the spring session on the Lisbon follow-up. Others are caused by external events like declarations on Afghanistan. It is hard to observe any special priority after accession.

Based upon Presidency conclusions, the European Council can be seen again and again to have taken up a role as steering body. During the period from 1975 to 1985, the European Council distributed over 100 assignments to EC institutions alone (cf. Wessels 2000, p. 229). This function continues to be used extensively. At the March summit 2007 the European Council in the 'Energy Policy for Europe' action plan 'invites' the Commission ten times and the member states four times to take up certain tasks (European Council, March 2007).

Overall, the European Council has established a programme for coordinating nationally located instruments in economic and employment policy, and foreign and security policy, as well as in Justice and Home Affairs.

Highest Decision-Maker

The European Council has not turned out to be merely an extraordinary 'summit', proclaiming general objectives for the Union. Rather, it has clearly expanded its decision-making role in policy processes. Beyond its originally

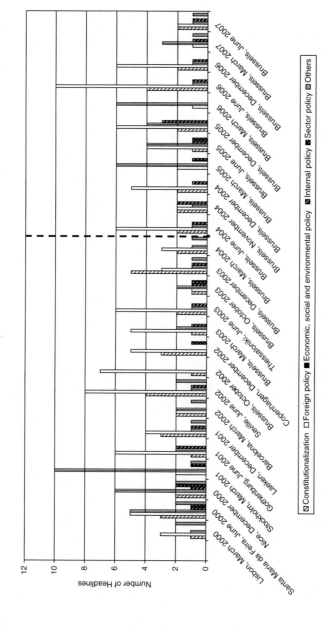

Source: Overview by Verena Schäfer, Jean Monnet Chair – Prof. W. Wessels, based on the headlines of the Presidency Conclusions, European Council 2000–2007.

Figure 2.1 Presidency conclusions and declarations of the European Council

intended role, this body has increasingly accepted – partly *contre cœur* and partly voluntarily – that it take up the task of highest and ultimate decision-maker, and in this sense the 'apex of the EU's institutional system' (Hayes-Renshaw and Wallace 2006, p. 173). This role includes the election and designation of persons belonging to leadership positions in the Community's institutions – such as the President of the Commission and of the European Central Bank. With accession we observe no major change in the practice of this function. The (s)election of the Commission in 2004 showed some problems but only to a very limited degree caused by expansion.

The European Council has been intensely concerned with decisions regarding the controversial mid-term Financial Perspectives. It has negotiated in great detail the sources of income and expenditure structures of the EC budget. Examples include the first 'summit of the calculators' in Dublin 1975, the Delors packages, 'Agenda 2000' drafted in 1999 and 'Agenda 2007' drafted in 2005. 'Agenda 2007' was an object of major disputes and intensive negotiations in the enlarged European Council. The new member countries became heavily involved and played a major role, but the basic pattern of cleavages between the net payers and the net receivers did not change dramatically. The results are rather typical. One might argue that the enlargement increased the number of special 'gifts', that is, soothing donations to individual member states, the so-called 'Additional Provisions' from seven in 'Agenda 2000' to 17 in 'Agenda 2007'. Of course, enlargement played a major role in the process leading to 'Agenda 2000', and will again do so in the budget review. However, the character of bargaining inside the European Council and the pivotal role of this body have not changed. It could even be argued that the accession countries were an important factor in bringing the European Council to an agreement in December 2005 after the failed referenda and in view of the marginalized position of the UK.

Directing Policies of Economic and Social Governance

Since 1975, the European Council has regularly delivered statements on economic and socio-political developments in the European Union. The founding fathers played pivotal roles in this regard. The heads of state or government later on assigned the European Council to direct the coordination of economic (cf. Art. 99 TEC) and employment (cf. Art. 128 TEC) policies. After accession the European Council has continuously dealt with questions surrounding economy policy and fiscal and employment policy, and in March 2005 introduced revised procedures (cf. European Council, March 2005). This body has thus remained a key in European economic governance without forming a 'gouvernement économique' (cf.

Linsenmann, Meyer and Wessels 2007). In this aspect there is no change which could be explicitly linked to accession.

Global Actor

The general role of the European Council in foreign affairs is rather clear (cf. de Schoutheete 2002, pp. 36–7). Since its creation, the European Council and its president have played a dominant role in shaping the EU's role(s) in the international system, regularly adopting statements on international developments and issues. Such positions have included developments in the Middle East, Eastern Europe and South-East Europe and the break-up of the former Soviet Union.

Even though the members of the European Council have frequently only signed texts prepared in advance by foreign ministers and diplomats, these texts form a major point of reference for the member states and for concerned third parties.

Time and again, the leaders of member states have used the European Council to jointly address unexpected crises in the international system. In serious historic events, for example the fall of the Berlin Wall, the terrorist attacks of 11 September 2001 and/or the Iraq conflict, the European Council convened to deal with crises in the international system, although they did not always successfully shape a common line for the EU.

With the latest round of enlargement, we would expect the Russian Federation to have become more important as a topic – partly owing to the worries of some new member countries with a different threat perception from that of some of the old members. The Ukraine and other crisis regions would likewise have been moved upwards on the list of the priorities of the European Council. The evidence provided by the Presidency conclusions (see Table 2.1), however, does not indicate any major change. Only the neighbourhood policy, a 'child' of the last enlargement, has – also in the interest of older members – drawn a higher degree of attention from the European Council.

Constitutional Architect

Over the course of its history the European Council has turned into the 'constitutional architect' of the EU system (cf. Wessels 2007, pp. 208–9); it has become the key body taking de facto decisions regarding deepening and widening of the Union in both procedure and substance (cf. Wallace 2000, p. 20).

At first glance, the assignment of this function might come as a surprise, given that the European Council is not mentioned in relevant treaty articles, especially in treaty revisions (Art. 48 TEU) and accession (Art. 49 TEU). In practice, however, the European Council has directly shaped essential features of the constitutional and geographic architecture of the Union. The quasi-constitutional acts of EU system-formation include decisions of the European Council regarding the initiation and completion of accession negotiations. The European Council has de facto made these decisions practically in every essential phase. Examples include the establishment of accession criteria (Copenhagen, 1993) and the final summit which concluded the largest accession round in Copenhagen in 2002 (cf. Lippert 2003a, 2003b). The European Council has also determined corresponding procedural steps in the accession process for Bulgaria and Rumania in 2004 and for Croatia and Turkey.

The latest round of enlargement has not changed this function (see Figure 2.2). The European Council was actively involved in dealing with the Treaty establishing a Constitution for Europe and its follow-up, leading to a decision on a Reform Treaty in June 2007. This quasi-constitutional process was launched by the European Council in reaction to the enlargement (see Declaration 23 in Nice) to make the institutional architecture 'fit' for an enlarged number of member states with a higher diversity of preferences and interests.

How did the accession then affect the making of a constitution? At first there seems to be a paradox in that it was two of the founding countries – not one of the newcomers – that put an end to the first round of the process, with the consequences of accession being a major point in their debates. At the opening of the second round – for what is now called the Treaty of Lisbon – the Polish government adopted a blocking position. However, we may argue – in some speculative fashion – that also among the 15, or even the six, no easy way to a consensus about the 'finalité' would have been found. In any case it is safe to say that the European Council has remained the central locus for dealing with these issues.

Also in terms of other issues linked in a broader sense to constitution-making, the European Council has remained the central body in dealing with institutional matters of the EU system and with budget and finance topics.

INTERNAL LIFE: FROM A CLUB TO A CHAMBER?

Decision-Making Modalities

The founding fathers of the European Council emphasized that these meetings should be confidential and informal. In their eyes, sessions should

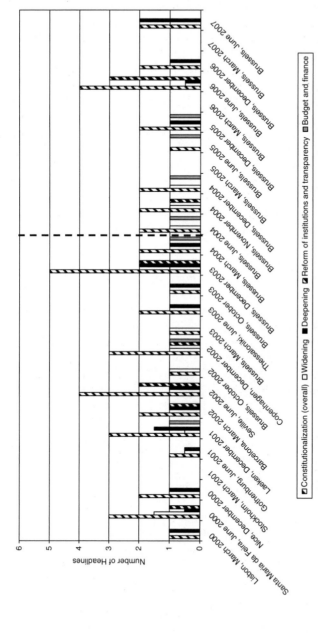

Source: Overview by Verena Schäfer, Jean Monnet Chair – Prof. W. Wessels, based on the headlines of the Presidency Conclusions, European Council 2000–2007.

Figure 2.2   The European Council as a constitutional architect

focus on high-level debates on vital issues, without papers and speeches prepared by civil servants.

Since its beginning there has been a trade-off between the informality which might lead to rather unfounded or uninformed decisions, and a too perfectly prepared session which turns the European Council into just a rubber-stamping machinery ratifying what has been formulated by other institutions before. With the expansion of the EU to 27 member states, the number of participants around the meeting table has risen to 56, reducing even more the opportunity of working in a 'club-like' atmosphere. A tendency towards a more formal chamber would be expected to be consolidated. In view of this fundamental dilemma and before the last round of enlargement the European Council has changed its way of working. The heads of state or government and the Commission President have tried to reinitiate the original concept of a 'fireplace meeting'.

Looking at the productivity of the European Council, here defined as output items per year according to headlines of the Presidency conclusions, the evidence shows that there is no major change (see Figure 2.3).

One question becomes evident: how can one explain the European Council's ongoing performance? According to conventional wisdom, the intergovernmentalist school of thought would expect that an ever more heterogeneous body of self-confident politicians, each focused on her/his national interests and armed with the power of veto, would feel little incentive to achieve sustainable decisions which might affect their position back home. Indeed, without a clear hierarchy, and in the absence of majority voting, the probability of achieving mutually accepted agreements is predicted to be low. Nevertheless, irrespective of these trends, a surprising dynamism of high productivity in regard to outcomes can be observed – including after expansion. This striking fact can be explained by a number of factors.

One major point is that the capacity of the European Council to reach consensus rests in the hands of the highest national decision-makers, who have developed their own specific 'rules of the game'. Such rules define the appropriate behaviour of these 'elite club' members.

Exploiting concepts and findings of constructivist approaches and of sociological institutionalism, we assume that the political leaders have, as a result of their regular and intensive exchanges, learned to adapt their preferences. Arguing in the 'club' has some lasting effects on each national position even if the impact may be only observed in a medium-term perspective. In this light, the European Council can be seen as more than an arena of power games, but a body which shapes the behaviour of its members in the medium term. In this respect there is another remarkable feature: as a general rule, with very few exceptions, newly elected heads of

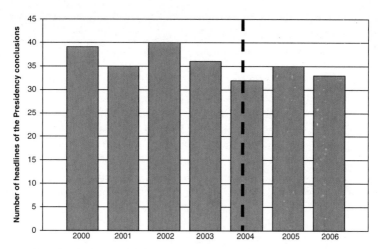

Source: Overview by Verena Schäfer and Niklas Helwig, based on the headlines of the Presidency Conclusions, European Council 2000–2006.

Figure 2.3   Productivity of the European Council

government quickly adopt the negotiation and consultation style of their more experienced colleagues. This is said also to be the case for the majority of the top politicians from the new members.

Beside the learning and socialization processes, the creation of comprehensive negotiation packages (i.e. 'big bargains', cf. Laffan 2005, p. 474; Moravcsik 1998) remains a prerequisite towards finding an agreement: only the top political level can settle demands and concessions over a broader scope of policy fields among the member states. In such 'horse-trading', the preferences of member states do not change considerably, but are rather combined in a laborious exchange process which usually results in an agreement which is mutually perceived as being positive (i.e. a 'win–win situation').

In order to obtain these results, considerable time is required. In addition to their role in the treaty texts as 'providers of impetus and definers of general guidelines' (see above) the members of the European Council must actually deal with concrete issues in detail when this is necessary to make 'hard' decisions. Major decisions are prepared in small steps and are then adopted in an intensive process over several levels and after several sessions. With a 'night of the long knives' (cf. de Schoutheete 2002, pp. 41–3) a negotiation dynamic is to be observed which often leads to ambiguous compromises coupled with some surprising agreements concerning even trivial points. It often appears that consent can only be reached by meaningless formulations ('consensus by nonsense') or by a respective increase in complexity ('consensus by complexity'). In ongoing controversies, new timetables with further postponements to later dates are arranged, referred to as 'left-overs' or 'rendezvous formulas'. Compromises often only become available if the majority of members respond to deviating interests with exception rules (i.e. 'opt-outs').

The European Council's working methods were also the subject of some conscious adaptations, notably the 'Rules for the Organisation of the Proceedings of the European Council' which were adopted at the summit in Seville in June 2002. These measures were intended to rationalize the agenda and improve the efficiency of meetings, in response to the difficulties in coordination caused by input from different Council configurations, as well as the pressures on time caused by the increase in the number of members. The preparation of meetings of the European Council was to be managed by the new General Affairs and External Relations Council, which would draw up four weeks in advance, on a Presidency proposal, an annotated draft agenda distinguishing between different classes of items proposed. Summits should normally last one day, and should not be disrupted by meetings in the margins with third parties. The Presidency was to ensure that business is conducted smoothly, taking measures to promote 'the best possible use of the time available, such as organising the order in which items are discussed, limiting speaking time and determining the order in which contributors speak'.

All these patterns have 'survived' the accession of 12 more members. Indeed, it can be argued that with more and different preferences the range of package deals has even been augmented. New members want to see their specific problems dealt with and have their 'voice' heard. Negotiations leading to the mandate for the 2007 Intergovernmental Conference again saw the use of all the conventional means to arrive at a consensus – thus the night of long knives, postponements in the QMV issue, 'opt-outs' for the Charter of Fundamental Rights and so on.

Power and Influence on Decision-Making

Considering the political leverage of the European Council, we need to look at the distribution of power and influence within this top body of the Union (cf. Tallberg 2007).

One major issue is the cleavage between 'large' and 'small' members. This divide between states was and is particularly important in the case of the Union's institutional architecture, in which the smaller aim at 'equal participation'. Overall, the historical record and some anecdotal evidence suggest that debates in the European Council have been more frequently led by the heads of government of larger member states (cf. de Schoutheete 2006, p. 46). Those members bring more resources and leverage into negotiation packages but, if a smaller country is serious about an issue it is – as a veto player – in a strong position. Although perhaps less obvious, the interests of smaller members are thus not marginalized. Depending on the matter, the European Commission President or single heads of government of smaller countries may also play an influential role next to the European Council President (cf. Christiansen 2002; Delors 2004, p. 219; Laffan 2005). There are good reasons to believe that these patterns have survived the last round of accession.

One issue in the power game is the pivotal role of the French–German tandem. In the past, intensive cooperation between the respective leaders has frequently led to the achievement of fundamental compromises which are accepted as useful by other members (cf. de Schoutheete 2006, p. 57). With enlargement, this two-party leadership is generally seen to have lost its energy for further steps and its impact on the other partners. As the French–German couple was, after the negative French referendum, hampered for two years by one 'lame duck', it is certainly too early to predict the final agony of this tandem. More interesting is to speculate as to how the need of the European Council for some kind of leadership is met: given insights of game theory there is an inbuilt demand for some kind of a 'cooperating or collective hegemon' or an informal 'directoire' among the 'great powers'. Such a leadership can only work, however, if it takes properly into account the overall interest of the European Union and the concerns of the smaller and less prominent members.

Independent from the matter of size, there have been recurring cleavages between groups of more progressive and more sceptical countries in terms of further integration. The conventional wisdom of the intergovernmentalist school expects that the new member countries – being sensitive to their newly acquired sovereignty – will be less integration oriented than at least some of the older members. Though some newer members have shown strong tendencies to reinforce the camp of sovereignty-oriented countries, it would be premature to claim that the whole direction of the European Council will change. So far, lessons of the past show that members who are generally more hesitant will nonetheless agree to steps upgrading the EU institutional architecture if the relevant package deals also include issues of their own vital national interests.

Individual capacities are also relevant for the power game. Frequently connected with the duration and participation of successful presidencies (cf. de Schoutheete 2006, pp. 46–7), influential participants have also come from smaller member states. A good example is the present Prime Minister of Luxembourg, Jean-Claude Juncker (cf. de Schoutheete 2002, p. 31). The

top politicians of new member states will have to earn such trust from their
colleagues.

The Presidency

A major issue for the internal life of the European Council is the performance of the president. This person and the machinery behind him/her
play a major role in the preparation, conduct and follow-up of the session.
The sessions of the European Council have often been referred to as the
'hour of the presidency' (Hayes-Renshaw and Wallace 2006, p. 178).
Politicians of the country holding presidency have often seized the opportunity to develop their own profile vis-à-vis their domestic voters as well as
internationally.

Aside from the usual tasks of the formal chairing of the sessions, the role
of the president is to reach consent among members. In controversial questions, the presidency uses the so-called 'confessional procedure' (cf. Hayes-
Renshaw and Wallace 2006). Given the increase in numbers and interest,
this brokering function of the chairperson has become even more important. Chancellor Merkel has used this procedure well before the Berlin
informal session and before and during the June summit.

CONCLUSIONS

Looking at the long-established functions and the internal life of the
European Council, therefore, the evidence collected indicates that enlargement has not led to blockage at the apex of the institutional architecture.
Assessment of the enlarged European Council so far – taking Polish opposition to the Reform Treaty well into consideration – cannot be dominated
by a 'gloom and doom' view pointing at new and inexperienced, sove-
reignty-driven, member states. In major decisions such as the Financial
Perspectives and the 'Energy Policy for Europe' action plan, the fusion perspective is more valid. The quantity of the output and its major substance
have not changed in a significant way, although the European Council continues to put vital national issues into the EU arena. No major new con-
stellations could be identified in terms of internal dynamics either.

It may simply be too early to make any definitive judgements, since only
a short time has passed. Moreover, there is one particular element arising
from enlargement which had not yet happened at the time of writing in
2007, namely the assumption of the presidency of the European Council
by a new member state. If the Lisbon Treaty is ratified, the result will be
that only Slovenia will have played this role, in the first half of 2008. The

proposal to create an elected president of the European Council, which was retained in the Lisbon Treaty, has responded to a variety of concerns. One of the main arguments for such a change, however, has related to the impact of enlargement. With a rotating presidency among the 27, 'conventional wisdom' doubted whether the European Council could always expect to have a professional and experienced chairperson, especially – so the argument went – from among the 'provincial' heads of government of the smaller new members. In fact, the new elected president will affect productivity and the internal dynamics only to a limited degree. It is possible that an ambitious incumbent might be tempted to distinguish him- or herself from the role of chairperson vis-à-vis the members of the European Council. In this case, and disregarding the treaty, he/she could place himself/herself in the position of 'president of the Union' (meaning not only of the European Council).

However, the most likely prospect, even with an elected president, is for 'business as usual' – or even more so. Overall, if we take lessons from the past and look at the experience of the last few years, no major changes in the role of the European Council are to be expected in a Union with 27 members, based on the Lisbon Treaty. If we follow the set of expectations elaborated above, moreover, the European Council will play an enhanced role in the future development of the EU system and its institutional architecture. It is not surprising that the European Council, and especially its leadership structure, should have become central points in the debates over the institutional architecture in the Constitutional and Reform Treaties. The heads of state or government have repeatedly confirmed de facto the tasks of the European Council as an agenda-setter, highest decision-maker, global actor and constitutional architect. Enlargement of the European Council will certainly not lead to a diminution of its institutional role – providing the central arena for dealing with essential common problems.

REFERENCES

Christiansen, T. (2002), 'The role of Supranational Actors in EU Treaty Reform', in G. Falkner and J. Richardson (eds), *Journal of European Public Policy, Special Issue: EU Treaty Reform as a Three-Level Process: Historical Institutionalist Perspectives*, Oxford, pp. 33–54.

Delors, J. (2004), *Erinnerungen eines Europäers*, Berlin: Parthas Verlag.

de Schoutheete, P. (2002), '*The European Council*', in J. Peterson and M. Shackleton (eds), *The Institutions of the European Union*, New York: Oxford University Press, pp. 21–46.

de Schoutheete, P. (2006), 'The European Council', in J. Peterson and M. Shackleton (eds), *The Institutions of the European Union*, New York: Oxford University Press, pp. 37–59.

European Council (2007), *Presidency Conclusions*, http://europa.eu/european_council/conclusions/index_en.htm, 6 November 2007.

Federal Constitutional Court (1993), BVerfGE 89, 155, Maastricht.

Hayes-Renshaw, F. and Wallace, H. (2006), *The Council of Ministers*, Houndsmill and New York: Palgrave Macmillan.

Hill, C. (1993), 'The Capability–Expectations Gap, or Conceptualizing Europe's International Role', *Journal of Common Market Studies*, **3**, 305–28.

Hill, C. (2006), 'The Directoire and the Problem of a Coherent EU Foreign Policy', *CFSP Forum*, **4** (6), 1–4.

Hoffmann, S. (1966), 'Obstinate or Obsolete: The Fate of the Nation-State and Case of Western Europe', *Daedalus*, **95** (3), 862–915.

Kassim, H. and Menon, A. (2003), *The Principal–Agent Approach and the Study of the European Union: A Provisional Assessment*, Working Paper Series, European Research Institute, University of Birmingham.

Laffan, B. (2005), 'Der schwierige Weg zur Europäischen Verfassung: von der Humboldt-Rede Außenminister Fischers bis zum Abschluss der Regierungskonferenz', in M. Jopp and S. Matl (eds), *Der Vertrag über eine Verfassung für Europa: Analysen zur Konstitutionalisierung der EU*, Baden-Baden: Nomos, pp. 473–92.

Linsenmann, I., Meyer, C. and Wessels, W. (eds) (2007), *Economic Government of the EU: A Balance Sheet of New Modes of Policy Coordination*, Houndsmill: Palgrave Macmillan.

Lippert, B. (2003a), 'Die Erweiterungspolitik der Europäischen Union', in W. Weidenfeld and W. Wessels (eds), *Jahrbuch der Europäischen Integration 2002/2003*, Bonn: Europa Union Verlag, pp. 417–30.

Lippert, B. (2003b), 'Der Erweiterungsgipfel von Kopenhagen: Abschluss der Beitrittsverhandlungen und Neubeginn für die EU', *Integration*, **1** (3), 48–65.

Lisbon Reform Treaty (2007), http://www.consilium.europa.eu, 24 October 2007.

Louis, J.V. and Ronse, T. (2005), *L'ordre juridique de l'Union européenne*, Dossiers de droit européen, 13, Genf: Helbing & Lichtenhahn.

Ludlow, P. (2005), Die Führung der Europäischen Union durch den Europäischen Rat: Übergang oder Krise?, *Integration*, **1** (5), 3–15.

Milward, A.S. (2005), *The European Rescue of the Nation-State*, 2nd edition, London and New York: Routledge.

Monnet, J. (1976), *Mémoires*, Paris: Fayard.

Moravcsik, A. (1993), 'Preferences and Power in the European Community: A Liberal Intergovernmentalist Approach', *Journal of Common Market Studies*, **31** (4), 473–524.

Moravcsik, A. (1998), *The Choice for Europe: Social Purpose and State Power from Messina to Maastricht*, London: Cornell University Press.

Morgenthau, H.J. [1948] (2005), *Politics among Nations: The Struggle for Power and Peace*, New York: McGraw-Hill Higher Education.

Paris summit (1972), *Commniqué*, http://aei.pitt.edu/1919/, 5 November 2007.

Pierson, P. (2000), 'Path Dependence, Increasing Returns, and the Study of Politics', *American Political Science Review*, **94** (2), 251–67.

Pollack, M. (2003), *The Engines of European Integration, Delegation, Agency, and Agenda Setting in the EU*, New York: Oxford University Press.

Pollack, M. (2005), 'Theorizing EU Policy-Making', in H. Wallace, W. Wallace and M. Pollack (eds), *Policy-Making in the European Union*, 5th edition, Oxford and New York: Oxford University Press, pp. 13–48.

Scharpf, F.W. (1997), *Games Real Actors Play: Actor-Centered Institutionalism in Policy Research*, Boulder, CO and Oxford: Westview Press.

Tallberg, J. (2007), *Bargaining Power in the European Council*, Report No. 1, Swedish Institute for European Policy Studies, Stockholm.

Tindemans, L. (1975), 'Die Europäische Union', in *EG-Bulletin*, Beilage 1/76, 29 December.

Treaty establishing a Constitution for Europe (2004), http://eur-lex.europa.eu/en/treaties/dat/12004V/htm/12004V.html, 24 October 2007.

Wallace, H. (2000), 'The Institutional Setting', in H. Wallace and W. Wallace (eds), *Policy-Making in the European Union*, Oxford: Oxford University Press, pp. 3–38.

Waltz, K. (1979), *Theory of International Politics*, New York: McGraw-Hill Higher Education.

Wessels, W. (1980), *Der Europäische Rat. Stabilisierung statt Integration? Gesichte, Entwicklung und Zukunft der EG-Gipfelkonferenzen*, Bonn: Europa Union Verlag.

Wessels, W. (2000), *Die Öffnung des Staates: Modelle und Wirklichkeit grenzüberschreitender Verwaltungspraxis 1960–1995*, Opladen: Leske & Budrich.

Wessels, W. (2005a), 'The Constitutional Treaty – Three Readings from a Fusion Perspective', *Journal of Common Market Studies*, Annual Review 2004/2005, 11–36.

Wessels, W. (2005b), 'Die institutionelle Architektur des Verfassungsvertrags: Ein Meilenstein in der Integrationskonstruktion', in M. Jopp and S. Matl (eds), *Der Vertrag über eine Verfassung für Europa: Analysen zur Konstitutionalisierung der EU*, Baden-Baden: Nomos, pp. 45–85.

Wessels, W. (2007), 'Europäischer Rat', in W. Weidenfeld and W. Wessels (eds), *Europa von A bis Z: Taschenbuch der europäischen Integration*, 10th edition, Baden-Baden: Nomos, pp. 207–11.

Wessels, W. and Schäfer, V. (2007), 'The European Council in Theoretical Perspectives: The Principals on a Fusion Path, Paper presented at the Tenth Biennial Conference of the European Union Studies Association in Montreal, 19 May.

3. Surviving enlargement: how has the Council managed?

Edward Best and Pierpaolo Settembri[*]

The Council of the European Union – the Council of Ministers – has been the subject of concerns about the impact of enlargement since before 1995. Indeed these have been more prominent and more focused than in the case of the other institutions, given that it is here that the increase in numbers is most directly and obviously reflected. Some issues have concerned perceptions of fairness, given the significant increase in the relative number of small countries enjoying over-representation in the institutional system. Most, however, have related to effectiveness. Would there not be a risk of paralysis if decisions had to be taken between 27 or more countries without major change in the rules? How would meetings be managed with so many delegations?

This chapter therefore looks at the Council, three years after the 2004 enlargement, in order to assess what has actually changed in how the Council does business, and what significance enlargement may have had. It first addresses the methodological challenges which are involved in identifying and evaluating the specific 'impact' of enlargement on the Council, and presents the data and parameters which are used in the present analysis. It then looks back at the initiatives taken by the Council to prepare for the enlargement with regard to decision-making rules, languages, the General Secretariat, and Council working methods. The third section assesses how the Council has 'survived' the doubling of membership, and whether this survival has been accompanied by qualitative changes in the nature of Council work, on the basis of original quantitative evidence and qualitative insights from interviews and case studies.[1] The conclusion reviews the salience of these results and sets out some next steps for further research.

THE METHODOLOGICAL CHALLENGE

We are cautious about simple measurements of the 'impact' of enlargement on the Council. There has been a tendency in recent years to embark on comparisons implicitly based on an assumption that the Council is facing essentially the same policy agenda, the main difference being the expansion of membership; to compare situations immediately before and after 1 May 2004; and to fail to take into account the influence of other actors. We argue that a more sophisticated approach to understanding change is required.

First, enlargement has not been a matter of overnight change. The EU had been talking about institutional reform in preparation for enlargement for almost a decade. The potential impact had already begun to shape debates over Council procedures in 1994. The accession of Austria, Finland, Sweden and, as it then seemed, Norway saw the beginning of wrangling over the system of qualified majority voting (QMV) (and of a remarkable boom in academic debate on the measurement of voting power) which has lasted until the present. Pre-accession cooperation began in the second half of the 1990s. The new member states were then 'phased in' to Council business, and there was significant anticipatory adaptation in terms of working methods and linguistic capacities, as described in the next section. Arrangements for the interim period consisted of an information and consultation procedure following formal conclusion of the negotiations, through an 'interim committee' in place as of 19 December 2002, and active observer status following signature of the Treaty of Accession on 16 April 2003.

Second, one must distinguish between *levels* where change occurs. The discussions about preparation for enlargement have taken place at two levels: first, the adaptation of the basic *rules* of legislative decision-making – primarily the scope and modalities of the system of QMV, as well as the scope of 'co-legislative' interaction with the European Parliament, which had to be pursued through treaty change; second, institutional *practice*, which was to be dealt with through an internal initiative (notably the adoption of a Code of Conduct). The renewed 'constitutional' debate is in part a continued discussion as to whether changes in practice within the current rules (i.e. first-order change) are proving sufficient to ensure continued performance at a generally satisfactory level in terms of quantity and quality, or whether change in the formal rules themselves (i.e. second-order change) is needed to guarantee continued stability of the system. The specificities of these two dimensions need to be taken into account while evaluating continuity and change.

Third, the work of the Council cannot be approached in isolation from other institutional *actors*. For example, a sound evaluation of its activities must take into account changes in the specific input coming from the Commission, notably the quantity and the quality of proposals. At the same time, in many areas the Council is nowadays a co-legislator with the EP, and its performance cannot be judged independently from that of the Parliament.

To respond to these challenges, the chapter tries to go beyond usual comparisons on institutional activity. On the one hand, it proposes a new way of using quantitative data to assess the nature of the post-enlargement Council and, in broader terms, the decision-making capacity of the EU.[2] On the other hand, it draws examples from across sectors in order to provide some qualitative observations, which can shed light on how the specific issues introduced by enlargement have been dealt with. The qualitative input focuses in particular on three sectors, which present both different procedures and different kinds of policy: agriculture; environment; and employment and social affairs. This consists of 24 interviews carried out with relevant officials in the Council Secretariat, Commission and Parliament, as well as particular member states.

ANTICIPATING ENLARGEMENT

Measures adopted in anticipation of enlargement have mainly concerned four aspects, at different levels: decision-making rules, the language regime, the staffing of the General Secretariat, and working methods within the Council.

Decision-Making Rules

Enlargement has had a major impact on decision-making rules, although these have been the subject of debate for other reasons since the 1960s. It has intensified pressures to extend further the *scope* of QMV as increasing numbers of Council members inevitably raise the spectre of paralysis under rules of unanimity. In terms of the *system* of QMV, it has invalidated the original principles by which votes were apportioned and the threshold was calculated. In the process, it has accentuated sensitivities about the relative influence of large and small countries and encouraged a more direct and explicit relationship between population and representation.

The original definition of the threshold and the distribution of votes reflected a set of equations concerning the implications for decision-making of different combinations of the three large, two medium and one small member states. The resulting threshold of around 71 per cent (12 out of 17 votes) was subsequently maintained, as was the principle of group-

Table 3.1 Relation between qualified majority threshold as share of total
weighted votes and as minimum share of total EU population
required to achieve that threshold

	EC6	EC9	EC10	EC12	EU15	'EU27'	EU25	EU27
Share of total votes	70.6	70.7	71.4	71.1	71.3	70.9	72.3	73.9
Share of population	67.7	70.6	70.1	63.3	58.2	50.2	55.5	58.2

Note: Column for 'EU27' represents an extrapolation of the system in force for EU15 to
EU27, with voting threshold set at 95/134.

Source: EC6 to 'EU27', Commission of the European Communities 2000, pp. 29–30;
EU25 and EU27, own calculations.

ing countries in rather loosely based clusters. The first political arguments
about continuing extrapolation came in the run-up to the 1995 enlargement, as the UK and Spain resisted the proportional increase of the blocking minority from 23 to 26.[3] The result was the Council Decision of 29
March 1994 containing the 'Ioannina compromise', by which it was agreed
that, if a group of countries representing between 23 and 25 votes were
opposed to a measure, discussion would continue.

In this context, as the prospect of eventual expansion across the continent was being digested, analyses began to be made concerning the impact
of enlargement. The implications of much greater numbers were openly
discussed, usually in terms of a possible negative impact. The relationship
between share of votes and share of population became explicit. The
Council Secretariat, as well as a growing mass of academics, produced
figures indicating that extrapolation beyond a certain level of enlargement
would, among other things, stretch beyond acceptable limits the relation
between the qualified majority threshold as a share of total weighted votes
and the corresponding minimum share of total EU population required to
achieve that threshold (see Table 3.1). This shift was primarily due to the
accession of an increasing proportion of smaller countries that are over-
represented in the system of 'degressive proportionality'.

The 1995 Report of the Reflection Group which was established in
advance of the 1996 IGC expressed concern about the consequences of
maintaining unanimity in a Union of 30 members, stressed the need to take
population adequately into account, and noted that '[f]or some there could
also be problems with the accession of very small States' (para. 108). These
issues were echoed in the Commission's Opinion for the 1996 IGC, which
was entitled 'Reinforcing Political Union and Preparing for Enlargement'.

The challenge concerned not only the apparent perspective of larger (and older) member states being outvoted by small newcomers. It also concerned the presidency. The sensitive question arose as to whether rotation should be maintained, given unspoken doubts as to the practical capacity of countries with relatively very small administrations to manage Council business. There was concern about how the EU would be represented under the pre-Amsterdam 'troika' system (current, previous and following presidencies) in a Union of up to 30 members. Even before the logical prospect of an alphabetical trio of Latvia, Lithuania and Luxembourg could come about, the new order of rotation adopted in 1994 for the period until June 2003 was therefore shaped so as to ensure that a large member state would be part of any troika.

By this stage, it was clear that the voting arrangements would have to be modified, either by re-weighting the votes or by introducing some new criteria reflecting population. The 1996–97 IGC did not take a final decision in this respect. Although the prospect of enlargement was the factor which made change unavoidable, the immediate reasons for the failure at Amsterdam to agree on what to do arose from the sensitivity of issues at stake between existing member states. On the one hand, there was resistance to demographically based re-weighting on the part of the smaller members of two pairs of countries which had traditionally enjoyed equal voting weight despite large differences in population (Belgium–Netherlands, France–Germany). On the other, there was the 'special situation' of Spain, which had entered the Community with a package of representation based on two Commissioners, like the biggest four countries, but only eight votes compared to their ten. If all of the largest five countries were to lose their second Commissioner – as was agreed at Amsterdam in principle in view of enlargement – what should happen to compensate Spain?

The arrangements agreed at Nice in December 2000 include three criteria. The first, adopted in advance without controversy, is that there must be a numerical majority of member states. Proposals for a dual majority of states and citizens, however, were not adopted. The votes were increased and re-weighted in a way that was strongly shaped by political equations. France insisted on retaining parity with Germany despite a notable difference in population. Demography was recognized explicitly in a third possible criterion. A member state can ask for verification that a coalition of countries representing a qualified majority of votes (in EU27 nearly 74 per cent) represents at least 62 per cent of the total EU population, whereas the minimum possible share of population for a winning coalition is around 58 per cent. As of late 2007 this has never happened.

Since it was felt that Spain could not be given the same number of votes as the biggest countries, the Spanish question was answered by giving Spain the same ability to block a decision as the biggest countries. The negotiations resulted in the following set of equations: if the blocking minority were to be set at 88, then any three of the biggest four countries plus the smallest, Malta, could block a decision $((3 \times 29) + 3 > 88)$ and so could a coalition of any two of the biggest countries plus Spain plus Malta $((2 \times 29) + 27 + 3 = 88)$ (Galloway 2001, p. 84). The Spanish government maintained a vigorous defence of this state of affairs in the Convention and the Intergovernmental Conference, but this was dropped with the change of government in March 2004. The Constitutional Treaty signed in October 2004 therefore included the provision for a shift to a double majority of 55 per cent of states and 65 per cent of citizens (with the additional condition that a blocking majority must consist of at least four countries, and a further qualification that discussions would continue during a transitional period if there was opposition to a proposal from countries representing three-quarters of the blocking minority).

The defence of Nice was then taken up in negotiations for the Lisbon Treaty, however, by Poland, which had received the same institutional representation as Spain in view of its similar population size. The detailed mandate adopted by the European Council in June 2007 not only put off the shift to the dual majority to November 2014 but provided for the Nice arrangements to be requested in particular cases until March 2017.

Languages

The number of official languages has risen from 11 to 23. In order to manage this increase, a series of preparatory measures was adopted.

Under the new language regime, full interpretation should be available at European Council and Council meetings, Conciliation Committee meetings and an agreed list of up to 20 preparatory bodies. Some 50 preparatory bodies would have no interpretation. For the rest, a request system was created: an envelope of €2 million per year per language was made available; countries requesting interpretation for a lower cost would receive part of the money as travel costs, and those requesting more would have to pay.[4]

The recruitment process, however, did not go as quickly as hoped, given a shortage of suitable candidates in most of the new languages. Indeed in the case of Maltese, the competitions for interpreters in 2003 and 2006 yielded no successful candidates at all. According to Commission figures published in February 2007, the level of satisfaction of demand in 2006 for interpretation into new member states' languages (excluding Maltese) at the Council was 85 per cent for active interpretation and 82 per cent for passive, only Polish being fully available.[5] Translation was managed by the decision only to translate 'core documents'[6] into all languages as well as

limits on length of documents. However, the insufficient number of trans-
lators in 2004 resulted in quality problems for translations into the EU10
languages, even as the new measures for control of translation led to some
over-capacity and low productivity for EU15 languages (ECA 2006; EP
2006).

One should note that the increase in the number of languages in use
has not only concerned the new member states. Irish became an official
and working language on 18 June 2005 (coming into practical effect on
1 January 2007) as requested by the Irish government in November 2004
and agreed in a Council Regulation of 13 June 2005. This was partly
influenced by enlargement. Although Irish is the first official language of
Ireland and English the second, Ireland had agreed in 1972 that Irish
should only be used for the European treaties and a few other special cases.
The fact that Malta (where Maltese is the national language but English is
likewise one of two official languages) was given the right to have official-
language status for Maltese encouraged the Irish government now to
request a change in the status of Irish.

The Council also adopted Conclusions in June 2005 on the use of languages other than the official languages of the Union 'whose status is recognised by the Constitution of a Member State in the whole or a part of its
territory or whose use as a national language is authorised by law'. This was
a response to the request of the Spanish government in December 2004 for
official recognition to be given to Basque, Galician and Catalan/Valencian.
The Council could authorize official use of such languages at the Council
on the basis of an administrative arrangement, with costs covered by the
requesting member state, for 'making public of acts adopted in codecision,
speeches to a meeting of the Council and possibly other Union Institutions
or bodies, and written communications to Union Institutions and bodies'.[7]
An agreement was reached with the Commission in December 2005, by
which these languages can be used by citizens in written communications to
the Commission, with translation carried out by the Spanish authorities.[8]
The Bureau of the Parliament initially voted against any such recognition
but very narrowly voted in July 2006 in favour of allowing citizens to com-
municate with the Parliament in their own language.

Moreover, the sensitivities which have manifested themselves about language usage arise primarily from some of the larger older member states.
For example, the Employment Committee had since its creation translated
documents into only English, French and German, provoking complaints
from Spain and Italy. Italy protested vociferously in early 2005 when Italian
seemed to be downgraded at Commission press conferences. In March 2006
the European Ombudsman, in response to a complaint from an association
for the defence of the German language about the non-availability of

German-language documents on the Dutch and Luxembourg Presidency websites, pressed the Council to promote the uses of German – a call immediately backed by the leaders, both German, of the two biggest political groups in the European Parliament.

The General Secretariat

The Secretariat has expanded gradually as a result of the expansion of the Union's activities and the successive enlargements. From 238 members of staff in 1958, it had reached 603 by 1970. It doubled in size with the accession of Denmark, Ireland and the UK, totalling 1475 in 1975. It then leapt again in the first half of the 1990s both as a result of the new responsibilities arising post-Maastricht in CFSP and JHA, and because of the accession of Austria, Finland and Sweden, reaching 2290 in 1995. Likewise, the increase to 3038 by 2005 is due not only to enlargement but also to the arrival of military personnel and the creation of specific structures for the Common Security and Defence Policy (Hayes-Renshaw and Wallace 2006, pp. 103–4).[9] This entailed the creation of two new directorates within DG E, a Situation Centre (which became operational in January 2007) and the INFOSEC office for the secure management of information, as well as support for the Military Staff and other new bodies connected with crisis-management operations.

The increase in staff related to the 2004 enlargement was proportionately lower than on previous occasions. A task force on administrative preparations for enlargement was set up in October 2001, reporting in March 2002 (Council 2002a). In terms of personnel, the Secretariat did not follow a simple extrapolation of the approaches adopted for preceding enlargements (which would have resulted in an increase of between 1320 and 1420 new officials) but a 'controlled approach' which made it possible to limit the increase to some 670 officials (25 per cent as opposed to 51 per cent) 'by limiting additional new posts to those which are strictly necessary for the new functions resulting from enlargement and by implementing an in-depth rationalisation of the translation services' (Council 2004, pp. 12–13). A further 97 posts were requested for the 2007 enlargement.

In July 2007, however, the Parliament and Council still expressed concern about the progress of recruitment in relation to the 2004 and 2007 enlargement across the institutions.[10]

Working Methods

The operation of the Council had been reviewed on several previous occasions, and enlargement has not been the only pressure for change. The need to manage the expansion of the Union's scope of activity, for example, had already in December 1988 prompted the Council to agree that each presidency should try to regroup subjects in order to limit the formations in which the Council had to sit. There were nonetheless some 22 formations in the 1990s (including such specialized areas as Youth Affairs, Tourism or Civil Protection). The number of authorized Council configurations was then formally reduced from 19 to 16 at the Helsinki European Council in 1999, and then to the current nine formal configurations agreed at Seville in 2002 (including a new General Affairs and External Relations Council). This was accompanied by a rationalization of Council working parties, from around 300 to the present formal figure of some 160 (plus subgroups).

A working party was set up with a broader agenda following the Amsterdam Treaty which in early 1999 presented a 'Report on the Operation of the Council with an Enlarged Union in Prospect' (Council 1999).[11] This process of reflection led to a series of decisions taken at the Seville European Council in June 2002 on the basis of a report from the Secretary-General (Council 2002b). In addition to changing the Council configurations, these included a multi-annual strategic programme for the following three years; an annual operating programme and new provisions for greater cooperation between presidencies; the chairing of certain working parties by the General Secretariat; new provisions on opening certain Council meetings to the public; and guidelines regarding the conduct of meetings. These guidelines were further developed in a 2003 Code of Conduct (Council 2003b), which then became an annex to the Council Rules of Procedure (Council 2006b, Annex V). With effective preparation of meetings becoming all the more essential, the Code suggested a rationalization of the referral of reports between Coreper and working parties; active preparation of meetings by the Presidency, including requests for written input in advance, whenever possible, on behalf of groups of like-minded countries; and maximum exchange of information in advance of Coreper meetings, including greater use of the groups that prepare Coreper's proceedings.[12] The guidelines for the efficient conduct of meetings included the rule not to place items on the agenda simply for presentation or information; the proscription in principle of full table rounds; the fixing of time limits by the Presidency; the avoidance of simple repetition of points made by previous speakers; the submission of drafting proposals rather than simple disagreement; and the principle that silence should to be taken as agreement.

These guidelines have been followed in different ways in different sectors, and under different presidencies. The Special Committee on Agriculture (SCA) adopted a text (revised in April 2005) highlighting relevant elements

of the guidelines and 'additional arrangements to make the principles operational' in tackling enlargement. For example, the Secretariat is encouraged
to use its judgement in listing the delegations which support different
options to help gauge support; working party chairmen are not to give oral
reports; 'targeted tasking' could be arranged by the Presidency between
meetings to consult on specific problems with concerned Agriculture
Counsellors/Attachés; and 'delegations are asked to exercise self-discipline
in requesting the inclusion of items under "other business" '.[13]

MEASURING THE IMPACT OF ENLARGEMENT

The evidence presented here is based on a comparison between the period
January–December 2003 and the period July 2005–June 2006. Most of the
changes in basic decision-making rules which were agreed in advance of
enlargement (i.e. scope and modalities of majority voting) had already been
adopted before the first period under consideration. The main exception is
the application since 1 January 2005 of codecision and QMV to most measures concerning asylum, immigration and the movement of persons
(except legal immigration and family law).[14] Otherwise, the decisions taken
by the Council in the two periods compared are therefore generally subject
to the same formal rules. The difference concerns internal and inter-institutional practice before and after enlargement.

Global Trends

The overall output of the Council in terms of acts adopted has remained
broadly similar in quantitative terms, dropping from a total of 479 in the
first of the two 12-month periods under consideration to 455 in the
second.[15] Comparison of the two periods indicates that there has not been
any major change with regard to the 'ease' with which decisions are taken
within the Council.

A partial exception to this is the reduction in the number of acts adopted
by unanimity. The overall amount of 'Community legislation' adopted by
unanimity is significantly lower (42 as compared to 63 acts) after enlargement, and the decrease is much greater than in the case of acts adopted by
QMV (down from 203 to 181). The difference between the two procedures
is even more striking if judged by the number of acts that are, in the
Council's definition, 'legally binding in or for the Member States': whereas
the number of acts adopted by QMV has remained almost identical (from
125 to 119), the number of acts adopted by unanimity has halved (see
Figure 3.1).[16]

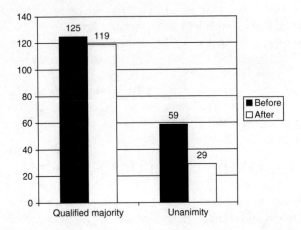

*Figure 3.1   Number of acts that are 'legally binding in or for the Member
              States' adopted before/after enlargement, by voting rule*

The change from unanimity to QMV for most of Title IV TEC (visas,
asylum, immigration and other policies related to free movement of
persons) as of January 2005 seems to have contributed marginally to this
shift. For the rest, it is not possible to establish from the data available to
what extent this reflects change in the underlying policy agenda and/or decisions not to submit proposals subject to unanimity in view of possible
blockage.

The contestation of Community legislation adopted under qualified
majority has increased very marginally and has remained stable for most
important acts (see Figure 3.2).[17] In fact, given the somewhat smaller
number of acts adopted after enlargement, the average number of times a
member state opposed (by voting against or abstaining) the adoption of a
legislative act subject to QMV has declined from 3.5 to 2.4.

Broadly speaking, enlargement has not entailed a slower decision-
making process: on the contrary, the adoption is, on average, more expeditious. Predictably, important legislation takes longer to be decided upon
than ordinary or minor, but there is no significant difference between the
EU15 and the EU25. Ordinary acts have actually been decided significantly
faster since enlargement (see Figure 3.3).

Interestingly, the situation changes if the data are presented by procedure
(see Figure 3.4): whereas acts under consultation are decided increasingly
rapidly, decisions under codecision take longer (22.7 per cent). In fact, it
took 4.5 per cent longer for the EU25 to adopt 69 codecision files than it
took the EU15 to adopt 81.

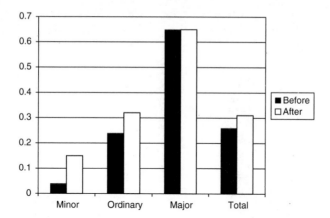

*Figure 3.2   Average number of states abstaining or opposing the adoption
of Community legislation under QMV, by importance*

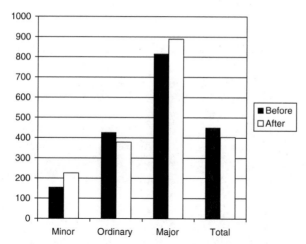

*Figure 3.3   Average number of days necessary to adopt Community
legislation by importance*

Evidence from Specific Policy Areas

The previous results suggest that the Council has rather successfully
adapted its own working methods. Yet, the modalities and the depth of this
adaptation may differ from one policy area to another.

In agriculture, there has not been an increase in the length of procedures:
adopting Community legislation in this area took 5 per cent less time after

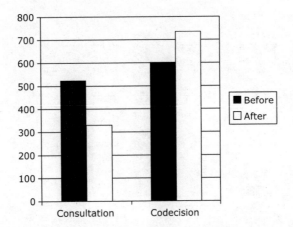

Figure 3.4   *Average number of days necessary to adopt Community legislation by procedure*

enlargement, and the process is consistently shorter regardless of the salience of the act under consideration. The increased number of languages may have caused delays in receiving the proposal and in carrying out the jurist-linguist work, but this has not resulted in a longer process. There could be various explanations for this: for example, there may be a slight increase in the number of meetings required to reach a conclusion since less can be achieved in each meeting (although the complexity of many recent dossiers may be just as important). Enlargement has further increased the importance of the Presidency and Council Secretariat, as well as the Commission, in preparing meetings and achieving results. Also, the average number of times that a file is discussed by ministers as a 'B point' has almost halved, from 1.26 to 0.68. Voting practices, and the importance of the 'shadow of the vote', are not felt to have changed significantly. Table rounds do still take place in the SCA and the Agriculture Council when there is an orientation debate, but these are generally avoided in working parties. While there has been an increase in written contributions, there are still few joint written positions or presentations on behalf of groups of 'like-minded' delegations.[18] Business is done in ways which are not fundamentally different from before.

The Council has adapted its ways of working without too much difficulty to enlargement in the field of the environment, but the difference with agriculture is striking: Community legislation in the field of environment takes almost one-third longer to be adopted since enlargement. Yet the political input by ministers is preserved, compared to agriculture: the average number of times that a file is discussed by ministers as a 'B point' has declined 'only' from 0.86 to 0.71. In terms of working practices, table rounds are rarely made, whilst written contributions have increased considerably. Joint presentations are made, but usually not on difficult points. Time limits are used in principle at Council level, at the discretion of the chair, but are rarely imposed in Coreper or working parties. There has been a certain change in the dynamics and the atmosphere of meetings. These have become a bit more formal, rather than less, given that it would be time-consuming and perhaps provocative to interrupt meetings in order to talk to two or three delegations. On the other hand, more contacts take place before meetings.

In the case of employment policy, it is harder to trace changes in how business is done. Most measures are not legislative[19] and the Employment Committee (EMCO) set up in 2000 has a distinct composition and nature within the Council system. EMCO operates by consensus, although simple majority voting is theoretically possible, and the minority group can state its views. EMCO documents are not publicly available. Moreover, unlike in legislative procedures documents do not indicate the positions of member states. Yet the overall impression is that enlargement has not caused major changes. More people may speak, but there is not necessarily any increase in the number of different positions. Moreover, most new member states have not been active in EMCO proceedings. There are no formal time limits but in practice they are applied: delegations know that they need to be brief and if need be the chair intervenes. This varies according to the presidency (the consensually oriented Finns, for example, tending to be more tolerant than some others). Table rounds do still take place for orientation debates. Language is an issue in EMCO, but not because of enlargement: documents are available only in English, French and German, but the complaints come from Spain and Italy, not the new member states.

Qualitative Changes

It appears from all the above that the Council has adapted to enlargement without major problems in terms of its internal procedures and practices. Nevertheless, certain qualitative shifts can be detected.

One is 'bureaucratization', in the sense of a further increase in the proportion of decisions which are reached below the ministerial level, and a decrease in the number of real debates which take place in the Council itself. In global terms, the overall number of Community acts adopted without discussion as 'A points' in the Council slightly increased after enlargement (from 76.9 per cent to 82.3 per cent). Conversely, the average

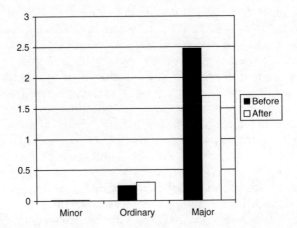

Figure 3.5   *Average number of discussions as 'B points' in the Council per*
Community act by importance

number of 'B point' discussions held per piece of Community legislation decreased significantly, from 0.69 to 0.40. The decline is particularly pronounced for major acts (see Figure 3.5).

The same trend is confirmed by more comprehensive information on the type of representation in the Council (see Table 3.2): 22.5 per cent of important acts are adopted in the EU25 without any discussion among ministers as compared to 3.7 per cent in the EU15. Moreover, none of the major acts adopted in the EU25 have been negotiated by ministers only, which happened in one-quarter of the cases in the EU15.[20]

Interviews confirm a partial trend toward a decreased relevance of ministerial meetings. This does have a certain enlargement dimension. It is partly a reflection of the reduced time available for individual ministers to speak, given the greater numbers involved. There may also still be a certain preference for some ministers from newer member states to avoid participating in negotiations. Yet the main issue seems to be the type of content. Debates still take place in, for example, agriculture or the environment, where difficult specific decisions need to be taken. Ministerial meetings are seen to have lost much of their added value at the general level (General Affairs and External Relations – GAERC) or where they tend to consist mainly of orientation debates or the adoption of conclusions, the extreme case being seen as Education, Youth and Culture.

The newer member states have been on a learning curve with regard to procedures and norms, including the rules of the European game when it comes to pursuing national interests. In many cases, they clearly suffer from

Table 3.2   *Type of representation in the Council when adopting Community acts, by importance*

		Minor %	Ordinary %	Major %
Before	Plenum of ministers	0.6	4.0	25.9
	Full ministerial	0.0	2.0	25.9
	Over 90 per cent ministerial	1.3	9.3	14.8
	Mixed ministerial – diplomatic	0.0	4.0	29.6
	Full diplomatic	98.1	80.7	3.7
After	Plenum of ministers	0.0	1.0	0.0
	Full ministerial	0.0	1.0	22.5
	Over 90 per cent ministerial	1.1	20.4	45.0
	Mixed ministerial – diplomatic	0.0	2.9	10.0
	Full diplomatic	98.9	74.8	22.5

a shortage of resources. Most of the new member states are seen as still remaining somewhat passive and cautious. Poland is seen to present a special case, not only in having a very assertive attitude but also in not seeming always to adapt to the norms.

The case of sugar reform is illuminating. Roughly equal proportions of old and new member states were initially opposed to the proposed measures: six of the 15 (Greece, Spain, Ireland, Italy, Portugal and Finland) and five of the ten (Latvia, Lithuania, Hungary, Slovenia and Poland). Poland and Greece opposed the 24 November 2005 compromise in the Council. When the SCA 'clarified and confirmed' the deal on 12 December, Latvia joined in opposing. In February 2006, negative votes in Council were recorded for Poland, Greece and Latvia. Declarations were made by Estonia, Sweden, the Czech Republic, Latvia, Finland, Lithuania, and France/Germany/Denmark/Netherlands. The Swedish declaration was a perfect example of what one might term the 'consensual complaint', in other words one of the ways in which member states have adapted to the increased constraints imposed by enlargement: 'By relying on formal statements to register their opposition instead of voting "no", governments are also able to affect a sense of the old culture of consensus without at the same time sending a political signal of having deviated from their initial policy preferences' (Hagemann and De Clerck-Sachsse 2007, p. 14). Sweden stated that it respected the political agreement of the Council. It 'deplored' that the change introduced subsequently regarding the level of price reduction had not been accompanied by corresponding modifications concerning isoglucose quotas but concluded that 'Sweden is nonetheless ready to accept this in a spirit of compromise'.[21] Poland, like Greece, presented rotund opposition to the whole package.

In the case of the spirit drinks proposal, similarly, a coalition of old and new member states even presented joint positions in defence of their definition of vodka.[22] Yet as negotiations proceeded, different styles were noted. Sweden and Finland began to adjust in order to 'sell' their preferences in the overall deal. Poland continued to hold out, not realizing that to end up in isolated opposition, under majority voting, is to have lost.

CONCLUSIONS

The enlargements of the EU in May 2004 and January 2007 have inspired a significant amount of academic work, as well as political debate, about their possible consequences for the functioning and further development of the EU's institutional system. Within this line of research, and with a special focus on the Council, this chapter has tried to contribute two additional dimensions of analysis: first, providing a new way of looking at quantitative evidence; and second, combining quantitative accounts with qualitative insights gathered from selected case studies. On this basis, the study has aimed to identify the kind of changes that can be observed to have taken place, and the significance of enlargement in initiating and shaping these changes. Since there has been only marginal change in decision-making rules since the entry into force of the Nice Treaty, the analysis has focused on Council procedures and practices.

The findings suggest that the Council has successfully assimilated the new members in its decision-making dynamics and has adapted its internal working methods to the new conditions: legislation is still adopted, and without greater political contestation. Beyond obvious changes such as the number of languages or the number of people round the table, or the need to deal with new substantive issues which have been specifically imported together with the newer countries, it is not easy to pin down the specific role of enlargement as an explanatory factor for changes. There are very rarely coalitions of 'new' versus 'old' member states. As demonstrated in the qualitative elements in this study, acceding countries have generally joined existing issue-based coalitions in which larger member states continue to play the leading role. In most policy questions, enlargement is only one among many other concurrent variables, and each issue has its own particular history.

Yet some qualitative changes can be detected in the process, with the Council becoming more 'bureaucratized': ministers, for example, become more and more 'excluded' from the decision-making process, to the benefit of officials. It may nevertheless be concluded that, when it comes to the 'ease' of decision-making, the Council has largely assimilated its new members and has successfully adapted its internal working methods to the new conditions. The changes observed are minor and can be seen as part of a more general evolution in procedures and the role of key actors. The increased length in procedures is notably greater in the case of codecision, suggesting that the continuing challenges are less to do with internal Council practices than its inter-institutional relations.

Where do we go from here? There are at least three aspects connected with this chapter that would deserve further attention in future research. The first one concerns time. Three years after enlargement is in many respects too short a period for a full appreciation of possible changes: the quantitative indicators and the selected case studies that have been presented will need to be analysed against a longer time frame. The second has to do with the role played by contingencies in EU politics and the connected challenge of reconciling global figures with individual stories: more sophisticated indicators and more representative case studies are needed to strengthen this link. Third, in addition to works focused on single institutions, such as this one, more needs to be done in appraising the inter-institutional or systemic dimension of change, an aspect that is partly dealt with in Chapter 10 on legislation.

NOTES

*   Pierpaolo Settembri writes in a personal capacity and the views he expresses in this book may not in any circumstances be regarded as stating an official position of the Council.

1.   The authors would like to thank Sarada Das (EIPA, Maastricht), for the invaluable assistance provided in the preparation of this work.

2.   The data used in this context are taken, unless stated otherwise, from a new dataset that contrasts Council and EU legislative activity in two comparable periods of decision-making, before and after enlargement. More details on the dataset are provided in the Appendix.

3.   The original figure was 27, but this was reduced to 26 following the negative result of the Norwegian referendum. The upper figure for application of the 'compromise' consequently became 25.

4.   For details, see Council 2006a, Annex 4.

5.   European Commission, MEMO/07/77, Brussels, 23 February 2007.

6.   The Council's core documents are defined as: draft legislation at certain milestone stages; agendas for the Council; 'A' item notes and their addenda; documents for adoption or discussion by the Council agenda; opinions of the legal service; Council minutes; Council replies to European Parliament written questions and oral questions with debate; declarations by the presidency on behalf of the Union; (where possible) press releases for sessions of the Council; written procedure telexes; manuals which are intended for use by national departments in member states; European Council Presidency Conclusions (Council 2003a, Annex).

7. *Council Conclusion of 13 June 2005 on the Official Use of Additional Languages within the Council and possibly other Institutions and Bodies of the European Union*, OJ C148 of 18 June 2005, p. 1. See also Presidency Note 9506/2/05 REV 2, Brussels, 13 June 2005. This could in principle also be requested for Luxembourgish, which is one of Luxembourg's three official languages together with French and German, or for Turkish, which is one of the official languages of Cyprus.

8. *Administrative Agreement between the European Commission and the Kingdom of Spain* (2006/C 73/06), OJ C 73 of 25 March 2006.

9. The Council's budget rose by 69 per cent between 1999 and 2005. Half of the increase was due to the 2004 enlargement, and half to the structures for the European Security and Defence Policy (Council 2004, p. 15).

10. Council Press Release 11630/07 (Presse 166), Brussels, 13 July 2007.

11. This was known as the 'Trumpf–Piris' report after its chairman, the then Secretary-General, Jürgen Trumpf, and the deputy chairman, Jean-Claude Piris, head of the Legal Service.

12. The original Code of Conduct referred explicitly to the so-called 'Antici' and 'Mertens' groups of officials tasked to support Coreper Part II (the Permanent Representatives) and Part I (their Deputies) respectively. The important role of these special groups was reflected in the informal version of the guidelines drawn up for the German Presidency by the German Permanent Representative in January 2007 as 'Wilhelm's 10 commandments for Coreper proceedings'. The tenth was 'For the sake of the efficient conduct of meetings the Permanent Representatives are welcome to sleep (quietly) but Antici members must always be awake.'

13. *Presidency Information Note to Special Committee on Agriculture*, Doc. 7783/05, 4 April 2005.

14. Some changes in voting procedure came into effect on 1 January 2007, following agreement of the new Financial Perspective.

15. These figures include 'Community legislation', 'other Community acts' and 'Intergovernmental acts', as defined in Chapter 10.

16. This category is established by the Council itself, to determine when it decides in 'legislative capacity'. Such acts are present in each of our three categories of acts (see previous note). In the rest of the chapter (and in Chapter 10) we will stick to our categories because, among other things, the Council's definition excludes important acts (such as provisions concerning internal administration, budget, and inter-institutional and international relations) and includes acts that, in our view, can hardly be considered 'legislative' (such as acts adopted on the basis of a piece of secondary legislation). Yet we did provide figures also for this category, in this particular case, to show that the decrease in the number of acts subject to the unanimity rule adopted after enlargement is not the product of our manipulation but also stems, even more clearly, from the official figures provided by the Council.

17. For a definition of 'minor', 'ordinary' and 'major' acts, please see Chapter 10 and the Appendix.

18. One exception was the joint written contribution of the Estonian, Latvian, Lithuanian, Polish, Finnish and Swedish delegations regarding the definition of vodka – Doc. 9871/06 of 21 June 2006. Earlier Poland also spoke on this issue on behalf of the same group of countries (e.g. Doc. 15902/05).

19. Only two legislative acts were adopted in this area in the two years considered in this study.

20. Depending on the exact number of ministers, deputy ministers or diplomats present when the Council reached political agreement on a proposal or when it discussed it for the last time as a 'B point', five different categories of representation in the Council have been created: 'plenum of ministers' (only ministers present), 'full ministerial' (only ministers and deputy ministers or equivalent), 'over 90 per cent ministerial' (ministers and deputy ministers account for at least 90 per cent of the total representation), 'mixed ministerial – diplomatic' (the sum of ministers and deputy ministers is less than 90 per cent of the total: the rest are diplomats) and 'full diplomatic' (only diplomats present). In the case of an act never discussed as a 'B point' in the Council, the act is considered as discussed only by diplomats (i.e. 'full diplomatic' representation).

21. Council of the EU, Doc. 6538/06 ADD 1, 3 March 2006.
22. See note 21 above.

REFERENCES

Commission of the European Communities (2000), *Adapting the Institutions to Make a Success of Enlargement: Commission Opinion on the Calling of a Conference of Representatives of the Governments of the Member States to amend the Treaties*, COM (2000) 34, 26 January.

Council of the European Union (1999), *Operation of the Council with an Enlarged Union in Prospect*, Report of the Working Party set up by the Secretary-General of the Council, SN 2139/99, Brussels, 10 March.

Council of the European Union (2002a), *Report on the Administrative Consequences for the General Secretariat of the Council of the Enlargement of the European Union*, 7301/02, Brussels, 19 March.

Council of the European Union (2002b), *Measures to Prepare the Council for Enlargement*, Report by the Presidency to the European Council, 9939/02, Brussels, 13 June.

Council of the European Union (2003a), *Guide for Producing Documents for the Council and its Preparatory Bodies*, Brussels, 28 March.

Council of the European Union (2003b), *Working Methods for an Enlarged Council – Code of Conduct*, 7105/03, Brussels, 11 March.

Council of the European Union (2004), *Report on the Management of the General Secretariat*, 12860/04, Brussels, 1 October.

Council of the European Union (2006a), *Council Guide, Presidency Handbook*, Brussels, February.

Council of the European Union (2006b), Council Decision of 15 September 2006 adopting the Council's Rules of Procedure (2006/683/EC, Euratom), OJ L 285 of 16 October 2006.

Court of Auditors (ECA) (2006), *Special Report No. 9/2006 Concerning Translation Expenditure Incurred by the Commission, the Parliament and the Council together with the Institutions' Replies*, OJ C 284 of 21 November 2006, p. 1.

European Parliament (EP) (2006), *Report on Special Report No. 9/2006 of the European Court of Auditors Concerning Translation Expenditure Incurred by the Commission, the Parliament and the Council (2007/2077(INI))*, Committee on Budgetary Control, Rapporteur: Alexander Stubb, A6-0215/2007, 8 June.

Galloway, D. (2001), *The Treaty of Nice and Beyond: Realities and Illusions of Power in the EU*, Sheffield: Sheffield Academic Press.

Hagemann, S. and De Clerck-Sachsse, J. (2007), *Old Rules, New Game: Decision-making in the Council of Ministers after the 2004 Enlargement*, CEPS Special Report, March.

Hayes-Renshaw, F. and Wallace, H. (2006), *The Council of Ministers*, 2nd edition, Basingstoke: Palgrave Macmillan.

4. The European Commission: enlargement as reinvention?*

John Peterson and Andrea Birdsall

Only the most courageous contemporary analyst could claim to know what significance will be attributed by future historians to the 2004–7 enlargements of the European Union (EU). Perhaps the radical expansion of the EU's membership will come to be seen as one of the most heroic and consequential steps ever taken towards the political unification of Europe. By this view, the EU system would absorb, without damaging itself, an 80 per cent increase in member states over three years. Specifically, enlargement would succeed in three different senses. First, the EU's institutions would smoothly integrate nationals from the new 12 member states. Second, the EU12 (as they have come to be called), many of which only recently regained their sovereignty, would grow comfortable with the idea of pooling it, thus enhancing the legitimacy of EU decisions and institutions. Third, the EU would continue to function without any 'seizing up' of its (already intricate) system of decision-making.

Alternatively, 1 May 2004 might mark the moment when the unique European post-war experience of pooling sovereignty and delegating authority to the EU's institutions became a sort of museum piece. A system designed during the Cold War for limited ends, and which (by some accounts) generated many unintended consequences, would finally lose its almost miraculous capacity for collective action. Especially in light of the rejection of the EU's Constitutional Treaty – a result sometimes blamed on enlargement itself (see Cohen-Tanugi 2005) – the competing demands of 27 governments would produce paralysis. The Lisbon Treaty[1] of 2007, regardless of its fate, cannot guarantee that paralysis is avoided. By this view, to borrow from a leading analyst of European foreign policy, the EU would stop being an 'action organization'. It would become more like other international organizations (such as the Organization for Security and Co-operation in Europe): a 'framework organization' in which governments debated and discussed issues of collective interest but engaged in little or no collective action (Hill 2004, p. 159).

The present volume is designed to give future historians a place to start.

It would be surprising if the analyses, collectively or even individually, pointed 'cleanly' towards either of the two scenarios we have sketched. It may be that some EU institutions absorb enlargement without much difficulty, while others struggle. Broadly, however, the EU's institutions tend to succeed or fail together (see Peterson and Shackleton 2006). Identifying the effects of enlargement on the EU *system* may be a different, trickier, but more important exercise than identifying its effects on individual EU institutions.

However, if our aim is to pinpoint enlargement's effects on the European Commission, we might start by considering the central dilemma the Commission has faced from its creation, namely 'between [the Commission's] duty to develop and apply common rules and continuous political pressure for deviation' (Christiansen 1997, p. 77). Living with this dilemma makes the Commission a uniquely 'politicized bureaucracy'. It seems uncontroversial to suggest that this dilemma stands to become *more* acute for a Commission that must now serve an enormously diverse Union of 27 states, nearly 500 million consumers, and unprecedented economic disparities.

Of course, the Commission, along with other EU institutions, is different from other international institutions in that it 'has the capacity and legitimacy to act relatively independently of member states' assent' (Christiansen 1997, p. 73), or at least in theory.[2] In practice, the Commission usually only succeeds when it works with the assent of a critical mass of member states. The problem is that a critical mass in an EU of 27 is now much bigger than before. Moreover, the view that the Commission has been in a state of steady institutional decline since its golden years under Jacques Delors in the 1980s has become something close to accepted wisdom amongst Commission-watchers (see Peterson 2005, 2006). Has enlargement made the Commission's job impossible? Or is the Commission capable of reinventing itself to show dynamism and leadership in the 'new Europe'?

In seeking to answer these questions, we confront the same issues that preoccupy other contributors to this volume. Specifically, we try to identify the main challenges and pressures for change in the role of the Commission, especially those arising from enlargement. We also consider the nature and extent of change in the Commission's working methods, the quantity and quality of its output, and its interaction with other EU institutions since 2004. The evidence on which we rely is, by nature, early in two different senses. First, the post-2004 enlargements are still recent phenomena whose effects will only be revealed in time; indeed, the possibility of a 'time lag' between cause (enlargement) and effect is a major theme of this volume. Second, we draw on material from interviews designed primarily to set the agenda for a forthcoming attitudinal survey of the

Commission (which itself investigates, *inter alia*, the effects of enlargement). Nevertheless, our argument is straightforward: enlargement has not fundamentally altered the role of the Commission, at least not thus far. But it has reinforced the impact of several other secular changes not exclusively or even specifically linked to enlargement. They include: the emergence of a younger and more flexible Commission, one that is more presidential (particularly under José Manuel Barroso), and one that can no longer rely as much on its traditional monopoly power to propose formal legislation as it seeks to influence EU policy debates. Enlargement is one, but only one, amongst multiple rationales being used by reformers to try to reinvent the Commission.

We proceed in four parts. Section 1 offers an overview of the lively politics of enlarging a politicized bureaucracy. Section 2 considers a second, major, life-changing event for the Commission: the 2000–4 reforms of its administrative code and working methods. In section 3, we consider how enlargement has, or has not, changed the Commission's role, work and methods. Section 4 considers where the Commission presently stands in the EU's institutional system.

1. 'ENLARGING' A POLITICIZED BUREAUCRACY

The accession to the EU of Bulgaria and Romania in 2007 completed what Nugent (2004) has labelled the '10 + 2' enlargement. Although undertaken in two waves over more than two and a half years, it was clear politically that the EU (of 15) was committed after 1999 to admitting all of a dozen new states, although the precise question of when was settled only in late 2006. After that, other candidates, particularly the Balkan states (especially Croatia) and Turkey, waited in the wings. But it was clear that there would be a pause of unspecified years before the EU enlarged again.

One effect was to remove – for the moment anyway – another big political project from the EU's agenda, along with the euro, the Constitutional Treaty, the development of a common foreign policy, services liberalization, and a new global trade round. All were either completed or stalled. As such, it might be thought that the Commission was set to become a more technocratic, apolitical body in an emerging 'post-vision' era[3] in European integration.

However, there are several reasons to think that the Commission will remain a uniquely politicized bureaucracy. It is worth revisiting Christiansen's (1997, p. 77) original elaboration of this typology:

What detracts from the bureaucratic element in the Commission's activity – what makes the Commission 'less bureaucratic' than other bureaux – is the nature of continuous bargaining in the Union. The major fields of Commission activity – proposing legislation and supervising the implementation of decisions – are highly politicized tasks. . . . the nature of much of the Commission's work – the overarching regulatory function it fulfills for the European Union, the large degree of symbolism that is often involved in EU decision-making, the continuing process of expansion of the EU's institutional framework, the ongoing process of 'constitutional reform' – has meant that numerous political forces take exceptional interest in the internal proceedings of the Commission.

This exceptional interest has been on prominent display in recent years, in large part because of enlargement. Consider the Commission's own composition and how any proposal to change it resonates at the highest political levels. Recall how bitterly fought was the debate about the size of the College (now 27) of Commissioners as designated in the Constitutional Treaty (Norman 2003). After the Constitutional Treaty was rejected by French and Dutch voters in 2005 referenda, the angst in European capitals was palpable after it dawned on governments that the Treaty of Nice, which remained in force, required that 'the number of members of the Commission shall be less than the number of Member States' (Art. 213.1) after the EU reached 27 member states. This provision had been agreed on the (arguably sensible) grounds that a College as large as 27 was unwieldy and inefficient. With the accession of Bulgaria and Romania, the Union had reached the magic number. It had to negotiate, eventually, some kind of rotation system to replace the one Commissioner per member state status quo.

Voices in the new member states began to suggest that a way around Nice had to found. The prospect of having no representative in the College who could appear in the national media, speaking the national language(s) and explaining to ordinary citizens why the EU did what it did, was daunting for states still adjusting to EU membership. One official in the cabinet of an EU12 Commissioner predicted that 'it will estrange the member states from the EU not to have a Commissioner. We must have one per member state.'[4] A leading member of the European Parliament from an EU12 state argued: 'it is far more important for the Commission to be legitimate than efficient'.[5]

By late 2007, the Commission itself was struggling to sound authoritative on the matter (apart from an obvious need for better website editing), while clearly implying that a smaller College was desirable:

A Commission with too many members will not work properly and, at present, there is one commissioner from each EU country. Since Bulgaria and Romania joined the European Union, the number has grown to 27 commissioners. This number was fixed by the Council by unanimous decision. But from the next Commission (i.e. in principle as of November 2009), following the accession of the 27th member state, the number of commissionners [*sic*] should be reduced. The final figure remains to be determined by a Council decision. Commissionners [*sic*] will then be appointed by rotation with care being taken to ensure that countries are represented fairly. The aim will be to ensure a clear reflection of the demographic and geographical range of all the Member States.[6]

Even at the level of the Commission's services, or Directorates-General (DGs, the Brussels equivalent of ministries), the newer member states took a keen interest in the intake of their nationals. The pace of absorbing EU12 officials remained slow: only 12 per cent of Commission officials hailed from the new member states by mid-2007. This figure represented a significant increase on the share – only 9 per cent – of late 2006.[7] But there remained few EU12 officials in high-ranking positions, with most in relatively junior posts. At the truly elite level of Directors-General and their deputies, only 9 of 75 officials hailed from EU12 states (and all were deputies) by mid-October 2007.

Recruitment to the Commission was closely monitored in eastern and southern national capitals, and its slow pace caused considerable agitation. To illustrate, when Poland's Prime Minister, Jaroslaw Kaczynski, made his first visit to Brussels in August 2006, the first meeting he held was with Polish European Commissioner Danuta Hübner, and the first issue discussed was the sluggish rate at which Poles were being recruited to the Commission.[8] With both subtlety and weariness, a member of the cabinet of the Commissioner for Administration, Siim Kallas, commented, 'we're trying to balance spread and quality [of EU12 officials] but politically, in terms of raw numbers, it is never enough'.[9]

In other ways, too, enlargement revealed the Commission to be a politicized bureaucracy. For example, in a climate of much-diminished political enthusiasm for further enlargement, the Commission remained an institutional activist for it. The Commission clearly took a sort of institutional pride in engineering the 10 + 2 enlargements.[10] Afterwards, multiple services – not only DG Enlargement – worked actively to prepare Croatia, Macedonia, Turkey and other candidates for membership. The Commission – whose College was nearly 45 per cent composed of new member state appointees by 2007 – showed itself to be more pro-enlargement than other EU institutions and governments. The College's handling of Bulgarian and Romanian accession provided clear evidence of the point: it recommended that more stringent post-accession obligations be imposed on them than had been imposed on any previous applicants, but recommended their admission nevertheless.

One logical reason for the Commission's support for further enlargement

Table 4.1 Trust in the European Commission

State(s)	Tend to trust %	Tend not to trust %
EU27	52	27
EU15	50	30
EU12	59	18

Source: European Commission (2007), Eurobarometer 67: Public Opinion in the European Union, Spring, http://ec.europa.eu/public_opinion/archives/eb/eb67/eb67_en.htm.

is that the 10 + 2 enlargement could be viewed, in headline terms, as boosting support for the EU generally and even the Commission specifically. The share of EU citizens reporting that they believed that their country had 'benefited from EU membership' jumped from 47 per cent before the 2004 enlargement to 54 per cent two years afterwards.[11] Majorities in all of the ten states that acceded after 2004 (except tiny Latvia) said they 'tended to trust the EU'. The composite total for the states that joined in 2004 was considerably higher than for the original EU15 (60 v. 45 per cent).[12]

Enlargement also appeared to make the Commission more 'popular', or at least less unpopular. Majorities in all EU12 states (except Latvia and Bulgaria) said they tended to trust the Commission by spring 2007, and significantly fewer reported 'tending not to trust' it than in the EU15 (see Table 4.1). In a sense, enlargement appears to be as pro-Commission as the Commission is pro-enlargement.

It was not always thus. The first Eurobarometer poll, taken in spring 1974 after the first enlargement, today looks Neanderthal – full of errors and apparently typed on numerous typewriters – on the Commission's website. It contains none of the now-familiar questions about the benefits of membership or whether respondents 'tend to trust' the EU or its institutions. However, nearly all questions – in the 1974 poll as well as those taken over the next several years – showed support for the European Economic Community (as it was then) and all the EEC did to be considerably higher in the original six member states than in the United Kingdom, Denmark or Ireland.[13] Similarly, the share of citizens who thought their state benefited from Community membership was higher in the original ten Community states than in Spain or Portugal for several years after the latter two joined in 1986.[14] Since the 1995 enlargement, relatively few Austrians or (especially) Swedes have reported trust in the EU generally or the Commission specifically compared to EU averages (which Finnish totals broadly match).[15] In short, the 10 + 2 enlargement is different from past enlargements in that it has given the Commission reason to be more, not less, self-confident.

However, a considerably more important factor is the Commission President's ability to give firm direction to such a strange, inchoate and politicized bureaucracy. The emergence of a more *presidential* Commission under Barroso – more dominated by the political and policy choices and preferences of its President – is a change that has been hastened, but in no sense exclusively driven, by enlargement. In some respects, enlargement made the Commission President's job – not an easy one to start with – almost impossible. Surely no political figure in the world had more 'constituents' than Barroso, including strong-willed ones within 27 different governments who considered themselves to have a legitimate claim on his time and agenda. One indicative barometer was the number of days Barroso was compelled to spend outside of Brussels: a total of 168 in 2006 alone.[16]

Moreover, the challenge of ensuring coherence in a College of 27 was daunting. In theory, the College is meant to uphold collective responsibility: all of its decisions, even those requiring a vote by simple majority, are collective (even, in formal terms, 'unanimous') ones that all Commissioners must defend publicly. If they cannot, they are expected (in theory) to resign. In practice, Commissioners frequently disagreed with each other publicly under Barroso's immediate predecessors, Romano Prodi and Jacques Santer, who usually simply tolerated or drew a veil over the splits. Enlargement of the College to 27 members, however, potentially marked a step-level change. Barroso thus had a rationale for insisting that his be the most presidential Commission since Delors'. One official in an EU12 Commissioner's cabinet observed that Barroso had shown that, if necessary, he was prepared to 'override and ignore and clash with individual Commissioners'.[17]

Enlargement also yielded two other major changes at the level of the College, both of which could be viewed as justifying or facilitating stronger presidentialism. First, the formal equality of all Commissioners became something close to an outright fiction. Prior to the 2004 enlargement, larger member states (France, Germany, Italy, the UK and Spain) always appointed two Commissioners. Under these conditions, the idea that all Commissioners were equal was plausible in principle (if not always in practice). After the 10 + 2 enlargement, each member state appointed one Commissioner. No one could pretend that Commissioners from (say) Germany and France carried the same weight as those from Malta or Latvia.

A second and related change was that, for the first time, the College resembled a Council working group with each EU member state represented by one member. The question of whether the College thus became a more *intergovernmental* institution was inevitable. More generally, even more than when Coombes (1970) made the point more than 35 years ago, it was unclear what was meant to hold the College together. Unlike members of a cabinet government, members of the College shared no nationality, ideology, party political affiliation or even – unlike the first Commissions – ties to a particular geographical corner of Europe.

The Commission had already become more presidential under Barroso's predecessor, Romano Prodi. This shift was prompted by changes to the EU's treaties in the 1990s that made it clear, for the first time, that the College worked under the political direction of its President, who shared responsibility with member states for choosing its members. But the most compelling factor pushing towards greater presidentialism was the perception that the Commission had become chaotic and rudderless under Santer's presidency, leading ultimately to the mass resignation of his College in 1999 amidst charges of nepotism and mismanagement (Peterson 1999, 2006).

Prodi headed a College of 20 members for most of his time as President. He took pains to reserve for himself the role of the main 'political voice' of the Commission. He also used the presidency to dispense patronage widely, ensuring that his hand-picked operatives occupied key, strategic posts. Yet, to his credit, Prodi clearly realized that his was probably the most talented and experienced College, across the full spectrum of EU competences, in the Union's history (see Peterson 2005). Thus, most individual Commissioners were given considerable autonomy in their own policy area and rarely faced meddling from the President. Prodi's Commission was thus more presidential but also more *ministerial* than past Commissions. One indicator, more than just symbolic, was that under Prodi individual Commissioners occupied offices in the same building as the DG for which they were responsible, for the first time in the Commission's history, *à la* ministers in ministries.

Under Barroso, Commissioners were re-housed together in the new, refurbished (de-asbestosed) Berlaymont building in central Brussels. There was little question that Barroso personally dominated his Commission far more than Prodi had dominated his. For one thing, Barroso's College was considerably less dynamic or experienced, and to some extent because of enlargement. EU12 states generally sent top members of their political or diplomatic classes to serve as Commissioners in Brussels (see Peterson 2006, pp. 90–91). Yet, one top Commission official, with experience of multiple cabinets, described the Barroso Commission as: 'not a political Commission in part because an intermediate generation of technocrats dominated the first post-Communist political classes in the new member states. One consequence is that there is not a lot of ideological debate in this Commission.'[18]

In the circumstances, Barroso found that he could both impose his authority and policy agenda on the Commission and justify strong presidentialism as a response to enlargement. With an expanded College of 27, particularly with one per member state, the Barroso Commission risked outright paralysis and descent to the level of an intergovernmental bargaining committee without strong presidential direction. One anti-paralysis measure was the so-called 'finalisation written procedure', whereby agreement on a proposed measure could be agreed by the heads of Commission cabinets, and effectively substitute for the prior approval of the legal service and/or the agreement of the DGs consulted in the inter-service consultation (Settembri 2007, p. 7).[19] Barroso's operatives claimed that the procedure shifted decision-making power from the services to the College while also freeing Commissioners to focus debate on more important proposals.

Another response to enlargement – and also a sign of a stronger President – was a new Impact Assessment Board, a review panel whose members were widely viewed as hand-picked by Barroso. It was empowered to block any Commission proposal whose assessment of impact was held to be incomplete or unsatisfactory. One long-serving EU15 official reckoned that the biggest change that enlargement had rendered was 'much more need for impact assessment with 27'.[20] But others saw the Impact Assessment Board as another sign of Barroso's own control and dominance. Whether it was because Barroso was an effective consensus-builder or an authoritarian, it was striking that the College had yet to vote on any proposed measure more than three years into his five-year term.[21]

Ultimately, it can be argued that other background changes were more important than enlargement in shifting the role of the Commission. A short list might include rising concerns about climate change, energy security, international terrorism, and the emergence of China and India. All were complicated, multi-dimensional issues which resisted simple legislative solutions and required strong coordination – even centralization – across the Commission. On all of these issues the Commission became potentially, at least, a stronger player precisely because it was so difficult to reconcile the needs and preferences of 27 states and their citizenries. At the same time, there was little question but that enlargement made the Commission's job both much tougher and – if the EU was to have ambitions and pursue them collectively – more consequential. The central point is that enlargement is one factor among many in determining whether or how the Commission reinvents itself in the new European Union.

2. REFORMING A POLITICIZED BUREAUCRACY

Of all angles from which the Commission might be studied, the administrative reform angle has spawned the largest academic mini-industry.[22] The so-called Kinnock reforms were a direct response to the management problems that sprouted during the Santer years (as well as before then). The reforms were widely viewed as a political necessity. They were piloted by the Vice-President for Administration under Prodi and former British Labour Party leader Neil Kinnock (2004), who had previously overseen the wholesale reform of his own party after years when it was widely viewed as unelectable.

The Kinnock reforms were announced as a package in March 2000. They were organized around three prongs: strategic priority setting and resource allocation, human resource management, and financial management. A progress report issued in early 2003 claimed that 84 out of 93 specific reform actions were complete or in the process of being implemented. Academic evaluations have varied wildly in their portrayals of the Kinnock reforms. Several (especially early) treatments lauded them as an 'historic accomplishment' (Kassim 2004a), which showed that the Commission could deliver on a 'heroic if thankless task' (Kassim 2004b). Others stressed that they were being applied in 'a very unpromising reform environment' (Levy and Stevens 2004, p. 2) and to a Commission that was overloaded and risk averse (Levy 2006).

We do not propose to offer yet another verdict here. Instead, we note that the Kinnock reforms were bound up with enlargement in at least three respects. First, and most simply, the reforms were a considerable shock to the Commission in close proximity to enlargement. Few administrations adapt smoothly and quickly to major changes in their working methods or the pool of applicants from which they recruit their officials. Having to cope with both in a relatively short period of time might be seen as a kind of 'perfect storm' for the Commission (see Peterson 2008).

Second, enlargement and the reforms were linked in the minds of many Commission officials. One reason why is that internal Commission communications about the reforms justified them as necessary in light of 'the forthcoming enlargement of the Union, which would have a major impact on the tasks of the Commission and on its internal make up and culture' (Bearfield 2004, p. 17).[23] Another is that personnel reforms were widely resented across the services, especially a new administrative statute unveiled (coincidentally?) at precisely the same time as the (1 May) 2004 enlargement became official. Especially younger officials, who were set to be disproportionately EU12 nationals,[24] felt aggrieved by a new promotion system that doubled the number of promotions needed to get to the same administrative grade, with only half as much additional pay per promotion compared to the system it replaced. One senior official described the decision to make the new system effective on 1 May 2004 as a 'huge political mistake, given that these new officials are coming from relatively poor countries'.[25]

Meanwhile, a complicated system linked appraisal to promotion and was based on a system of awarding points that was neither understood nor trusted. A senior official involved in personnel issues admitted that the system, which was being revisited, was 'widely-hated. . . . The best case would be that the top 10 per cent could fly through the ranks. We are clearly not there yet.'[26]

In fact, the view that the purpose of the Kinnock reforms was to economize on the cost of enlargement, while reining in the Commission by creating a growth market in scrutiny, was widely shared across the Commission. Kinnock (2004, p. 11) himself perhaps lives up to his reputation for saying more than is really necessary by pointing out that the EU's administration is inexpensive, costing only 5 per cent of the Union's budget, and that enlargement will make it even cheaper because of the reduced salary bill that comes with lowering the average age of officials (as well as, in the event, the implementation of a new pay scale). Further fuelling perceptions of a Commission under siege was a proposal (eventually rejected) by the 2006 Finnish Council Presidency to cut around 1700 Commission posts as part of a drive to 'improve productivity'.

Third and finally, it is worth asking whether the Commission – even after reforms designed (at least) to make it a more professional, meritocratic, high-performance administration – has in fact been made an even more politicized bureaucracy by enlargement. Generally, EU12 governments seem far less concerned about making the Commission a meritocracy than ensuring that they retain 'their' Commissioner and are allotted what they consider a fair share of posts (especially senior ones) in the services. Moreover, it might be hypothesized that the more member states there are admitted to the EU, the more concern and emphasis there must inevitably be on control: particularly, ensuring that EU funds are spent correctly and the Union's rules applied correctly by a larger number of national administrations, including many with limited capacity for management or audit. A revealing comparative study stacks up the Kinnock reforms against recent reforms of national administrations and concludes:

> The rhetorical flourishes concerning decentralization seem to have lost out to a strong bureaucratic logic of further centralization in the name of tighter control. . . . There is a sense in which the reforms have themselves been bureaucra-

tized during implementation, so that the original rhetorical emphasis on a more performance-oriented approach has somewhat evaporated under the welter of new rules on financial procedure, internal audit, and personnel management.
(Pollitt and Bouckaert 2004, p. 236; see also Levy 2003)

The same study notes that two features of the Kinnock reforms make them unique amongst public management reform programmes, which have sprouted globally (Pollitt and Bouckaert 2004; see also Pollitt and Talbot 2004; Pollitt *et al.* 2007). First, the Commission reforms were a response to a perceived crisis following the scathing indictment of the Santer Commission by the Committee of Independent Experts in 1999. Arguably, this contingency 'biased attention towards an agenda of control (tightened procedures and audit) and away from the agenda of efficiency and perform-ance' (Pollitt and Bouckaert 2004, p. 234). Again, enlargement could well be viewed as reinforcing the 'control agenda' even if the reforms themselves were driven by the debacle of 1999 rather than enlargement per se.

Second, Pollitt and Bouckaert (2004, p. 234) observe that, compared to other public administrations, the Commission has 'few direct contacts with citizens'. As such, it lacks 'clients' who can be relied upon to defend it from this and future waves of reform that – whatever else they are designed to do – may have the effect of limiting or reducing its autonomy, prerogatives or dignity. As such, a Commission that sees an increase in citizen trust in an EU27 as a reason to be more self-confident could be accused of grasping at straws. A politicized bureaucracy that lacks a polit-ical constituency seems a strange anomaly. But that is precisely what the Commission is.

3. HOW THE 'ENLARGED' COMMISSION WORKS

The question of how and how much enlargement has induced change in the way that the Commission works is a complicated one for which we lack precise metrics. Yet there is evidence to suggest that it is at least one factor inducing change, in ways that are subtle more than they are sharp, in the Commission and the way it works. One of the Commission's most experienced officials explained:

> The Commission is now less cosy. Enlargement has brought us new blood and enthusiasm and people who are open to change . . . and that has contributed to change in our working methods, especially in terms of policy design and imple-mentation. Both are now more difficult because we face much more diversity [in an EU27]. Designing anything that is legally binding is much harder. We inevitably look to more flexible, framework approaches.[27]

Under Barroso, there were clear signs that the Commission was becoming less suspicious of new types of policy instruments such as voluntary regulatory agreements, co-regulation, the 'open method' of coordination, and so on (see Windhoff-Héritier 2002; Windhoff-Héritier et al. 2004; Citi and Rhodes 2006; Szyszczak 2006). Of course, the EU had been experimenting with new policy instruments for years prior to 2004 as part of the Commission's embrace – half-hearted or otherwise – of a new 'governance' agenda (see below). Yet, experimentation with non-traditional, non-legislative modes of regulation became a much clearer priority for the Commission under Barroso than it had been previously, especially in view of the commitment of the President and his key allies to a programme of 'better regulation' (see Radaelli 2007).

But enlargement was a factor, too, and in two specific ways. First, the Commission's administrative culture was subject to a 'push' effect from the recruitment of new, reform-minded EU12 officials, even though the pace of recruitment (again) was well behind schedule. Second, the 'pull' effect of having to design policy suitable for all member states in an enormously diverse EU of 27 was even more powerful. Even the most committed defenders of the Commission's trump card in institutional power games – its monopoly over the right to initiate formal legislation – could not deny that it was much more difficult to design one legislative solution in Brussels to solve problems that were manifest in many different permutations in the EU's now considerably larger and more diverse heartland. Accordingly, as part of the better regulation agenda, the Commission engaged in a retrospective screening of pre-2004 legislative proposals that led 68 proposals formally to be withdrawn in 2005–6, with another ten similarly abandoned after that.[28]

As a caveat, framework approaches were far more common in some sectors – such as environmental and enterprise policy – than in others, such as police and judicial cooperation in criminal matters, or what used to be called Justice and Home Affairs (JHA). In fact, the pace with which the Commission produced formal legislative JHA proposals in the early years of the Barroso presidency was sometimes breathtaking and often seemed designed to make political points. The Constitutional Treaty had proposed to increase significantly the number of legislative decisions, particularly related to JHA, that could be endorsed by the EU Council of Ministers by qualified majority voting (QMV). After the Constitutional Treaty was put on hold in 2005, Barroso argued that it was time to employ the so-called *passerelle* clause of the existing treaties, which allowed the Council of Ministers to make decisions by QMV without any treaty change. But multiple member states, particularly Germany, remained cool to the idea. By way of response, one analyst claimed that 'the Commission keeps cramming the [JHA] agenda with proposals to highlight how little consensus there is in this area'.[29] In short, the 'new' Commission in an enlarged EU had by no means retreated entirely from inter-institutional power games.

Still, Barroso enhanced his credibility with EU member governments by insisting that the Commission should be less obsessed with its own institutional position under his presidency. Under Prodi, the Commission had expended significant administrative resources as well as political capital in debates on institutional reform, with effects that hardly seemed to maximize its credibility or influence within the EU system (see Norman 2003). The Commission's (2001) White Paper on Governance heaped criticism on the member states and 'intergovernmental' EU institutions and was decidedly cool towards new policy instruments, stubbornly defending the traditional Community method of legislating and its own monopoly on the right of initiative. Wincott's (2001, p. 897) verdict was that it reflected 'neither good politics nor a full response to the questions raised' about governance given the EU's imminent enlargement.

Prodi also made shaping debates on the Constitutional Treaty a central priority for his Commission. The final result was not unfavourable to the Commission, but far more in spite of than because of its efforts. Multiple units across the Commission worked on the Constitutional Treaty, leading to considerable duplication and waste (see Peterson 2006, pp. 88–9). It was unhelpful to Prodi, as well as a sign of his weak leadership, that the College under his presidency could not agree a unified position on its own composition. Of course, the Commission had failed to agree such a position during three previous rounds of debate on institutional reform in the 1990s (see Gray and Stubb 2001). In all of these cases, including that of the Constitutional Treaty, the Commission's inability to decide how its own house should be ordered marginalized it in debates on institutional reform.

Here, we spot one reason why Barroso decided to prioritize policy and what he labelled 'a Europe of results'. Barroso clearly shared the distaste of key members of the Prodi Commission, particularly Pascal Lamy and Chris Patten, for what the latter termed the Commission's 'dogmatic insistence on institutional prerogatives over substance' (quoted in Peterson 2005, p. 507). In terms of policy priorities, Barroso insisted that the Commission focus on the Lisbon agenda on economic reform, launched in 2000 (see Dehousse 2004), although eventually 'backed up' by measures on climate change and energy. Perhaps ironically, the most oft-heard criticism of Lisbon was that it itself lacked priorities, originally containing 28 policy objectives divided into 120 sub-goals with 117 policy indicators to be monitored. A 2004 panel review of Lisbon chaired by the former Dutch Prime Minister Wim Kok poured scorn on the programme generally and on member states specifically for failing to deliver on their earlier promises to make the EU 'the most dynamic economy in the world'.[30] At the same time, the Kok report gave Barroso ammunition for a White Paper in early 2005 that sought to give fresh impetus, via annual progress reports, to Lisbon[31] and became a precursor to a 2007 European Council statement on the programme.

Despite all of this, the verdict of one Lisbon-watcher was that a strategy of pursuing reforms in an array of diverse policy fields via the open method of coordination in 27 different member states was 'highly flawed' (Groenendijk 2006, p. 3). Barroso's supporters were forced to play down the Commission's lack of formal legislative powers in key areas of Lisbon, insisting that its concern should be bringing the greatest good to the greatest number of Europeans, regardless of what it meant for the position of the Commission in the EU system. These arguments were by no means universally supported within the Commission. But it was widely acknowledged that, as one senior Commission official put it, 'the growth and jobs agenda feeds into all else the Commission does. It has given political coherence to the College.'[32]

One reason why (amongst others) was enlargement. An economic reform agenda seemed a natural one to many EU12 Commissioners. Commissioner Dalia Grybauskaite, a Lithuanian, insisted that Commissioners from the new EU states were usually 'on the side that is most supportive of reforms because we know what it means not to do that'.[33] There was also evidence that a proportionately large share of EU12 officials – especially from the larger states among them – were being recruited in the first years after the 2004 enlargement to services with a natural affinity for economic reform, such as DG Trade, Enterprise, and Internal Market (see Table 4.2). Again, we find the Commission's emphasis and outlook evolving partly – but only partly – because of enlargement.

4.   WHERE DOES THE COMMISSION STAND?

It is never easy to get a clear read on the standing of the Commission in the EU system, for at least three basic reasons. One is that the Commission inevitably finds it expedient to hide its light under a bushel: specifically, to allow member states, especially the holder of the Council presidency, to take political credit for agreements that it helps to broker. When the Commission does so, it often finds the next deal easier to broker. The Commission thus may be more powerful than it wishes to appear to be.

Second, the Commission is, as Christiansen (1997, p. 82) shows, not just a supranational administration but 'also an intergovernmental body' (even though some of his evidence, such as national 'flags' on senior posts, is no

Table 4.2   EU12 and EU15 in 'economic' DGs

	Total EU12 officials in all DGs	Total EU12 officials in economic DGs*	Total percentage of state's officials in economic DGs*
BG	89	5	5.6
CY	77	10	13.0
CZ	329	43	13.0
EE	151	11	7.3
HU	451	75	16.6
LT	186	17	9.1
LV	143	6	4.2
MT	86	6	7.0
PL	809	138	17.1
RO	148	23	15.5
SI	226	10	4.4
SK	124	21	16.9
Total EU12	2819	365	12.9
Total EU15	20462	2196	10.7

Note: * DGs Trade, Internal Market, Economic and Financial Affairs, Competition, and Enterprise

Source: Bulletin Statistique, http://ec.europa.eu/civil_service/docs/bs_dg_nat_en.pdf (data as of September 2007).

longer relevant). It is probably more accurate to say that every interest, including national ones, with a stake in any EU policy is represented within the Commission than to say that the Commission internalizes and defends some composite, supranational, 'general European interest'.

Third, and very simply, the Commission is deeply enmeshed in the EU system, as one of its main legislative bodies alongside the Council of Ministers and Parliament. The system tends to succeed or fail as a system. At the end of the policy process, only rarely does anyone remember which institution was responsible for which policy detail for the simple reason that the system is designed to achieve collective responsibility (see Peterson and Shackleton 2006).

Nevertheless, we have early results on which to gauge how and how much patterns of the Commission's interactions with other EU institutions have changed since 2004. The most data-rich treatments of post-2004 EU decision-making focus mostly (perhaps inevitably) on the Council, not the Commission. Logically, the Council is where the addition of 12 member states would be expected to have the biggest impact. But these works also highlight the earlier point about 'enmeshing', and generally find more continuity than change (European Commission 2006; Mattila 2006; Maurer 2006; Hagemann and De Clerck-Sachsse 2007; Heisenberg 2007).

Specifically, it appears that the pace of legislating fell immediately after 2004, but 'recovered' to roughly where it was prior to enlargement by 2006. There was no clear change in the frequency or pattern of opposition to Commission proposals, although member states used formal statements to signal their opposition more often (as opposed to actually voting no). Larger EU member states were the main dissidents less frequently than they were before enlargement. Predictably, far more got done in areas where qualified majority voting (QMV) applied than where unanimity was the decision rule in a radically enlarged Council. In fact, a record high was registered in 2006 in the use of the so-called codecision procedure, under which the Council legislates on the basis of QMV.[34] However, there is little evidence to suggest a need to put more proposals to actual votes post-enlargement.

The biggest change from the Commission's point of view may be in patterns of mediation and brokership. Of course, the Commission has always shared these functions with the Council Presidency and Council General Secretariat. Maurer (2006) suggests that one of the most important changes in EU working methods is that Council Presidencies can no longer maintain oversight of potential deals between so many small countries. However, Heisenberg (2007, p. 81) claims that the main effect is to create 'greater room for large countries to "organize" the groups before Council meeting', as opposed to enhancing the role of the Commission.

In fact, the role of the Commission in an enlarged EU is a matter on which insiders 'have very different views' (Hagemann and De Clerck-Sachsse 2007, p. 25). Some claim that the Commission wields more influence than ever before, as revealed in (say) the higher frequency with which agreement is brokered at the first reading stage in codecision, which occurred nearly 50 per cent more frequently in the first year and a half after the 2004 enlargement than in the few years before (Hagemann and De Clerck-Sachsse 2007, p. 25). Others see the Commission doing basically what it has been doing for years: patiently and quietly coaxing compromises and trying to help build coalitions, usually in the background and between formal meetings of the Council and its offshoots.

The most important difference between how the Commission works now and how it worked before 2004 may arise from what Hagemann and De Clerck-Sachsse describe as (2007, p. 25) 'its recent strategy of introducing less legislation with the intention of dedicating more rigorous attention to the individual proposals'. The Barroso Commission claimed that the most important difference in the way that the EU legislated before and after the 10 + 2 enlargements actually had little to do with enlargement per se: it resulted from the Commission's stricter scrutiny of its own proposals. It was unclear whether the result was truly fewer legislative proposals than was the case before 2004, since the data is 'incomplete in many ways' (Heisenberg 2007, p. 80).[35] But there seemed a general consensus that the Commission was tabling fewer poorly prepared proposals than in the past, and indeed was withdrawing past proposals that it judged to be unnecessary, overly burdensome, or inappropriate for an EU of 27.

Some EU insiders viewed the Commission's claims with scepticism, suspecting it of dredging up and withdrawing long-dormant proposals on which no one was actively working anyway. Still, the Barroso Commission could at least claim to be delivering on Santer's pledge of the mid-1990s to get the Commission to 'do less but do it better' (Peterson 1999). Here, again, we find a more or less secular change to which enlargement has probably had some stimulus: designing *any* legislation for an EU of 27 requires 'rigorous attention', and the Barroso Commission no doubt could find at least some proposals that shifted from being difficult for an EU15 to being entirely implausible for an EU27.

Legislating in the new EU also requires significant give and take with the European Parliament (EP). Broadly speaking, Barroso was unpopular in the EP. Arguably, he got off to a bad start over *l'affaire* Rocco Buttiglione – when Barroso stood by the original Italian nominee to his Commission even after Buttiglione aired ultra-conservative views on homosexuality and women in the EP (see Peterson 2006, p. 93) – and never recovered. More generally, Barroso was viewed in the EP as lacking ambition, not least because he showed himself to be considerably less committed to reviving the Constitutional Treaty than were most MEPs. Barroso went as far as to label the decision to abandon it in favour of the Lisbon Treaty a 'rational choice' on the grounds that 'one of the biggest reasons we needed this Treaty was to put an end to all of this discussion about a Treaty'.[36]

Moreover, Barroso's better regulation agenda and embrace of non-legislative policy instruments met with a considerable lack of enthusiasm amongst MEPs. The Commission's embrace of new, non-legislative policy instruments forced Barroso to defend his Commission from charges that it lacked legislative ambition, particularly from the European Parliament.[37] 'It's a myth', Barroso claimed in late 2006, 'that this Commission is not legislating: 45 per cent of our work in 2005–6 involved new legislative proposals.'[38]

Yet, there was no question but that the Commission showed a stronger predisposition towards non-traditional, non-legislative modes of regulating, not least in response to enlargement. There was also strong evidence in a 2007 working group report on parliamentary reform that the EP was having to find its own issues to debate in the absence of 'enough' legislative proposals: the study showed that MEPs were spending nearly 22 per cent of their debating time on 'own-initiative reports', or papers written by MEPs on matters on which the EP had few or no powers, and only 19 per cent of its debating time on legislative proposals.[39] The Parliament, an essential cog in the EU's legislative machine, could hardly be expected to welcome a Commission committed to feeding less legislative 'throughput' into it (even if the pace of legislation appeared only marginally slower than pre-Barroso). More generally, relations between the Barroso Commission and the EP were troubled but (again) not exclusively or directly because of enlargement.

Nevertheless, enlargement did not help. Somewhat perversely, the College was larger in an EU of 27 but also less politically representative than in the past. Since large member states post-enlargement nominated only one Commissioner, it meant that they no longer nominated a second Commissioner to represent (usually) the political opposition in their country (see Wonka 2007). Large numbers of MEPs thus found that they lacked 'one of their own' – a member of their own political family from their own member state – in the College. A member of a senior Commissioner's cabinet summed up the state of Commission–EP relations:

> One of the effects of having no French Socialist or German CDU [Christian Democratic Union] member in the Commission is that it weakens the Commission's relationship with the European Parliament. And the political dominance in Brussels of the EP is unbelievable. It accentuates the disconnect between Brussels and the rest of Europe.[40]

If there is such a disconnect, an important mechanism for closing it is the Commission President's membership of the European Council. In fact, one of the most important determinants of the Commission's standing in the EU system generally is its President's standing in this institution. A Commission President lacks any power base comparable to those of European heads of state and government and so must 'derive his authority from other sources' (Crum *et al.* 2004, p. 2). Of all of Delors' political assets while he was Commission President (1985–95), none was more important than the respect he commanded at this level, where he became viewed (at least for a time) as an equal by heavyweights such as Helmut Kohl, François Mitterrand and even Margaret Thatcher (Peterson 2006, p. 85). Delors' capacity for hard work was legendary, and it was rare that anyone in the room at a European Council meeting knew the details of any dossier better than the Commission President.

In contrast, both Santer and Prodi often appeared lackadaisical in

European Councils and were frequently bullied by EU heads of state and government, despite each himself being a former prime minister (of Luxembourg and Italy respectively). For his part, in the words of a very senior Commission official, Barroso showed himself to be a 'player' in the European Council.[41] Several EU summits towards the middle of his term agreed policy statements – no mean feat in itself in an enlarged EU – in which Barroso invested heavily, particularly the 2005 Hampton Court summit statement on globalization and the March 2007 Brussels European Council agreements on the Lisbon agenda on growth and competitiveness and (especially) climate change. Arguably, Barroso showed himself able to perform the three tasks required of an effective 'technocrat politician': mastering his brief (*à la* Delors), leading the Commission, and communicating 'convincingly as the permanent credible voice of the general EU interest' (Crum *et al.* 2004, p. 2). While there was no intrinsic connection between his effective performance and enlargement per se, there was possibly more receptiveness to a Commission President who, amidst the cacophony of an EU of 27, seemed able to articulate the 'general EU interest'. But here, again, cause and effect cannot be linked directly or unambiguously.

CONCLUSION

There are many different ways in which we might seek to gauge the impact of the 10 + 2 enlargement on the Commission. They include numerous devices that have *not* been employed here such as individual policy case studies. Yet, whatever method is employed, it is impossible to measure precisely how much the Commission has been changed by enlargement, or to isolate the effect(s) of enlargement from other factors. Besides, it remains early days in the life of the 'enlarged' Commission: it will be years before any judgement could be definitive. It may be the case that problems for the Commission stemming from enlargement have yet to reveal themselves and will only do so years from now. The Commission may be better organized and managed as a consequence of administrative reform, less self-obsessed, and doing less but doing it better. But it has only very limited control over its own fate. By nature, a politicized bureaucracy always runs the risk of being overwhelmed or marginalized by broader political developments, including a general loss of faith in the EU as a source of solutions to policy problems that have wildly diverse origins and manifestations.

Amidst such uncertainty, what *is* clear is that our knowledge of the effects of enlargement, on the Commission or more generally, remains quite primitive. So does our knowledge of the Commission itself, which has never collected very systematic data on who works in the administration, how the administration itself actually works, and what are the attitudes of its officials towards their work. Too often, the Commission is considered to be an institution that operates quasi-independently of the EU's member states, as opposed to being fully integrated into the EU system.

These points were illustrated by the first-ever *Economic Survey of the European Union* carried out by the Organisation for Economic Co-operation and Development (OECD) in 2007. The report was no doubt welcomed within the Commission itself, since it concluded that Europe's future economic prosperity depended on much faster progress towards a truly single market. In unveiling the report, the OECD's Secretary-General commented that 'The European Commission is making tremendous efforts to get rid of barriers to trade, and we fully support them', but admonished member governments to make more of an effort themselves.[42] Revealingly, one analysis of the study highlighted its conclusion that 'indigestion caused by the recent addition of 12 new members to the bloc' was a 'roadblock' to a stronger EU capable of generating superior economic performance. But it offered no clues as to what such 'indigestion' entailed or precisely how it was manifest, in the Commission or anywhere else.[43]

To try to enhance our knowledge beyond its primitive state, we and a wider research team have advanced plans for a large-scale attitudinal survey (in 2008) of the Commission. Some of the most important questions that we aim to answer concern the effects of enlargement on the Commission. As such, a final quarry to be mined for evidence of how the Commission's role has changed as a consequence of enlargement is a series of semi-structured interviews with Commission officials in 2006–7, the main purpose of which was to probe perceptions in the administration (particularly at its highest levels), in advance of our survey about specific questions that might appear on a questionnaire.[44] One question was left open-ended, and simply asked officials to identify 'the main effects of enlargement on the Commission'. The results shed interesting light on perceptions within the institution about how and how much enlargement is perceived to have changed the Commission.

. Table 4.3 seems to reveal a basic split between the view that enlargement had brought 'fresh blood, energy, enthusiasm and youth' to the Commission, and the view that it had not changed it very much. However, given the limited number of officials from the new member states who had been recruited at the time of research, we might expect that any respondent's answers to be determined by whether or not they had encountered significant numbers of EU12 officials in their work. It might even be possible to hold these two views simultaneously.

We also find support for the view that enlargement has made the

Table 4.3   *What have been the main effects of the 2004–7 enlargements on the Commission? (n = 26)*

	Services EU15	Services EU12	Cabinet EU15	Cabinet EU12	TOTAL	%
New blood, energy, enthusiasm, youth	5	2	2	3	12	22
Not fundamentally altered Commission	3	4	1	3	11	20
Less cosy, more diverse perspectives/views/ policy	5	2	1	2	10	19
More unwieldy College	3	1	1	2	7	13
Large, old member states less engaged	1	2	1	1	5	9
More use of English	4			1	5	7
More reform-minded	1	1		1	3	6
Empowers Commission	2				2	4
TOTAL					54	100
Respondents by category	12	4	2	8		26

Commission less 'cosy' and brought new perspectives to it. Perhaps most interestingly, there appears to be a widely held view that one consequence of enlargement is that older, larger EU15 member states are no longer as engaged at the EU level, with France and Germany mentioned most often in this context.

Still, on balance, there is little evidence here as elsewhere to suggest that enlargement has fundamentally altered the role of the Commission (at least not yet). At most, enlargement seems to have had a sort of *homoeopathic* effect. Homoeopathic remedies mostly work by applying small doses to 'multiply' already occurring body processes. Similarly, enlargement has reinforced or accentuated the impact of secular changes that are not exclusively or even specifically linked to enlargement. They include the emergence of a younger and more flexible Commission, one that is more presidential, and one that is no longer as reliant on its traditional monopoly power to propose formal legislation as leverage in EU policy debates. We have considered how the Kinnock reforms are linked in time and space to enlargement, at least in the minds of many officials, and how they may end up having effects that were not highlighted or even intended by their designers. We obviously lack counterfactuals, but there is little to suggest that the reforms were a response to the enlargements that were on the horizon as they were being designed, as opposed to the circumstances that led to the Santer Commission's resignation in 1999.

As a broad conclusion, there is certainly evolutionary change amidst the continuity in the Commission's role. Perhaps the single most important factor in provoking change is Barroso's strong stamp on his Commission and the stark contrast between its priorities and those of the Prodi Commission. There are clear reasons to believe that the Commission has become more hierarchical and presidential, if perhaps also more intergovernmental. Yet, it may be time to revise what we mean by 'intergovernmental' (see Peterson 2008). The Commission may now be less independent and unique as an institution, with (say) one member (Commissioner) per member state just like most offshoots of the Council. But it also may now be more intimately enmeshed in an EU system in which bargaining and coalition-building have become considerably more complicated, developments themselves that may make the position of the Commission stronger. If indeed these changes are taking place, enlargement has a place in the chain of causation. Yet, in the end, enlargement is one, but only one, amongst multiple rationales being used to try to reinvent the Commission.

NOTES

* Earlier versions of this paper were presented to the European Union Studies Association conference in Montreal, a workshop held at the European Institute for Public Administration (EIPA), and the Harris seminar of the Institute of Governmental Studies (IGS) at the University of California (Berkeley) in May 2007. We are grateful to colleagues who attended these sessions, and especially to Elizabeth Bomberg, Richard Doherty, Sonia Piedrafita Tremosa, and the editors for helpful comments. John Peterson wishes to thank colleagues at IGS for hosting him while work was done on this paper in early 2007.

1. The Lisbon Treaty was agreed by EU leaders in outline form in June 2007. Its provisions for institutional reform, such as reducing the size of both the (College of the) Commission and the European Parliament, were very similar to those of the Constitutional Treaty, but the new Treaty eschewed all the 'constitutional' trappings (mention of flag, anthem and so on) of the earlier one. The Lisbon Treaty still faced an uphill ratification process after its rejection in a June 2008 referendum in Ireland.

2. The Commission also has considerable independence in legal terms in specified policy areas, such as competition policy. For an overview, see Spence (2005).

3. We found this phrase was used by several senior Commission officials who were interviewed for this project in late 2006.

4. Interview, Brussels, 4 July 2006.

5. This claim was made by an MEP (from an EU12 state) at a private meeting in Edinburgh on 26 June 2006.

6. Text from http://www.europa.eu/institutions/inst/comm/index_en.htm (accessed 22 September 2007).

7. These figures are published (and regularly updated) in the Commission's *Bulletin Statistique*, and are available at http://ec.europa.eu/civil_service/docs/bs_dg_nat_en.pdf

(accessed 3 December 2006 and 22 September 2007). The share we cite for 2006 is for EU10 officials.

8. Interviews Brussels, 12 September 2006, and Edinburgh, 21 September 2006.
9. Interview, Brussels, 12 September 2006.
10. This pride shines through in many of the Commission's publicly stated positions on enlargement. A prime example is European Commission (2006), which spins a very upbeat story of the effects of the 2004 enlargement, and is full of pronouncements such as: '[e]nlargement has shown its enduring value as one of the EU's most effective policies, successfully contributing to peace, stability and democratic development throughout the continent' (European Commission 2006, p. 4). The same could be said about 'Myths and Facts about Enlargement', a web page maintained by DG Enlargement (http://ec.europa.eu/enlargement/questions_and_answers/myths_en.htm, accessed 30 November 2006). It boasts that 'the European Union is peacefully unifying Europe. ... A carefully managed enlargement process extends peace, democracy, the rule of law and prosperity across Europe. . . . The 2004 enlargement was the best-prepared in the history of the EU.' It is notable that Jan Truszczyński, a native Pole, was named Deputy Director-General of DG Enlargement in late 2006, a post which carries responsibility for the DG's information and communication strategy (see http://europa.eu/rapid/pressReleasesAction.do?reference=IP/06/1462&format=HTML&aged=0&language=EN&guiLanguage=en, accessed 30 November 2006).
11. These 'headline figures' are reported in the spring 2006 Eurobarometer poll (number 65), p. 12, available at http://ec.europa.eu/public_opinion/archives/eb/eb65/eb65_first_en.pdf (accessed 4 May 2007). As caveats, it should be noted that different questions (such as 'Do you think your country's EU membership is a good/bad thing?' or 'Does the EU conjure up for you a very positive/fairly positive/neutral/fairly negative/very negative image?') produced more sceptical views. A later (autumn 2006) poll generally suggested rising Euroscepticism in the new member states. See spring 2006 Eurobarometer (number 65), pp. 9–17 and autumn 2006 Eurobarometer (number 66), available from http://ec.europa.eu/public_opinion/archives/eb/eb66/eb66_highlights_en.pdf (accessed 4 May 2007).
12. These results are from the spring 2006 Eurobarometer (number 65), pp. 18–19. This question was not included in the autumn Eurobarometer poll (number 66), but reappeared in the spring 2007 poll (number 67), which generally showed less of a differential as support for the EU (especially in the EU15) rose in the midst of an economic recovery (results available at http://ec.europa.eu/public_opinion/archives/eb/eb67/eb67_en.htm, accessed 22 September 2007). See also 'Support for EU rises after economic recovery', *Financial Times* (UK edition), 20 June 2007, p. 6.
13. Eurobarometers 1, 3 and 4 (such as they are) are available at http://ec.europa.eu/public_opinion/archives/eb_arch_en.htm (accessed 1 May 2007).
14. See the spring 1988 Eurobarometer (number 29), available at http://ec.europa.eu/public_opinion/archives/eb/eb29/eb29_en.pdf (accessed 1 May 2007), pp. B72–3.
15. The trend can be observed by consulting any post-1995 Eurobarometer (at http://ec.europa.eu/public_opinion/standard_en.htm), although the specific question on trust in the Commission has been asked only since 1999.
16. Interview, Edinburgh, 28 November 2006.
17. Interview, Brussels, 2 October 2007.
18. Interview, Brussels, 2 October 2007.
19. The new rules are spelled out in Article 12 of the Commission's rules of procedure (which came into force in January 2006): '(Decisions taken by written procedure) 1. The agreement of the Members of the Commission to a draft text from one or more of its Members may be obtained by written procedure, provided the prior approval of the Legal Service and the agreement of the departments consulted in accordance with Article 23 has been obtained. Such approval and/or agreement may be replaced by an agreement between the Heads of Cabinet under the finalisation written procedure as provided for in the implementing rules.'

20. Interview, Brussels, 2 October 2007.
21. This point was confirmed in multiple interviews conducted with members of cabinets in late 2007.
22. The recent literature on the administrative reform of the Commission is larger than on any other topic. See the sources listed in Szarek and Peterson (2007, pp. 6–9).
23. The author cited here is a Commission official in DG Administration.
24. It should be noted that the Kinnock reforms included provisions for early retirement that lowered the average age of Commission officials by about two years (from 44 to 42) even before enlargement.
25. Interview, Brussels, 2 October 2007.
26. Interview, Brussels, 11 September 2006.
27. Interview, Brussels, 5 July 2006.
28. See the Commission's 'Legislative and Work Programme 2007', available from http://eurlex.europa.eu/LexUriServ/site/en/com/2006/com2006_0629en01.pdf (accessed 10 October 2007).
29. Hugo Brady, research fellow at the Centre for European Reform, quoted in *European Voice*, 16–22 November 2006, p. 21.
30. See 'Facing the Challenge: the Lisbon Strategy for Growth and Employment', Report from the High Level Group chaired by Wim Kok, November 2004, available from http://ec.europa.eu/growthandjobs/pdf/kok_report_en.pdf (accessed 13 December 2006).
31. See European Commission, 'Time to Move Up a Gear: The European Commission's 2006 Annual Progress Report on Growth and Jobs', available at http://ec.europa.eu/growthandjobs/annualreport_en.htm (accessed 13 December 2006).
32. Interview, Brussels, 4 July 2006.
33. Quoted in Peterson (2005, p. 9).
34. Codecision is increasingly the EU's template decision rule. It makes the European Parliament (EP) a politically and legally equal co-legislator with the Council (see Burns 2004).
35. Heisenberg (2007, p. 69) provides a general portrait of the EU's legislative pace over time as well as pre- and post-enlargement: the EU agreed an average of 46 directives in 1999–2005, compared to an average of 48 in 1974–95; and 15 during the first five months of 2006 compared with eight in the same months of 2005. She also explains why no straightforward measure of the number of Commission proposals exists (Heisenberg 2007, p. 80).
36. See the transcript of an interview with Barroso conducted within the framework of the EU-CONSENT Network of Excellence, available at http://www.eu-consent.net/library/BARROSO-transcript.pdf (accessed 27 September 2007); the quote is from p. 9.
37. See for example the barbed comments of EP political group leaders Martin Schulz and Graham Watson in response to Barroso's unveiling of his Commission's 'citizens' agenda', available from EuropeanVoice.com, http://www.europeanvoic.com/archive/article.asp?id=25407 (accessed 1 December 2006).
38. Quoted by EuropeanVoice.com, http://www.europeanvoice.com/archive/article.asp?id=26699 (accessed 1 December 2006).
39. See *European Voice*, 20–26 September 2007, p. 2.
40. Interview, Brussels, 12 September 2006.
41. Interview, Brussels, 5 July 2006.
42. Angel Gurría quoted in 'Faster Integration Key to Stronger European Growth, Says OECD report', available at http://www.oecd.org/document/37/0,3343,en_2649_201185_39335333_1_1_1_1,00.html (accessed 29 September 2007).
43. Lorraine Mallinder, 'EU Could Do Better, Says OECD', *European Voice*, 20–26 September 2007, p. 3.
44. The interviews were conducted mostly with senior officials, who were presented in advance with a standardized list of (pre-tested) questions. There was no prompting of responses, thus necessitating the codification of answers, and respondents were allowed to identify more than one 'effect'. The sample (n = 26) consisted of two cabinet chiefs and eight cabinet officials, the Secretary-General, two Directors-General, one Deputy

Director-General, three Directors, five Heads of Unit, three Policy Officers and one Programme Manager. Care was taken to construct a sample that included EU15 and EU12 nationals in the services, as well as officials in the cabinets of Commissioners from both categories of member state. The sample over-represents officials from EU12 Commission cabinets. However, officials who are nationals of EU15 states are, unsurprisingly, over-represented in EU12 Commission cabinets. In fact, four of eight officials in the cabinets of EU12 Commissioners interviewed for this analysis were nationals of EU15 member states. Interviews were conducted in Brussels on 4–5 July, 11–13 September, 20–22 November 2006, and 11 January, 3 July and 2 October 2007.

REFERENCES

Bearfield, N.D. (2004), 'Reforming the European Commission: Driving Reform from the Grassroots', *Public Policy and Administration*, **19** (3), 13–24.

Burns, C. (2004), 'Codecision and the European Commission: A Study of Declining Influence?', *Journal of European Public Policy*, **11** (1), 1–18.

Christiansen, T. (1997), 'Tensions of European Governance: Politicized Bureaucracy and Multiple Accountability in the European Commission', *Journal of European Public Policy*, **4** (1), 73–90.

Citi, M. and Rhodes, M. (2006), 'New Modes of Governance in the European Union: A Critical Survey and Analysis', in K.E. Jorgensen, M.A. Pollack and B. Rosamond (eds), *Handbook of European Union Politics*, London and Thousand Oaks, CA: Sage.

Cohen-Tanugi, L. (2005), 'The End of Europe?', *Foreign Affairs*, **84** (6), 55–67.

Coombes, D. (1970), *Politics and Bureaucracy in the European Community*, London: Allen & Unwin.

Crum, B., Davignon, E., de Schoutheete and Micossi, S. (2004), *Three Theses for the New Commission President*, CEPS Policy Brief, Brussels: Centre for European Policy Studies.

Dehousse, K. (2004), *La Stratégie de Lisbonne et la méthode ouverte de coordination: 12 recommandations pour une stratégie á plusieurs niveaux plus efficace*, Paris: Notre Europe.

European Commission (2001), *European Governance: A White Paper*, Brussels: European Commission.

European Commission (2006), *Communication on Enlargement Strategy and Main Challenges 2006–2007*, 8 November, Brussels, available at http://ec.europa.en/enlargement/pdf/key_documents/2006/Nov/com_649_strategy_paper_en.pdf.

Gray, M. and Stubb, A. (2001), 'Keynote Article: The Treaty of Nice: Negotiating a Poisoned Chalice?', The European Union: Annual Review of the EU 2000/2001, *Journal of Common Market Studies*, **39**, 5–23.

Groenendijk, N. (2006), 'Is Lisbon Not Delivering?', *EUSA Review*, **19** (4), 4–7.

Hagemann, S. and De Clerck-Sachsse, J. (2007), *Old Rules, New Game: Decision-making in the Council of Ministers after the 2004 Enlargement*, CEPS Special Report, available at http://shop.ceps.eu/BookDetail.php?item_id=1470 (accessed 6 May 2007).

Heisenberg, D. (2007), 'Informal Decision-making in the Council: The Secret of the EU's Success?', in S. Meunier and K. McNamara (eds), *Making History: European Integration and Institutional Change at Fifty*, Oxford and New York: Oxford University Press.

Hill, C. (2004), 'Rationalizing or Regrouping? EU Foreign Policy since 11 September 2001', *Journal of Common Market Studies*, **42** (1), 143–63.

Kassim, H. (2004a), 'A Historic Accomplishment: The Prodi Commission and Administrative Reform', in D.G. Dimitrakopoulos (ed.), *The Changing European Commission*, Manchester and New York: Manchester University Press.

Kassim, H. (2004b), 'The Kinnock Reforms in Perspective: Why Reforming the Commission Is an Heroic, but Thankless, Task', *Public Policy and Administration*, **19** (3), 25–41.

Kinnock, N. (2004), 'Reforming the European Commission: Organisational Challenges and Advances', *Public Policy and Administration*, **19** (3), 7–12.

Levy, R. (2003), 'Confused Expectations: Decentralizing the Management of EU Programmes', *Public Money and Management*, **23** (2), 83–92.

Levy, R.P. (2006), 'European Commission Overload and the Pathology of Management Reform: Garbage Cans, Rationality and Risk Aversion', *Public Administration*, **84** (2), 423–39.

Levy, R. and Stevens, A. (2004), 'The Reform of EU Management: Taking Stock and Looking Forward', *Public Policy and Administration*, **19** (3), 1–6.

Mattila, M. (2006), *Voting and Coalitions in the Council – Two Years after the Enlargement*, EUI Discussion Paper 2005–6, Florence: European University Institute.

Maurer, A. (2006), 'How Does the Council Work (or Not)?', in G. Durand (ed.), *After the Annus Horribilis: A Review of the EU Institutions*, EPC Working Paper 22, available at http://www.isn.ethz.ch/pubs/ph/details.cfm?lng=en&id=16977 (accessed 28 September 2007).

Norman, P. (2003), *The Accidental Constitution: The Story of the European Convention*, Brussels: EuroComment.

Nugent, N. (2004), *European Union Enlargement*, New York: Palgrave Macmillan.

Peterson, J. (1999), 'The Santer Era: The European Commission in Normative, Historical and Theoretical Perspective', *Journal of European Public Policy*, **6** (1), 46–65.

Peterson, J. (2005), 'Where Does the Commission Stand Today?', in D. Spence (ed.), *The European Commission*, London: John Harper.

Peterson, J. (2006), 'The College of Commissioners', in J. Peterson and M. Shackleton (eds), *The Institutions of the European Union*, Oxford and New York: Oxford University Press.

Peterson, J. (2008), 'Enlargement, Reform and the Commission: Weathering a Perfect Storm?', *Journal of European Public Policy*, **13** (6), 797–816.

Peterson, J. and Shackleton, M. (eds) (2006), *The Institutions of the European Union*, Oxford and New York: Oxford University Press.

Pollitt, C. and Bouckaert, G. (2004), *Public Management Reform: A Comparative Analysis*, Princeton, NJ and Oxford: Princeton University Press.

Pollitt, C. and Talbot, C. (eds) (2004), *Unbundled Government: A Critical Analysis of the Global Trend to Agencies, Quangos and Contractualisation*, London and New York: Routledge.

Pollitt, C., Van Thiel, S. and Homburg, V. (eds) (2007), *New Public Management in Europe: Adaptation and Alternatives*, Basingstoke and New York: Palgrave.

Radaelli, C.M. (2007), 'Whither Better Regulation for the Lisbon Agenda?', *Journal of European Public Policy*, **14** (2), 190–207.

Settembri, P. (2007), 'The Surgery Succeeded: Has the Patient Died? The Impact of Enlargement on the European Union', mimeo, available at http://nyugloballaw.org/fellowsscholars/documents/gffsettembripaper.pdf   (accessed   10 October 2007).

Spence, D. (ed.) (2005), *The European Commission*, London: John Harper.

Szarek, P. and Peterson, J. (2007), 'Studying the European Commission: A Review of the Literature', EUCONSENT Working Paper, available at http://www.euconsent.net/library/deliverables/D17_Team7_Szarek-Peterson.pdf (accessed 4 May 2007).

Szyszczak, E. (2006), 'Experimental Governance: The Open Method of Coordination', *European Law Journal*, **12** (4), 486–502.

Wincott, D. (2001), 'The Commission and the Reform of Governance in the EU', *Journal of Common Market Studies*, **39** (5) 897–911.

Windhoff-Héritier, A. (2002), *Common Goods: Reinventing European and International Governance*, Lanham, MD and Oxford: Rowman & Littlefield Publishers.

Windhoff-Héritier, A., Stolleis, M. and Scharpf, F. (2004), *European and International Regulation after the Nation State: Different Scopes and Multiple Levels,* Baden-Baden: Nomos.

Wonka, A. (2007), 'Technocratic and Independent? The Appointment of European Commissioners and its Policy Implications', *Journal of European Public Policy*, **14** (2), 169–89.

5. The European Parliament and enlargement

Brendan Donnelly and Milena Bigatto

This chapter considers from a number of related perspectives the interaction between the recent enlargement of the European Union and the workings and role of the European Parliament (EP). It concludes that the objective impact of enlargement upon the Parliament has been slight, but that the Union's enlargement has crystallized differing views about the Union's future, differences which bear and will continue to bear particularly on the development of the EP over the coming years.

THE NEW PARLIAMENTARIANS

The Quantitative Impact of Enlargement

A number of factors have combined to ensure that the impact of the European Union's enlargements in 2004 and 2007 would be less pronounced in the EP than in the European Commission or the Council of Ministers. The first and most obvious – as the Parliament relates to the Council – is purely quantitative in nature. While at plenary meetings of the Commission the number of decision-making participants has increased since 2004 from 20 to 27 (plus 35 per cent) and the European Parliament's membership has increased by around the same proportion as a result of those countries joining the Union in 2004 and 2007, from 570 to 785 (plus 38 per cent) (see Table 5.1), the Council's plenary meetings now have 27 members, where previously they had 15, an increase of 80 per cent. The enlargements of 2004 and 2007 embraced a number of small and very small member states, the limited population of which is reflected in their representation in the EP. The capacity of the parliamentarians in question to change significantly (even if they wished to) the workings and attitudes of the EP was always likely to be constrained by their limited numbers, whatever their personal and political qualifications for their new positions.

Table 5.1   MEPs from the 12 new member states

Country	EPP	PES	ALDE	UEN	Greens / EFA	EUL / NGL	ID	ITS	Non-attached	Total	Total %
BG	5	5	5					3		18	2.29
CY	3		1			2				6	0.76
CZ	14	2				6	1		1	24	3.06
EE	1	3	2							6	0.76
HU	13	9	2							24	3.06
LT	2	2	7	2						13	1.66
LV	3		1	4	1					9	1.15
MT	2	3								5	0.64
PL	15	9	5	20			3		2	54	6.88
RO	9	12	8					6		35	4.46
SI	4	1	2							7	0.89
SK	8	3	2						3	14	1.78
Total EU12	79	49	33	26	1	8	4	9	6	215	27.39
Total EU15	199	167	71	18	41	33	20	14	7	570	72.61
Total EU27	**278**	**216**	**104**	**44**	**42**	**41**	**24**	**23**	**13**	**785**	**100**

Source: Data from www.europarl.europa.eu (1 November 2007).

Table 5.2   Degree of education of first-time MEPs

	MEPs EU10		First-time MEPs EU15		All first-time MEPs	
	(nominal)	%	(nominal)	%	(nominal)	%
Postgraduate education	134	83	110	45	244	60
Doctorate	76	47	45	18	121	30

Source: Bale and Taggart (2006).

These qualifications are in many cases impressive. A study undertaken by Bale and Taggart (2006) sheds some light on the profiles of the MEPs from the ten new member states which joined in May 2004. The vast majority of this new intake of MEPs exhibit an exceptionally high degree of education, expressed in a striking number of holders of postgraduate qualifications (83 per cent) and even doctorates (47 per cent) (see Table 5.2). This compares to 45 per cent of first-time MEPs from the 15 'old' member states holding post-graduate qualifications and 18 per cent holding a doctorate. The remarkable educational background of MEPs from the new member states is no doubt linked to the high proportion of them whose previous professional occupa-tion was in education. The educational sector forms by far the largest occu-pational background of this group of MEPs (38 per cent), followed by public administration (12 per cent) and the sectors of industry, media and health and social services (11 per cent respectively) (see Table 5.3).

Regarding their previous political experience, Bale and Taggart's findings show that a significant number of MEPs of the ten new member states also have previous experience in the world of politics. As many as three-quarters of MEPs from this group have had experience as holders of an elected office, whether in their national parliament (60 per cent) or in government (33 per cent) (see Table 5.4). A number of MEPs from these countries have had extensive experience of the EU before entering the EP, gained for example when serving on the EU committee of their national parliament or even in the role of observers in the run-up to accession. Others again have gained experience in a multinational environment by working for international organizations such as the NATO or OSCE assemblies.

The arrival of a number of new national parties within the European Parliament has slightly changed the number of political groups. After the election, there were seven groups – one fewer than during the previous term. After the appointment of MEPs from Bulgaria and Romania the number increased temporarily to eight with the creation of the Identity, Traditions, Sovereignty group (ITS), which however ceased to exist in November 2007.

Table 5.3   Occupational backgrounds: sectors of previous employment of first-time MEPs

	MEPs EU10 %	First-time MEPs EU15 %	All first-time MEPs %
Education	38	29	32
Public administration	12	11	12
Industry	11	15	13
Media	11	10	10
Health and social services	11	3	6
Legal	4	8	7
Banking, finance, insurance, property	2	7	5
Agriculture, fishing, hunting, forestry	1	2	2
Security services (e.g. police, armed forces)	1	1	1

Source: Bale and Taggart (2006).

Table 5.4   Previous political experience of first-time MEPs

	MEPs (EU10)		First-time MEPs (EU15)		All first-time MEPs	
	(nominal)	%	(nominal)	%	(nominal)	%
EU institutions	18	11	22	9	40	10
International organizations	43	26	29	12	72	18
Elected office	120	74	168	68	288	71
Local council	47	29	124	50	171	42
Regional government	9	6	43	18	52	13
National parliament	96	60	89	36	185	45
National government	54	33	41	17	95	23
High position in national party	86	53	120	49	206	50
High position in regional party	11	7	49	20	60	15

Source: Bale and Taggart (2006).

Most MEPs from the new member states have joined the existing political groupings. Most joined the Christian Democrats (Group of the European People's Party and European Democrats, EPP), socialists (Socialist group, PSE) and liberals (Group of the Alliance of Liberals and Democrats for Europe, ALDE). Some joined the nationalistic group

Table 5.5   Measure of fragmentation (1979–2007)

	1979	1981	1984	1987	1989	1994	1995	1999	2004	2007	2007*
Countries (α)	9	10	10	12	12	12	15	15	25	27	27
Number of MEPs (β)	410	434	434	518	518	567	626	626	732	785	785
Political groups (γ)	7	8	9	9	11	10	10	9	7	8	7
γ/α	0.778	0.800	0.900	0.750	0.917	0.833	0.667	0.600	0.280	0.296	0.259
γ/β	0.017	0.018	0.021	0.017	0.021	0.018	0.016	0.014	0.010	0.010	0.009
$\Sigma\%$ (PSE + EPP)	53.7	55.3	55.3	54.1	58.1	62.6	63.2	65.9	64.2	63.2	63.2
Rae index	0.806	0.801	0.812	0.810	0.738	0.783	0.775	0.758	0.767	0.770	0.768

Note: * 14 November 2007: breaking up of ITS group.

Source: Revision of Verzichelli and Edinger 2005, p. 262.

(Union for Europe of the Nations Group, UEN), which doubled its membership; the accession of Bulgaria and Romania encouraged the creation of a new right-oriented group; a small number of deputies joined the Parliament's left-wing grouping (Confederal Group of the European United Left – Nordic Green Left, GUE/NLG) and one MEP joined the Greens (Group of the Greens and European Free Alliance, V/EFA). This distribution of MEPs from the new member states between the EP groups reflects the current political cultures in these transition democracies, but at the same time supports the idea that the European Parliament's traditional groups are well able to incorporate young political parties (Verzichelli and Edinger 2005). In fact, only ten MEPs in the first part of the legislature and nine in the second part (after the enlargement to Bulgaria and Romania) are in the group of Non-attached Members. After the breaking up of the ITS this number increased automatically to 34; it will be interesting to see which group the 23 ex-members of ITS will join. This legislature is certainly not more fragmented than the previous parliament, but on the contrary confirms the recent tendency of the European Parliament to reduce its fragmentation (see Table 5.5 and Figure 5.1).

Enlargement has not led to any restructuring of the European Parliament's committee structure, although the number of vice-Presidents

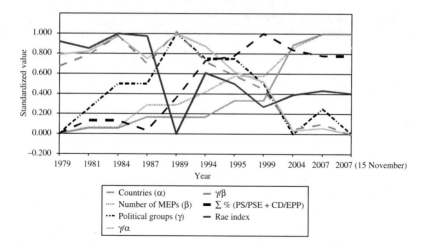

Figure 5.1   Measures of fragmentation within the EP (1979–2007)

on each committee has been temporarily increased from three to four to reflect the larger overall number of MEPs. In the first part of the legislature, MEPs from the new member countries held three not particularly prestigious committee chairmanships and that of the Budget Committee, although the role of this traditionally prestigious committee was to some extent reduced over this period by the Parliament's special temporary committee on the EU Financial Perspective for 2007–13. There was at least one vice-chairman in a majority of the committees from the new accession countries (not including the Employment, Fisheries and Civil Liberties Committees). In the second part of the legislature new MEPs have maintained four committee chairmanships, two of them being among the most important, the Foreign Affairs Committee (AFET) and the Environment Committee (ENVI). In the second part of the term the percentage of vice-chairmen from the new member states increased from 23 per cent to 30 per cent.

MEPs from the countries which have most recently acceded to the European Union have made less headway in being appointed the co-ordinators for their political groups within the individual committees. In the first part of the legislature in the three major groups, there was not a single coordinator from the new member states; in the second period, only one coordinator (in the PSE group) came from a new member state, but is responsible for one of the less important committees, the Petitions Committee. As to rapporteurships, MEPs from the new member states had been appointed until 2006 as rapporteurs for only 6.8 per cent of European parliamentary reports allocated since 2004 (Szczepanik 2006).

Qualitative Impact of Enlargement

The potential impact of parliamentarians from 12 new countries on the EP can neither be assessed in exclusively numerical terms nor be linked solely to the personal background of the elected individuals. The internal structures of the EP and its specific position within the institutional interplay of the European Union's political system create for the Parliament an idiosyncratic organizational and intellectual context which might well have been able rapidly to accommodate a much larger number of new parliamentarians than it has over the past five years with no fundamental change to its underlying aspirations and ethos. It has often been remarked that the turnover of members in the EP from one set of European elections to another is greater than in many national parliaments. Very rapidly, most of these new members undergo an integrative process within the Parliament which goes well beyond the self-confidence arising from growing familiarity with the voting procedures or the geographic peculiarities of the Parliament. Indeed, it is no exaggeration to say that the EP has always had a noticeably more profound effect on the great majority of its new members than they have had on it. It would have been distinctly surprising if the new parliamentarians from the 12 new member states had proved an exception to this rule.

Two defining characteristics of the European Parliament contribute particularly to its traditional ability to integrate within its political culture and norms a wide spectrum of new members from different political backgrounds. These are the political and administrative structuring of the Parliament around multi-national political groups and the essential nature of the Parliament as a legislative (not executive) body, which can make its strongest contribution to the European Union's legislative agenda only through its relationships with the other main elements in the Union's legislative structure, namely the European Commission and the Council of Ministers. Both these facts create for MEPs powerful political and functional identities which are specific to their role as European parliamentarians, and which in the vast majority of cases shape the developing political consciousness of MEPs when they go about their parliamentary business in Brussels or Strasbourg. This political and functional consciousness is of course not universal within the European Parliament, but the notable exceptions to this rule are in any case instructive, deriving usually from a radical rejection of the current constitutional structures of the European Union. Such a pre-existent and thorough-going rejection of existing structures seems almost to be a precondition for the resistance of individuals or political groupings to any internalization of the European Parliament's dominant ethos.

The transnational political group structure of the EP creates for any new MEPs or groups of new MEPs two contrasting sets of pressures, one of differentiation and the other of collaboration. The first of these derives primarily from ideological and electoral considerations, the second from the EP's recurrent need, under the current institutional structure of the EU, to obtain for its legislative proposals in particular as large a consensual majority as possible among the Parliament's 785 members. Both of these pressures are central to the working life of any MEP who wishes or is at least prepared to work within the conventional self-understanding of the EP. Both of these pressures work inevitably to dilute and disaggregate any united impact that might otherwise have been discerned arising from the arrival in the EP over the past three years of the MEPs representing the 12 new member states of the European Union. Where the EP political groups are in dispute among themselves, the default reaction of Maltese, Slovak, Polish and Estonian members will be to vote in disparate, non-national ways reflecting their group affiliations. Where there is a consensus, negotiated or spontaneous, between a number of parliamentary groups, then the great majority of parliamentarians from these groups will normally associate themselves with this consensus, and there is no obvious reason why parliamentarians from the new member countries should systematically fall outside this general rule.

A recent study by Hix and Noury (2006) has shown that party cohesion in the EP, reinforced by the pressures described above, has indeed remained strikingly stable after the enlargement of 2004. This statistical analysis, based on roll-call votes in the plenary meetings, demonstrates that MEPs from the new member states do indeed correspond in their recorded votes to the voting patterns deriving from their group affiliations rather than their national origins and that the primary motor of voting choices by European parliamentarians is political and not national. Occasionally, a shared national approach to a particular European issue generates a consensus between political opponents of the same nationality, and this is reflected in a specifically national voting pattern which ignores the normal discipline of the political groups to which the members in question are affiliated. But such events are very much exceptions that mark the rule, and by no means confined to MEPs from the newest member states. Equally, there are national delegations within the Parliament's political groups which are more prone than others to transgress in the interest of national positions the voting discipline of their groups. But such differences are differences normally only of degree between the components of the Parliament's groups. It might be that further statistical analysis could provide findings which, in isolation, could be regarded as illuminating or surprising about the behaviour of individual national parliamentary cohorts in the EP. It would not necessarily follow that such statistics would be significant for the functioning of the EP as a whole.

The application of this general analysis to the case of the 215 newest members of the EP is clear. These members constitute just over 27 per cent of the MEPs, and this percentage will persist after the adoption of the Lisbon Treaty and the consequent decrease in the number of EP seats to 751 (750 MEPs plus 1 president). For them to make any significant statistical impact on the characteristic and well-established voting patterns of the European Parliament, it would be necessary for all of them (or at least a large proportion of them) radically to depart from the norms and patterns of their predecessors and for them to structure these departures in similar ways among themselves. There would need to be a consistent and regular pattern of voting along specifically national lines, not merely by individual national delegations, but by all or the great majority of the national delegations concerned. It seems clear that no such radically atypical behaviour has been manifested by the new members in question. At most, there have been some suggestions that, among the Polish and Czech MEPs, there is a greater willingness to embrace specifically national positions on questions relating to the European Constitutional Treaty. This has and can only have a very limited significance for the overall work of the EP. The general stance of the EP on these questions remains clear and at wide variance from the 'national' stances of the Czech and Polish MEPs. Moreover, for all the political polemic which surrounds in the EP the sort of institutional questions treated by the Constitutional Treaty, these are issues where the role of the Parliament is indirect and declaratory. No serious case can be made for the proposition that the underlying political culture of the Parliament has been changed by enlargement.

THE POLITICS OF THE NEW EUROPEAN PARLIAMENT

The new members of the European Parliament have been elected by a variety of systems of proportional representation, from 12 new countries of the EU with widely differing recent histories of economic and political development. The spectrum of political views and economic analyses they represent is correspondingly variegated. Their distribution among the political groups has not altered the fundamental balance of voting majorities, whether conflictual or consensual, within the EP (see Table 5.1). On any plausible statistical review, the EP remains a body with a centre-right majority for most contested votes and one with a potential centrist majority in cases when there are institutional incentives for the Parliament to achieve an absolute majority of its members to give itself more purchase in its dealings with the Council and Commission. (For the latter phenomenon, see the interesting analysis by Neuhold and Settembri (2007), bringing out the high level of consensus attained in the Parliament's committee votes, both before and after enlargement.) If there is a discernible political impact which enlargement has had on the EP, it certainly falls far short of any kind of restructuring of its underlying political composition.

Much comment has been generated by the recent establishment of a new right-wing group made numerically possible by the participation of Bulgarian and Romanian MEPs. For some commentators, this development is evidence of a worrying prevalence in Eastern Europe of the disagreeable and dangerous nationalism the EU was founded to combat. For others, it is more generally indicative of a political volatility, even instability, of political attitudes in some countries formerly within the Soviet bloc and now full members of the EU. Such arguments and perceptions are worth considering in some detail, not necessarily to establish their objective truth or otherwise, but to locate more precisely their relevance for the functioning of the EP.

It should not of course be forgotten that the newly established right-wing group is not the first such alliance in the European Parliament's history. Unsurprisingly, in a parliament largely elected by proportional representation, there has always been a numerically limited stratum of extreme right-wing MEPs, who sometimes have had the numbers and administrative cohesion to form an independent group of their own and sometimes not. If on this occasion it happens to be an accretion of right-wing Bulgarian or Romanian MEPs who allow the formation of a new political group, then it would be premature indeed to conclude that the enlargement of the EU will generally impart to extreme right-wing views within the EP a reinforcement and momentum which they did not previously possess. Given the present electoral system and Rules of Procedure for the EP, neither the emergence nor the disappearance of an extreme right-wing group will ever be a surprising phenomenon. That the elections in Bulgaria, Poland or the United Kingdom should tip the balance in one direction or another is of some limited significance for the propagation of extreme right-wing views within the EU. But the real institutional and political context within which the EP operates would only genuinely be changed by the emergence of an extreme right-wing group in the Parliament considerably greater than that which has now come to exist. There is as yet no significant reason to believe that such a development is in immediate prospect, or that the likelihood of its coming to pass has been greatly affected by enlargement.

None of this is to deny that, on a number of issues, the political centre of gravity of the EP has somewhat shifted at the margins in recent years.

There is unanimous agreement among observers that the present EP is more sympathetic than some of its predecessors to the rhetoric and policies of the free market, more inclined to be suspicious of Russian attitudes and of its leading politicians, and that there is a noisy strain of social conservatism, even reaction, which is to be found among the new MEPs from the former Warsaw Pact countries in particular. But the significance of these observations must not be overstated, either in the short or in the long term. There are many MEPs from former Warsaw Pact countries who are bitterly critical of what they see as reactionary social attitudes exemplified by their compatriots in the EP; and there is every reason to believe that the passage of time will soften rather than exacerbate any particularly flagrant contrasts of rhetoric and political approaches between the great majority of the European parliamentarians (from wherever they come) and the small minority who, as new members of the Parliament, understandably attract to themselves a disproportionate amount of short-term attention.

Nor should it be forgotten that parliamentarians from the Union's newest countries will rightly demand of their colleagues that they take seriously the new insights and experiences coming from the political systems of the new member countries. If, as a result of enlargement, the EP centre of political gravity moves a little towards free market political preferences or towards a less accommodating view of the present Russian government, then such developments can hardly be regarded as unreasonable or anomalous in an enlarged EU. Parliamentary representatives from new member states are not likely to be those individuals most likely to take advantage of occasions offered them to say nothing. It is difficult to avoid the impression that some at least of the unfavourable comment directed towards the attitudes or utterances of individual MEPs from the new member states of the Union reflects the general concerns of the commentator about the overall question of enlargement, rather than the real significance for the EP of such attitudes or utterances.

THE EUROPEAN PARLIAMENT AND EUROPEAN DEMOCRACY

Ever since the first direct elections to the Parliament in 1979, the European Parliament has been that institution of the European Union most in developmental flux. Many hoped in 1979 that the very fact of direct elections to the Parliament would rapidly call into being a powerfully legitimizing new element of the Union's political structure, exercising increasingly salient powers in the Union's continuing institutional and political evolution. Some but not all of these expectations have been fulfilled. Over the past 28 years, the formal powers of the European Parliament have dramatically increased, to the point where it can properly claim to be a co-legislator over great swathes of new legislation from the Union. On the other hand, the Parliament cannot reasonably claim that for anything other than a small majority of the European Union's citizens it enjoys a democratic legitimacy or political salience easily comparable to that of national parliaments. The following paragraphs will consider the question of whether enlargement is likely to change, and if so in what direction, this uneasy present equilibrium of the European Parliament as a European institutional giant and a political pygmy.

For those who accept in its purest form the traditional integrationist analysis of the European Union, the directly elected European Parliament is one important focus of the democratic legitimacy of the Union, the other being the democratically elected members of the Council of Ministers. Between them, and particularly when they work together in the codecision procedure, the Parliament and Council constitute on this analysis an unanswerable rebuttal of sceptical questioning or doubts about the democratic credentials of the Union. Whether the Council fulfils quite the democratically legitimizing role attributed to it in this context is a moot question. National elections, which dictate national representation in the Council of Ministers, are only rarely shaped or decided by European topics and, if they are, then it is even more unusual for detailed questions of pending European legislation to figure in domestic campaigning. On the face of it, the European Parliament, issuing from specifically European elections, has a better claim to be regarded as the carrier of the Union's democratic legitimacy. Even this claim, however, needs qualification and perhaps more vigorous qualification in the light of the enlargement of the European Union since 2004. The dramatically low participation of voters from the Union's newest members in the European elections of 2004 does not suggest any widespread recognition in these countries of the European Parliament's legitimizing role within the Union.

Confronted with the low and generally decreasing participation of voters in successive European elections, Members of the European Parliament often and rightly point to low turnout in other large political units such as the United States. It is not generally held that the legitimacy and legitimizing function of the Congress is destroyed by this low turnout. This is only a partial answer to the Parliament's critics, since American democracy rests on a number of related foundations, of which elections to Congress form only one, together with presidential elections, gubernatorial elections, state elections and local elections. None of these elections have obvious equivalents within the European Union, where national and local elections form no part of the European Union's institutional fabric. Moreover, democratic legitimacy in the United States is sustained by an almost universal sense of shared American political identity, the central role of which in American political culture is well illustrated by the social pressure exercised upon new American citizens to revere the symbols of shared American political identity. The sense of American political identity is in its turn reinforced by a lively and polemical civil society, an American 'public space' in which the polity's common problems and concerns are debated. The majoritarian decisions of the American Congress would not be accepted as democratically legitimate without this pre-existing (or at least coexisting) sense of American political identity, from which the rights and obligations of minorities and majorities within the American political system flow. The European Union at its present stage of development has little resemblance to the real democratic circumstances of the United States of America. This fact is particularly pertinent for the real democratic possibilities and constraints under which the European Parliament has operated, both between 1979 and 2004 and from 2004 to the present. Whether the enlargement of the Union in 2004 significantly changed these possibilities and constraints is not a question capable of a single answer.

Since the Treaty of Rome, differences of view have coexisted on the institutional model of integration towards which the European Community and (later) European Union were tending. These differences are sometimes described as those between the 'intergovernmentalist' model and the 'federalist' model. A more precise description of the debate might be as one between those who foresee the European Union as acquiring a substantial and increasing range of state-like attributes and those who believe its existing state-like attributes are already sufficient or even excessive. The implications of this debate for the standing and future role of the European Parliament are evident. A powerful and politically highly visible European Parliament, with an autonomous and widely recognized democratic legitimacy, would itself be a striking state-like attribute for the European Union. For reasons described above, however, such a European Parliament will never exist in isolation from other state-like elements of the Union, which either do not currently exist or exist only fragmentarily. Until the Amsterdam Treaty of 1997 it was possible to believe, or to fear, that the work of state-like construction in the European Union was proceeding consistently. The Amsterdam Treaty itself marked an important further step in the state-like characteristics of the Union, with the substantial pruning back of the 'intergovernmentalism' which until then had characterized the Justice and Home Affairs pillar of the Maastricht Treaty.

But if there is reason to say that the enlargement of the European Union in 2004 has made it somewhat more difficult to envisage the continuing construction of such a network of state-like attributes for the Union, it cannot be claimed that the 15 member states of the Union between 1997 and 2004 were pursuing this path with any great enthusiasm. The enlargement of the Union in 2004 took place at a time when the 'state-building' aspect of European integration was anyway quiescent, with the important exception of the single European currency. The late 1990s were not a period when the member states were eager to construct new state-like functions for the European Union. Indeed, the European single currency itself has a structure of governance as un-'state-like' as possible at the European level. If it is to be argued that enlargement made 'state-building' within the European Union more difficult, it must be precisely specified what were the new elements in this equation arising from enlargement. Two possible elements present themselves, namely the difficulty of agreement on constitutional innovation among 25 member states rather than 15 and the potentially looser sense of a binding political identity engendered in some longer-standing member states of the Union by enlargement.

The first of these elements does not need extended discussion, being little more than a mathematical self-evidence. While many of the day-to-day decisions of the Union are taken by majority voting, the new treaties which are central to the continuing constitutional innovation on which the European Parliament in particular depends need to be agreed by unanimity. To steer 27 national governments to such unanimity must always be more difficult than to do the same for 15. Less tangible, but just as important for the short- and medium-term institutional development of the Union, are the changes arising for the Union's political meteorology from the accession to the Union of 12 new countries between 2004 and 2007.

Ever since the end of the Cold War and the emergence of the real possibility that the European Union would expand to include in particular the countries of the defunct Warsaw Pact, debate has raged within the Union on what relationship there might be between the institutional deepening and the geographic widening of the Union. An often-expressed expectation has been that the workings of the European institutions in an enlarged European Union would be so inefficient and tardy that the case for institutional reform would be thereby reinforced. It cannot be claimed that events in the European Parliament have yet followed this course. On the contrary, it would be difficult to argue that the European Parliament has been so hamstrung in its regular activities since 2004 as to reinforce the case for the extension of the codecision procedure which was so important a feature of the European Constitutional Treaty. In any event, the principal argument for that extension was always one of democracy rather than efficiency. It is in the context of the democratic self-understanding of the European Union that enlargement has made at least in the short term a difference to the European Parliament's possible evolutionary path.

Rightly or wrongly, the enlargement of the European Union in 2004 has been associated in the minds of many ordinary electors in the European Union with a sense that the political identity of the Union was being diluted, in the interest of a purely economic Union geared around the values of economic liberalism and globalization. This sense was crucial to the rejection in both France and the Netherlands of the European Constitutional Treaty. The much-quoted figure of the 'Polish plumber' was at a superficial level pure caricature. At a deeper level, it reflected concerns in France and elsewhere that the enlarged European Union is so politically and economically disparate that further progress along the route sketched out by the Single European Act, the Maastricht Treaty and the Amsterdam Treaty is no longer possible or desirable. These concerns have been sustained and reinforced in particular by some of the social attitudes which the former Polish government embraced and for which it had on occasion even sought to proselytize. More than any other institution of the Union, the European Parliament depends in the medium to longer term on the continuation of the state-like integration which found its highest point until now in the Amsterdam Treaty. If enlargement poses in the coming years, for whatever reason, a barrier to the resumption of this process, the European Parliament will be a particular loser. The vexed question of relations between the European Parliament and national parliaments is a powerful illustration of the new challenges which the European Parliament is coming to face in its quest for a democratically legitimizing role.

THE EUROPEAN PARLIAMENT AND NATIONAL PARLIAMENTS

A specific and significant theatre over which the debate about the future institutional structure of the European Union has ranged in recent years is that of the role of national parliaments in the Union's institutional architecture. This argument has been exacerbated by the Union's enlargement, since to involve national parliaments from 27 countries in the legislative and other work of the Union presents even more of a political and administrative challenge than to involve the national parliaments of 15. The role of national parliaments in the European Union was a much-debated one in the European Constitutional Convention. The terms of that debate were highly illuminating and potentially disquieting for the European Parliament.

In the Convention, two contrasting views of democratic legitimacy in the European Union clashed: that of the 'federalists', who argued that only the European Parliament had the expertise, focus and specifically European democratic legitimacy to perform with any credibility the central parliamentary role within the European Union; and on the other hand that of the so-called 'intergovernmentalists', who doubted the aptness of the European Parliament for any such role and believed that democratic legitimacy speaks rather out of the barrel of national parliamentary weaponry. (It may incidentally be doubted whether in this context the often self-attached designation 'intergovernmentalist' was wholly appropriate. The real contrast was surely that observed between those content with the state-like evolution of the European Union and those hostile to any such evolution.)

The compromise achieved by the Convention and incorporated into the Constitutional Treaty (with only marginal changes in the Lisbon Treaty) was one which should rationally have satisfied neither party. The logic of the 'statelike-building' European Union had traditionally ascribed to national parliaments only the role of scrutinizing the European policies of the national governments with which they were associated. By appearing to give a new, European role to national parliaments in the Union's legislative procedures, it implicitly cast doubt upon the democratically legitimizing role of the European Parliament and sought to reintroduce into the Union's legislative procedures the approximately 40 varied national parliaments of the Union. Intellectually and politically, this was a damaging breach in the philosophical and institutional rationale of the European Parliament, made all the more damaging by the nonchalant claims of some national politicians that 'democratic legitimacy' could only be assured for the European Union by national parliaments. The 'federalist' side of this argument, however, could draw comfort from the hollow, restricted and incoherent nature of the new power given to national parliaments. It was not long before Eurosceptic critics in the United Kingdom and elsewhere were claiming (with some plausibility) that the European Constitutional Treaty's institutional structure was in at least one respect demonstrably untransparent and dishonest, appearing to involve more fully national parliaments in European legislative procedures but in reality not doing so.

It is not, of course, by chance that the compromise elaborated by the Constitutional Convention was so indefensibly incoherent. It was an attempt to marry two wholly incompatible views of the current and future institutional rationale of the European Parliament and indeed of the European Union. Both views have persuasive elements to their argumentation. The European Parliament is not in most member states of the Union a substantial legitimizing factor for the Union's decision-making. But it in no sense follows that the greater involvement of national parliaments in this decision-making, anyway bringing with itself enormous practical problems, will enhance the Union's democratic legitimacy in the minds of its citizens either. The European Parliament is today uncomfortably poised between impractical and incoherent notions of national democratic legitimization for European decision-making, on the one hand, and as yet implausible and fragmentary accounts of itself as a supporting column of the Union's democratic legitimacy. There must be considerable doubt as to the long-term sustainability of this position. Since direct elections to the European Parliament began in 1979, the formal powers of the European Parliament have increased exponentially, and the Lisbon Treaty is likely to continue this process. But the formal powers of the European Parliament should not necessarily be equated with political legitimacy and its essential concomitant in a modern democracy, high public profile. The capacity of the MEPs who served on the Convention to set the agenda of the Convention in a way so favourable to their institution was in no sense a response to public pressure for an enhancement of the Parliament's role. It was rather a consequence of the (wholly legitimate) negotiating skill shown by the Parliament's representatives in the Convention.

CONCLUSIONS

The specific impact of the European Union's enlargement upon the European Union has been limited, because of both the modest numbers of new parliamentarians involved and their dispersal within the pre-existing political groups of the Parliament. Other than on institutional questions, where the role of the European Parliament is in any case restricted, MEPs from the newest member states of the Union have followed the example of their predecessors and voted in a manner more easily explicable by their political rather than their national affiliations. To a limited extent, the prevalence of certain political views within the Parliament has been rein-forced by the influx of new members (as it has in the Council and Commission), and some marginal political views have become slightly less marginal. The European Parliament remains however confronted with its fundamental existential question, whether it can substantially contribute to the democratic life of the European Union. This was a question which already was posing itself in sharper tones as the 1990s progressed. Enlargement has certainly not rendered this question less acute. If the European Union, or a substantial portion of its members, is prepared to resume that institutionally integrative path on which it seemed irrevocably set until the Amsterdam Treaty, the future role of the European Parliament will be a clearer and securer one. If not, it may well be that the growing calls for national parliaments to provide the democratic legitimacy of the Union, in spite of all the practical difficulties involved, will become irresistible. In those circumstances, the question could not be avoided as to the sense and future of the directly elected European Parliament itself. In the twentieth century, the British House of Lords reinvented itself as essentially a highly qualified revising chamber for the legislation of the House of Commons. It must be doubtful whether the European Parliament would wish or be able in the long term to content itself with such a role. The years leading up to the European elections of 2009 will be particularly important in this regard. The process of ratification of the Lisbon Treaty and the capacity or otherwise of the Parliament to take advantage of the new possibilities given to it by the Treaty, particularly in the election of the President of the Commission, will provide important clues about the future likely evolution of the (enlarged) European Parliament.

BIBLIOGRAPHY

Bale, Tim and Taggart, Paul (2006), 'First-Timers Yes, Virgins No: The Roles and Backgrounds of New Members of the European Parliament', *SEI Working Paper*, **89**.

Corbett, Richard, Jacobs, Francis and Shackleton, Michael (2007), *The European Parliament*, London: John Harper Publishing.

Hix, Simon and Noury, Abdul (2006), 'After Enlargement: Voting Behaviour in the Sixth European Parliament', Paper presented at the Federal Trust conference on 'The European Parliament and the European Political Space', 30 March, London.

Judge, David and Earnshaw, David (2003), *The European Parliament*, London: Palgrave.

Kaeding, Michael (2005), 'The World of Committee Reports: Rapporteurship Assignment in the European Parliament', *Journal of Legislative Studies*, **11** (1), Spring, 82–104.

Neuhold, Christine and Settembri, Pierpaolo (2007), 'Achieving Consensus through Committees: Does the Sixth European Parliament Continue to Manage?', Paper presented to the EUSA Tenth Biennial International Conference, 17–19 May, Montreal.

Pasquinucci, Daniele and Verzichelli, Luca (2004), *Le elezioni politiche europee e classe politica sovranazionale 1979–2004*, Bologna: Il Mulino.

Szczepanik, M. (2006) 'The European Parliament after Enlargement: Any Different?', Paper prepared for presentation at the Federal Trust conference on 'The European Parliament and the European Political Space', 30 March, Goodenough College, London.

Verzichelli, Luca and Edinger, Michael (2005), 'A Critical Juncture? The 2004 European Elections and the Making of a Supranational Elite', *Journal of Legislative Studies*, **11** (2), 254–74.

Whitaker, Richard (2006), 'New Kids on the Brussels Block: Committee Assignments in the European Parliament before and after Enlargement', Paper prepared for the Federal Trust conference on 'The European Parliament and the European political space', 30 March, Goodenough College, London.

6. EU enlargement and the European Court of Justice

Caroline Naômé[1]

On 11 May 2004, ten new members of the European Court of Justice (here-after, the 'Court')[2] took the oath before a court composed of 15 judges and eight advocates-general. On the next day, nine[3] new members of the Court of First Instance (hereafter, the 'CFI') took the oath before a court composed of 25 judges and eight advocates-general. The bench had been adapted during the night in order for the members of the Court to sit in two rows. The reason for the organization of two different formal sittings may have been that it would have taken too long to listen to introductory speeches, presentations and oaths of 20 persons. Yet this distinction between the members of the two Courts allowed the new members of the Court to be immediately involved in the judicial activity and gave the new members of the CFI the opportunity to be sworn in before the members of the Court from their own member states. This is a good example of the effects of enlargement on the Court: material adaptations, immediate involvement of the new members and preservation of the substance.

The Court has had to adapt its structure, increase the number of cham-bers and reduce the amount of documents to be translated. The judicial activity of the Court between 2004 and 2007 shows that the Court has over-come the difficulties related to the enlargement and even used it as an opportunity to improve its working methods and reduce its backlog.

The preparations naturally did not start in May 2004, and not all the changes that have taken place at the Court are the results of enlargement. After explaining the decision-making process, this chapter therefore looks at the evolution of the Court during the years before the enlargement before trying to analyse the consequences of the enlargement on the deci-sion-making process and judicial activity. Some brief reflections are then added about the linguistic aspects of the enlargement and the other depart-ments of the Court.

This chapter is focused on the Court of Justice, for which changes in time are well documented, of which the scope of activity has not changed much during the period of time examined, and of which the author has a better knowledge.[4]

THE DECISION-MAKING PROCESS OF THE COURT

The Court of Justice consists of a number of judges corresponding to the number of member states,[5] assisted by advocates-general. The judges elect one of their number as president for a term of three years. The advocates-general appoint the first advocate-general for a period of one year.

The Court sits in plenary sessions (now Full Court or Grand Chamber), or in chambers of five or of three judges. Most of the work is done in chambers of five. Important cases are dealt with in the plenary sessions. Technical cases or orders are mostly decided by chambers of three.

After a case has been registered, the first important decision is the designation by the President of the Court of a judge to act as rapporteur in the case. He will analyse the documents submitted to the Court by the parties and write the preliminary report, which should contain recommendations as to how the case should be dealt with, whether a preparatory inquiry or any preparatory step should be undertaken, and to which formation the case should be assigned.

The advocate-general responsible for the case will be designated by the first advocate-general as soon as the judge-rapporteur is designated by the President. After the hearing, if it takes place, the advocate-general will present an opinion, in which he will propose a decision and the legal reasoning that supports it. After the opinion has been delivered, the judge-rapporteur sends a note to the judges composing the chamber dealing with the case. He can propose to follow the solution and the reasoning developed by the advocate-general. He can, however, disagree with the advocate-general on the solution and/or on the legal reasoning proposed.

Only the judges sitting in a case take part in the deliberation. No legal secretary, interpreter or agent from the registry is present. Although the judges try to reach a consensus in the decision, they may have to vote if there is a clear difference of opinion or if the President feels it appropriate. The decision is taken by a simple majority.

Some deliberations are short; others are more difficult and take time. However, the length of time that elapses between the last stage of the procedure (general meeting, hearing or opinion) and the delivery of the judgment is not a good indicator of the difficulty of the deliberation, as the discussion begins only with a proposition or a draft from the judge-rapporteur. More important are the number of times a case is discussed and the length of time spent in discussions. These elements, in turn, depend on the predictability of the legal reasoning that will be accepted by the court and of the quality of the draft. A well-written opinion of an advocate-general makes things easier. Stability in the composition of the deliberating body is also a factor of predictability.

It is therefore important to know the composition of chambers and, when the number of judges sitting in a case is smaller than the number of judges composing a chamber, how they are selected to sit in the case.

Before 2004, the Court (14 judges without the President) composed two chambers of five, each composed of seven judges. These seven judges, in turn, composed two chambers of three, one composed of four judges and the other one of three. The assignment of judges to chambers is decided by the Court upon proposition of the President.

In order to determine which judges sit in each case and to respect the principle of the 'legal judge', well known to German lawyers, lists are drawn up for the purpose of determining the composition of the chambers. The President excepted, the first on the list is the most senior one in office (or age, where there is equal seniority), the second on the list is the last one in seniority, the third one on the list is the second in seniority, etc., the objective being to have a mix in experiences at the Court. The composition of a chamber dealing with a case is determined according to those lists, at the general meeting of the Court, when a case is assigned to a chamber.

THE EVOLUTION OF THE COURT DURING THE TEN YEARS PRECEDING THE ENLARGEMENT

The ten years preceding the 2004 accession can be described as a permanent effort by the Court to improve its efficiency and its effectiveness. The steady increase in the number of cases led to the creation of the CFI in 1989, which consists of one judge per member state.[6] The idea was to relieve the Court of cases in which facts are important, such as competition cases and staff cases. The jurisdiction of the CFI was subsequently extended several times.[7]

Despite the creation of the CFI and the efforts of the Court to deal with more cases by reasoned orders and through chamber decisions (instead of plenary sessions), the number of cases kept on rising, as well as the average length of the procedure. There were preliminary references related to the abundant new legislation adopted in order to complete the internal market. There was also an unexpectedly high number of references coming from the new member states of the 1995 enlargement. The Court tried to deal with this by asking the member states for changes in the judicial structure or in the Rules of Procedure, so as to change its working methods and to use all the possibilities it had to handle the cases quickly.

The issue became serious after the signature of the Treaty of Amsterdam conferring new competences on the Union and the Community, and as the prospect of further enlargements became clearer. In a report asked for by the Commission and adopted by the working party, presided over by the former President of the Court, M.O. Due, on the future of the European Communities' court system (the so-called 'Due Report'), the working party stressed three foreseeable challenges: the expansion of the litigation volume, the difficulty for the Court of Justice to operate satisfactorily with a greater number of members and the aggravation of the language problems.

Some improvements were introduced by a modification of the Rules of Procedure in May 2000.[8] There was greater scope for disposing of cases by order and to dispense with the oral part of the procedure, which saves time. The Council also accepted the introduction of an accelerated procedure in references for a preliminary ruling, when the circumstances mean that a ruling on the question is a matter of exceptional urgency. It also agreed on the possibility of the Court issuing practice directions relating in particular to the preparation and conduct of the hearings before it, and to the lodging of written statements of cases or written observations.

Essential changes were introduced by the Treaty of Nice, signed on 26 February 2001 and in force since February 2003, which reorganizes the provisions on Community courts. Some rules are transferred from the treaties into a new statute of the Court, replacing the former ones. Most of the provisions of the statute may be amended by unanimous vote in the Council, i.e. without the need for a new treaty. As was requested by the courts, the Rules of Procedure may now be amended by qualified majority in the Council instead of unanimous vote. Concerning the judicial structure, the new treaty provisions provide for a further extension of the CFI's jurisdiction in direct actions (with the possibility of an appeal) and the creation of judicial panels to hear and determine at first instance certain classes of action or proceedings brought in specific areas (with the possibility of an appeal before the CFI and of a review of the CFI's decisions by the Court 'where there is a serious risk of the unity or consistency of Community law being affected'). According to Article 225 of the EC Treaty, the CFI could also have jurisdiction to hear and determine questions referred for a preliminary ruling (subject to review by the Court). The treaty established the principle of one judge per member state and maintained the number (eight) of advocates-general. However, should the Court so request, the Council may increase the number of advocates-general. Also, the new Statute introduced the possibility of the Court delivering judgments without an opinion from the advocate-general 'where the Court considers that the case raises no new point of law'. According to Article 221 of the EC Treaty, the Court shall sit in chambers or in a Grand Chamber, which consists, in 2007, of 13 judges and has a quorum of nine judges. When the Court considers that a case before it is of exceptional importance, it shall sit as a full Court (all the judges). As proposed by the working party in the Due Report, the presidents of the chambers of five judges are elected by the judges for three years and sit in all cases dealt with by the Grand Chamber. As for the composition of the CFI, Article 224 of the EC Treaty provides that it shall comprise at least one judge per member state and that the precise number of judges should be fixed by the statute.

In October 2003, immediately after the partial renewal of the Court and the election of M.V. Skouris as its new president, the Court started discussing the changes that would be necessary in order to implement the new provisions introduced by the Treaty of Nice, to improve the efficiency of its working methods and to be ready for enlargement. Without questioning the use of French as the working language, the Court decided important changes aimed mainly at reducing the volume of translations: shortening of the reports prepared by the rapporteur and of the judgments, as well as selective publication of the judgments (which means that they do not have to be translated in all official languages). Also, the advocates-general are invited, but not obliged, to draft their opinions in one of the five main languages (English, French, German, Italian and Spanish) selected by the Translation Directorate to be used as 'pivot' (relay) languages.

Besides those measures having a direct impact on translation, the Court adopted a number of measures aimed at improving efficiency and shortening the length of the proceedings: better respect of internal timetabling, better and quicker use of reasoned orders, shortening of the reports prepared by the rapporteur, better use of the work in chambers, reduction of the 'semaines blanches' (i.e. the weeks when no hearings or deliberations are organized), and an increased number of general meetings.

Immediately after the entry into force of the Treaty of Nice, the Court, which for a long time had two chambers of five judges and four chambers of three judges, kept the same structure. After the partial renewal of the Court in October 2003, however, the judges elected two presidents of chambers of five judges for three years. In May 2004, following enlargement, the increased number of judges made it necessary to create an additional chamber of five judges and to reduce the number of chambers of three judges. A third president of a chamber of five judges was elected. The composition of the chambers, adopted by the Court on a proposal by the President, was of course new, in comparison to October 2003. Given the amount of work they would have, the presidents of the chambers of five judges were not appointed as members of any chamber of three judges. All the cases which had already been dealt with by the general meeting of the Court but in which no hearing had taken place were reallocated by a next general meeting to the chambers in their new composition, in order to involve the new members immediately in the judicial work.

Further changes took place in the following period. By a decision of 26 April 2004,[9] the Council transferred some jurisdiction from the Court to the CFI. By a decision of 2 November 2004,[10] it made use of the possibility, introduced by the Treaty of Nice, of creating judicial panels to hear certain classes of action and established the European Union Civil Service Tribunal. On 12 July 2005,[11] the Council approved amendments to the Rules of Procedure proposed by the Court with the view of shortening the duration of proceedings. On 18 October 2005,[12] the Council adopted other amendments to the Rules of Procedure aimed at sharing more equitably the judges' participation in the Grand Chamber and other formations of the Court. As explained earlier, according to the Rules of Procedure and in order to respect the principle of the 'legal judge', the judges sit in rotation in the Grand Chamber and in the chambers of five or three, following lists of names established according to the Rules of Procedure. Before the amendment, the same judges would sit in all cases assigned to a formation at a specific general meeting. After the amendment, the composition would change in each case dealt with by the general meeting, accelerating the rotation and thereby ensuring a better participation of the judges.

Before summer 2006, the Court decided, in view of the accession of Bulgaria and Romania, to create an additional chamber of five judges and an additional chamber of three judges. After the partial renewal of the Court, in October 2006, the Court re-elected M. Skouris as President, elected the four presidents of the chambers of five judges and decided the composition of the chambers, upon a proposal by the President. The change in the number of chambers caused a modification of their composition.

In June 2006, the Commission sent the other institutions a communication proposing an extension of the Court's jurisdiction (visas, asylum, immigration, judicial cooperation in civil matters) in preliminary rulings.[13] In view of this extension which could bring cases requiring urgent or priority treatment, the Court proposed the establishment of an urgent preliminary ruling procedure with specific rules of procedure. It seems that the member states prefer that the Court changes first the procedure before agreeing on the extension of its jurisdiction. However, the extension should happen anyway according to the Lisbon Treaty prepared in 2007.

At the end of an afternoon on a Friday in January 2007, at the same formal sitting, the new judges of the Court and of the CFI from Bulgaria and Romania took the oath before the Court.

CHANGES DUE TO ENLARGEMENT HAVING AN IMPACT ON THE DECISION-MAKING PROCESS

The main change affecting the decision-making process was of course the arrival of ten new judges. The consequences of the increase in the number of judges – from 15 to 25 in 2004 and 27 in 2007 – are numerous. Some are linked to the fact that a great number of newcomers arrived at the same time. Others are linked only to the number of judges, whether or not those judges were newcomers.

The new judges helped to make the Court slightly younger. In 2004, the average age of the 15 judges before enlargement was 61.5 years, with a range from 50 to 73. For the ten new judges, the average age was 57.5, with a range from 49 to 66. The average age of the 25 judges became 59.8 years.

Among the 15 judges in 2004, only three were women. The ten new judges were all men. The three previous women judges then left, with the result that after October 2006, following the partial renewal, there were only two women judges at the Court, three after the arrival of the Rumanian judge.

The experience of the new judges before taking the oath was comparable to that of the 15 who were already there. Although it is very difficult to classify the experience of judges appointed to the Court, as all of them had a rich and varied experience before becoming judges and could be classified in several categories, we have tried to place them in three main categories according to the function they had before arriving at the Court: judiciary (including the European Court of Human Rights), academic and administrative (international, European or national). Among the 15 judges present in January 2004, and if we except M. La Pergola, who could be better classified as a politician, we could say that eight judges had worked in the judiciary (MM. Puissochet and Jann, Mrs Macken and Mrs Colneric, MM. Von Bahr, Cunha Rodrigues, Lenaerts and Schiemann), four in an EC/state administration (MM. Schintgen, Timmermans and Rosas, Mrs Silva de Lapuerta) and two in a university (MM. Skouris and Gulmann). Of the ten new judges, seven had worked for the judiciary (MM. Kuris, Arestis, Borg Barthet, Malenovský, Klucka, Lohmus and Levits), two for an international/state administration (MM. Makarczyk and Juhász) and one for a university (M. Ilesic).

The composition of the chambers of five gives an idea of how the new judges were integrated. As explained earlier, a proposal is made by the

President but, according to Article 9(1) of the Rules of Procedure, it is the Court which decides which judges shall be attached to each chamber.

In October 2003, M. P. Jann (AT, former judge at the Constitutional Court, judge at the Court since 1995) and M. Ch. Timmermans (NL, former Director-General of the European Commission Legal Service, university professor, judge at the Court since 2000) were elected presidents of the two chambers of five. The composition of those chambers was as follows:

First chamber (M. Jann, AT)	Second chamber (M. Timmermans, NL)
IT, UK, SE, BE, FI, ES	DK, FR, LU, IE, PT, DE

After the arrival of the ten new judges, the Court decided to form three chambers of five judges and elected M. A. Rosas (FI, former Deputy Director-General of the European Commission Legal Service, university professor, judge at the Court since 2002) as the third president of a chamber of five. The composition of the three chambers was as follows:

First chamber (M. Jann, AT)	Second chamber (M. Timmermans, NL)	Third chamber (M. Rosas, FI)
DE, PT, BE, UK, HU, SI, LV	DK, LU, ES, PL, LT, CY, SK	IT, FR, IE, SE, MT, CZ, EE

After the partial renewal of October 2006, the Court decided to create a fourth chamber of five, in view of the accession of 2007. MM. Jann, Timmermans and Rosas were reelected and M. K. Lenaerts (BE, judge at the CFI since 1989, university professor, judge at the Court since 2003) was elected. The composition of the four chambers (since January 2007) is as follows:

First chamber (M. Jann, AT)	Second chamber (M. Timmermans, NL)	Third chamber (M. Rosas, FI)	Fourth chamber (M. Lenaerts, BE)
LU, IT, MT, SI, LV	UK, PL, LT, DK, FR, RO	PT, SK, EE, IE, SE, BG	ES, HU, CY, CZ, DE

In January 2007, the judges of the new member states were thus spread evenly in the four chambers, three of them belonging to each chamber. The rules on the appointment of the judges sitting in a case mean that judges from new member states could form a majority in a chamber. Since the renewal of October 2006 and the arrival of new judges from old member states, this could also be the case in the Grand Chamber.

In the redesign of the chambers in May 2004, the chambers of five and the chambers of three which were linked to them were supposed to be the working units of the Court, with the purpose of facilitating the integration of the newcomers: judges, legal secretaries and assistants. However it was left to the judges already in office, with a special responsibility of the presidents of the chambers of five, to adopt initiatives to that end.

Since the Treaty of Nice, the presidents of the chambers of five judges have a special position. They participate in all cases of the Grand Chamber and, of course, in all cases of the chamber over which they preside. Given the surplus of work due to this participation in cases, they are assigned fewer cases as rapporteurs. Since the renewal of October 2006, they no longer preside over any committee of the Court. They have an authority linked to the management of the work of the chamber and the procedural problems related to the cases dealt with by the chamber. However, they do not have any administrative power, as it is the registrar who is responsible, under the authority of the President, for the administration of the Court. As far as judicial work in the deliberations or in the general meetings is concerned, the presidents of the chamber of five only have their persuasive force, like any other judge.

The existence of four chambers of five judges, in which most of the work is done, increases the risk of contradictory judgments. As deliberations are secret, only the judges sitting in a case know the arguments exchanged and the decision adopted in a case. A judge belonging to another chamber has to wait until the judgment is definitive (a few days before its delivery) to know its content. In the Due Report, the working party proposed that the presidents of the chambers of five judges 'should verify, at frequent and regular meetings, the consistency of the draft judgments prepared by the various sessions of the Court and should decide whether certain cases should be referred to the plenary session, where necessary'. However, the Court has always been very strict about the secrecy of deliberations, and the judges of a chamber do not have access to the drafts discussed by another chamber. Also, a discussion of drafts by the presidents could be felt by the other judges as a violation of their independence and of the collegiality of the chamber.

If the increase in the number of chambers of five is a first risk for the coherence of the case law, the composition of the Grand Chamber is a second one. On the one hand, only about half the judges participate in a specific case of the Grand Chamber (13 out of 27). This creates the risk that judges who do not participate in a certain case do not take into consideration, in the drafts they propose for deliberation in a chamber, the result of discussions taking place at the same time in the Grand Chamber. All the judges in the chambers, and particularly the presidents of the chambers of five judges, therefore have to be vigilant. On the other hand, two different compositions of the Grand Chamber could lead to two different majorities in similar cases; the presence of the presidents (of the Court and of the chambers of five) is not a guarantee of consistency: they do not have the majority in the Grand Chamber and, in any event, they are not expected to agree on all points of law.

As soon as the new judges arrived, they were designated by the President to act as rapporteurs in a few cases where the written procedure was completed and in some other pending cases. As is usual also after a partial renewal, the very first cases received by new judges are of minor importance, in order to allow them to get used to the procedure and to the technicalities of the preparation of documents. However, there are no genuinely 'easy' cases at the Court, and the new judges have immediately been involved with complex issues of Community law. By the beginning of 2007, almost all the judges who arrived in May 2004 had had one or more cases decided by the Grand Chamber.

The judges from the new member states were thus immediately and fully integrated in the decision-making process of the Court, with an equal right to decide. There are more risks than before for the consistency of the case law. However, the cause of these difficulties affecting the number of chambers and the composition of the Grand Chamber is the number of judges rather than the fact that they come from new member states.

One difficulty that the new judges faced when they arrived at the Court was to find experienced legal secretaries. When a new judge arrives, he often keeps some of the legal secretaries of his predecessor. When a new legal secretary arrives at the Court, he will be coached by a senior one in the same chamber, who will teach him how things are supposed to be done. In 1995, the new chambers were partially filled with former legal secretaries or persons who had worked in departments of the Court and who knew the work. In 2004, it was not possible to find enough experienced people, and in some of the chambers all three legal secretaries were newcomers. In order to help these new legal secretaries, a number of training and information seminars were organized. The chambers of the judges of old member states organized some 'parrainage' (or 'technical assistance') with chambers of the judges of the new member states. This helped explain as quickly as possible the working methods of the Court to the newcomers.

THE JUDICIAL ACTIVITY OF THE COURT

The statistics on the activity of the Court suggest that there has been a clear increase in the number of cases decided each year since 2004, compared to

Table 6.1   Judicial activity of the Court, 2000–2006

	2000	2001	2002	2003	2004	2005	2006
Cases completed	526	434	513	494	665	574	546
New cases	503	504	477	561	531	474	537
Cases pending	873	943	907	974	840	740	731

*Table 6.2   Average length of Court proceedings (preliminary rulings),
2002–2006*

2002	24.1 months
2003	25.5 months
2004	23.5 months
2005	20.4 months
2006	19.8 months

the previous years (see Table 6.1). This is due to the increase in the number of judges and chambers dealing with the cases.

Those numbers are gross figures, i.e. without account being taken of the joinder of cases on the grounds of similarity. Statistics should always be viewed with caution, and here it should be remembered that, in 2004, jurisdiction and 25 cases were transferred from the Court to the CFI (appeal before the Court). Furthermore, in 2005, jurisdiction and cases were transferred from the CFI to the Civil Service Tribunal (appeals before the CFI). The number of new cases is therefore difficult to interpret. However, there is a clear trend showing an increase of the cases completed and a decrease of the number of pending cases.

Statistics about the length of the proceedings also reveal a clearly decreasing trend. If we take references for a preliminary ruling, from 2002 to 2006, the average length of the proceedings is shown in Table 6.2.

It can be said that the Court took advantage of the 'window of opportunity' to reduce its backlog, making good use of the increase in the number of judges and chambers before the expected increase in new cases coming from new member states and before any possible broadening of its jurisdiction. However, given the fact that the Court also adopted new working methods, it cannot be determined exactly how much of the improvement is due to these new working methods and how much is due to enlargement and the increase in the number of judges and chambers.

Some jurisdiction was transferred from the Court to the CFI. However, this transfer concerns cases involving decisions of the Commission, and not

Table 6.3 *Distribution of compositions dealing with Court cases,*
2000–2006 (by number of cases)

	Full Court/Small Plenary/ Grand Chamber	Chamber of five	Chamber of three	Total
2000	128	165	90	383
2001	59	168	101	328
2002	83	187	87	357
2003	85	208	78	371
2004	54	275	174	503
2005	60	250	154	464
2006	57	278	108	443

Table 6.4 *Distribution of compositions dealing with Court cases,*
2000–2006 (in percentages)

	Full Court/Small Plenary/Grand Chamber %	Chamber of five %	Chamber of three %
2000	33.4	43.1	23.5
2001	18.0	51.2	30.8
2002	23.2	52.4	24.4
2003	22.9	56.1	21.0
2004	10.7	54.7	34.6
2005	12.9	53.9	33.2
2006	12.9	62.8	24.4

of the Council and the Parliament. Also, all cases introduced by institutions remain within the jurisdiction of the Court, leaving it in the role of a constitutional court. Given the reduction in the Court's backlog and the difficult situation of the CFI concerning the number of pending cases, no proposal has yet been made to transfer part of the jurisdiction to deal with preliminary rulings (questions from national courts), still considered as the 'jewel in the crown' of all proceedings.

One interesting phenomenon is the change in the compositions dealing with cases. From 2000 to 2006, the cases were dealt with by the Full Court/Grand Chamber and the chambers of five and three judges as shown in Tables 6.3 and 6.4.

The percentage of cases dealt with by chambers of three was more or less the same between 2000 and 2006. However, the Full Court/Small Plenary/Grand Chamber has reduced its share from 2000 to 2006, not only in percentage (from 33.4 per cent to 12.9 per cent) but also in the number of cases dealt with (from 128 in 2000 to 57 in 2006). The work is now concentrated in the chambers of five judges, which increase their share from 43.1 per cent to 62.8 per cent of the cases.

The rhythm of the production has changed. Each case has a specific duration depending on whether it will be dealt with by a reasoned order or a judgment, with or without oral hearing, with or without an opinion of the advocate-general. This diversity in the number of stages of a proceeding, together with the new working methods and, in particular, decisions increasing the number of general meetings and decreasing the number of weeks without hearings ('semaines blanches'), resulted in a better distribution of the work during the year.

It is difficult to say how many new cases an enlargement brings to the Court. The number of references for a preliminary ruling coming from each member state is published each year in the Annual Report, but one should add to those references all cases (actions for annulment, actions for failure of a member state to fulfil its obligations, etc.) that could clearly be linked to a member state. Even the number of references is very difficult to interpret. In some member states, such as Italy, the courts are obliged to refer several identical cases, in order for all the parties to be able to plead their arguments before the Court, which will join the cases and deliver only one judgment. In other member states, however, the court selects a 'pilot case' or sends to Luxembourg only the first one in time, and suspends all its other cases while waiting for the answer from the Court. All that can be said is that the number of references from new member states remains insignificant for two or three years, the time it takes for the national courts to get used to the procedure. When the working party wrote its report (January 2000), however, there was a clear link between the number of cases and the new member states from the 1995 enlargement, and Austria in particular, as Austrian courts sent two cases in 1995, six in 1996, 35 in 1997, 16 in 1998 and 56 in 1999, i.e. more than German or Italian courts, considered as the courts referring the most. Compared to earlier enlargements, the number of Austrian references was a surprise.

Table 6.5 shows the number of requests for preliminary rulings coming from the new member states during the year of the enlargement and the two following years. Even if it is difficult to compare the numbers relating to these years (1973–75 for DK, UK and IE; 1980–82 for EL; 1986–88 for ES and PT; 1995–97 for AT, FI and SE; 2004–06 for CZ, EE, CY, LV, LT, HU, MT, PL, SI and SK), as the enlargements did not have effect at the same time of the year, Table 6.5 shows that the specific phenomenon of the 1995 enlargement has not been repeated so far.

Table 6.5   *Requests for preliminary rulings in the first three years after accession, by member state*

	DK	IE	UK	EL	ES	PT	AT	FI	SE	CZ	EE	CY	LV	LT	HU	MT	PL	SI	SK
First Year	0	0	0	0	1	0	2	0	6	0	0	0	0	0	2	0	0	0	0
Second Year	0	0	1	0	1	0	6	3	4	1	0	0	0	0	3	0	1	0	0
Third Year	0	0	1	0	1	0	35	6	7	3	0	0	0	1	4	0	2	0	1

It has to be noted that the Court judged it had no jurisdiction to answer five of the requests coming from the new member states joining in 2004. In some of them, the facts of the litigation occurred prior to the accession of the state to the European Union. In others, the questions asked to the Court did not have any relationship with Community law.

Enlargements have always brought cases related to the enlargement itself or its consequences. Most of them were technical cases. Cases arriving after the 2004 enlargement are not to be considered as 'technical'. We shall give a few examples.

In two judgments of 28 November 2006,[14] the Court annulled a regulation and a directive of the Council granting temporary derogations in favour of Estonia and Slovenia in the field of electricity. According to the Court, the measures contested were not 'adaptations' of acts of institutions existing prior to accession that could be adopted by the Council at a qualified majority according to the Act of Accession, but derogations to a Community act adopted between the date of the signature of the 2003 Treaty of Accession and that of its entry into force. Those derogations had to be adopted by the Community legislator. Future member states had the opportunity to assert their interests through an information and consultation procedure (observer status). The Act of Accession of Bulgaria and Romania contains different provisions, in order to avoid the same problems.

In a judgment of 23 October 2007,[15] the Court dismissed the action by which Poland sought the annulment of a Council decision of 22 March 2004 adapting the Act of Accession following the reform of the Common Agricultural Policy, which had as its result a restriction of payments to agricultural producers. The main problem was one of admissibility, Poland having introduced its action on 28 June 2004, i.e. too late according to the provisions of the treaty. Poland defended itself on that point, saying that the regulation was not immediately published in Polish and, in any event, that the period allowed for commencing proceedings could not start running before 1 May 2004, when it became a member state. The Court did not take a position on the admissibility, considering, quite unusually, that it was 'necessary to rule at the outset on the substance of the case'.

Two cases also still pending are about collective actions and conditions of employment. In the Laval un Partneri case,[16] questions from a Swedish court concern the right of Swedish trade unions to take collective action in the form of a blockade at building sites where Latvian posted workers were supposed to work. In the Viking Line case,[17] the International Transport Workers' Federation opposed the reflagging of a loss-making ferry by a Finnish ferry company that wanted to register the ship in Estonia so as to be able to employ an Estonian crew according to the lower Estonian wages and to be able to compete with other ferries operating on the same route. Questions were asked by the Court of Appeal of England. Although these two cases concern different legal aspects of similar problems, the President of the Court appointed two different judges-rapporteur, one from an old member state, one from a new one. The first advocate-general also appointed two different advocates-general to deal with the cases. The hearings in the two cases were held on the same day, and both advocates-general delivered their opinions on the same day.

In the Skoma-Lux case, still pending,[18] a Czech court asks whether the Act of Accession can be interpreted as meaning that a member state may apply against an individual a regulation which at the time of its application had not been properly published in the EU *Official Journal* in the official language of that member state.

In the Vajnai case,[19] a Hungarian court asked the Court of Justice whether the principle of non-discrimination precludes a national provision, such as the relevant article of the Hungarian Criminal Code, which imposes sanctions on the public display of a five-point red star, considered as a 'totalitarian symbol'. By an order of 6 October 2005, however, the Court declared it had no jurisdiction to answer the question, as Mr Vajnai's situation was not connected in any way to any of the situations contemplated by the provisions of the treaties.

THE LINGUISTIC ASPECTS OF THE ENLARGEMENT

Owing to the linguistic aspects of the enlargement, many changes occurred in 2003 and 2004. The aim of reducing the number and the length of documents having to be translated concurred with the aim of speeding up the proceedings. Early on, the Translation Directorate started to prepare itself for enlargement. As it was impossible for each linguistic division to have specialists in all the official languages, a system of relay translation through the main languages was planned. Lawyers-linguists took intensive language courses in the nine new languages, with the aim of specializing lawyers-linguists of the 'pivot' language divisions in the languages they were supposed to relay. The advocates-general were invited to draft their opinions directly in one of the 'pivot' languages. Lawyers-linguists of the new member states were immediately trained in French and in the 'pivot' languages. The proposal was made to the Council to suppress the translation of the reference for preliminary ruling. The Council did not accept this proposal but agreed that, in specific circumstances, a summary of the reference could be drafted and translated.

The shortening of the reports prepared by the judge-rapporteur, mentioned above as a measure to speed the proceeding, can also be seen as having an objective of reducing translation. The same could be said of the absence of an opinion of an advocate-general in cases that raise 'no new point of law', as already proposed in the Due Report. To do away with an opinion reduces the length of the proceeding by one or more months, but it also reduces the amount of pages to be translated. However, it makes the work of the judge-rapporteur more difficult and can have as a result an increase in the length of the deliberation process.

The measure that had the greatest impact on the workload of the Translation Directorate was the decision not to publish all judgments in the Report, as judgments which are not published do not need to be translated in all official languages. The proposal had already been made in the Due Report not to publish repetitive cases or cases of minor importance. The positive impact of such a measure on the work of the services of the Court has, however, to be weighed against the negative consequence for a citizen's access to the text of a judicial decision in a language that he understands.

The most important decision concerning languages was a non-decision. Many expected the Court to adopt English as a working language, but the Court keeps on working in French, a language used as the working language for historical reasons. The topic is discussed once in a while but the conclusion of the discussion is always the same. It would be too difficult to have two working languages. In order to use English, the whole chain of production would have to be changed, starting with the Translation Directorate, where the French division is about double in number of the other linguistic divisions. English-speaking lawyers-linguists are not attracted by the work at the Court, compared to the work as a lawyer knowing several languages in their own countries. The Court has always had difficulties recruiting them. The problem has been made worse by the new Staff Regulations, in force since May 2004, which provide for lower wages for newcomers in the European civil service. Besides the lawyers-linguists, the rest of the chain of production would have to be adapted (trained) or replaced: officials in the registry, legal secretaries in the chambers, the 'lecteurs d'arrêts' and officials in the Research and Documentation Service and in the other linguistic divisions. The documentary databases would have to be in English. As, for the moment, those databases are unique and exist only in French, the change of the working language would mean a complete loss of those searching tools. These different difficulties, added to the interest of those who are French-speaking or already have made the effort to master this language, explain that the Court has never seriously considered changing its working language. New judges either know French before they arrive at the Court or learn it intensively as soon as they arrive. It is not a problem linked to enlargement, but arises at any partial renewal of the Court.

As a result of the increase in the number of official languages, there is a lower probability that the judge-rapporteur, the advocate-general or their legal secretaries will be able to understand the language of a case. It will make their work more difficult, as not all documents of a file, for instance annexes, are translated into the working language.

THE DEPARTMENTS OF THE COURT

The Court consists not only of chambers with judges, advocates-general, legal secretaries and assistants, but also of departments, which are each very important for the adequate functioning of the whole system. The departments form a pyramid, on top of which is the Registrar.

The Court being a small institution, the 2004 enlargement caused a relatively important increase (around 50 per cent) in the number of people working for it in 2004 (1087 posts in 2003, 1641 in 2004). The number kept on rising: 1717 in 2005, 1757 in 2006 and around 2000 after the 2007 enlargement. Of course, the increase was substantial in the Translation Directorate, as nine new divisions had to be created. It increased the relative importance of that directorate, as in 2003 it represented 38 per cent of the Court (435 posts/1087), while in 2006 it represented 46 per cent (803 posts/1757).

The first consequence was the problem of offices. The Translation Directorate was already in a separate building, to which a complement was added. In 2004, the administration (Personnel Division, Finances, Interior Division) had to move away from the main building, as well as the Research and Documentation Service, which therefore was away from the Library, making work more difficult for the researchers. The new Civil Service Tribunal was established in offices rented in a building on the Kirchberg, which the interpreters joined in 2006, leaving their offices in the main building, as these had to be prepared for the new judges from Bulgaria and Romania. The increase in the number of officials and this spreading out of the departments have the result that people in the departments are far away from the visible work of the Court (the hearings) and that it is more difficult for the officials to know each other. The situation should change soon, as the new building – which should bring everybody together – should be ready in 2008.

Each department has had to adapt to an increase of the workload and to integrate and train new colleagues. By way of example, the Interpretation Division had difficulties in recruiting its officials, because of a shortage on the market of interpreters from the new member states. Officials of the Court had to spend time in competition juries in order to recruit their new colleagues. And the increase in the number of chambers caused an increase in the number of hearings. Therefore, the Division had to resort more to freelances than before, which meant an increase in the management work.

The enlargement does not seem to have caused insuperable difficulties in the departments. It could be said that the structure and the processes of the Court were strong enough to cope with the increase of the workload and of the staff. Another reason may be that many of the newcomers are lawyers and that the common legal culture may be stronger than the various national cultures. Newcomers understand the role of the Court, see the final product (the judgments), and all know what they are there for.

CONCLUSION

As can be seen from the description above, the Court constantly tries to adapt itself to the changing environment of the European Union: new competences of the Union and of the Community, new jurisdiction of the Court, changes in the judicial architecture, enlargements, general increase of the legal proceedings in the modern society and so on. The 2004 enlargement, because of its extent, may have been a problem, but it was also an opportunity to reduce the backlog before new cases came from the new member states and before the jurisdiction of the Court was enlarged.

The decision-making process is well regulated in the Court and allows a full and equal participation of each judge in the decision-making process. As soon as they arrived, the judges from new member states received cases to prepare as rapporteurs, had an equal right of decision in the general

meeting, sat in the cases coming before the Court for a hearing and participated in deliberations when they were members of the composition in
charge of the case.

Changes in the working methods have occurred because of the enlargement, but many of them are interlinked with changes aiming at improving
the efficiency of the Court. The result is therefore difficult to analyse, and
the multiplicity of new external factors of change will not make such an
analysis easier.

The increase in the number of people working for the Court and the fact
that the various departments work in different buildings have meant that
people from two different departments may not know each other any more,
whereas, in the past, social activities or eating in the same cafeteria made it
possible to know who was doing what in the institution. As far as the
members of the Court are concerned, however, they still form a close group
of persons, who meet and discuss regularly. The weekly general meeting
brings together all judges and advocates-general, and it is a place where
many questions are discussed, before the cases are sent to a specific chamber.

The near future will bring an increase in the number of cases, with the
arrival of more cases connected to the new member states. But it will also,
possibly, bring adoption of measures, decisions or a new treaty, extending
the jurisdiction of the Court. The Court has taken advantage of the
enlargement to prepare itself for the increasing role it is ready to play.

NOTES

1. Legal Secretary at the Court of Justice of the EC. This chapter expresses the views of
    the author and not of the institution to which she belongs.
2. The expression 'Court of Justice' refers to the institution as mentioned in Article 7 of the
    EC Treaty, but also to one of the courts that is part of that institution, together with the
    Court of First Instance and the Civil Service Tribunal.
3. The tenth member, whose appointment by his member state was challenged in front of
    a national court, was sworn in on 7 July 2004.
4. The situation of the Court of First Instance after enlargement is described in detail in
    the Report with Evidence 'An EU Competition Court' of the European Union
    Committee, House of Lords, 15th Report of Session 2006–07.
5. When six, ten or 12 states were members of the Community, an additional judge was
    appointed in order to avoid a tied vote.
6. Council Decision 88/591/ECSC, EEC, Euratom of 24 October 1988 establishing a Court
    of First Instance of the European Communities (OJ L 319 of 25 November 1988, p. 1
    and OJ L 241 of 17 August 1989 (corrigenda)).
7. Council Decision 93/350 Euratom, ECSC, EEC of 8 June 1993 (OJ L 144 of 16 June
    1993, p. 21); Council Decision 94/149/ECSC, EC of 7 March 1994 (OJ L 66 of 10 March
    1994, p. 29); Article 17 of the Act of Accession 1994 in the version set out in Article 10
    of the Decision of the Council of 1 January 1995 (OJ L 1 of 1 January 1995, p. 1); and
    Council Decision 1999/291/EC, ECSC, Euratom of 26 April 1999 (OJ L 114 of 1 May
    1999, p. 52).

8. Amendments to the Rules of Procedure of the Court of Justice of 16 May 2000, OJ 24 May 2000, L 122, p. 43. See the proposals of the Court as sent to the Council in document 9803/99 of 12 July 1999, available on the website of the Council.
9. Council Decision 2004/407/EC, Euratom of 26 April 2004 amending Articles 51 and 54 of the Protocol on the Statute of the Court of Justice (OJ L 132 of 29 April 2004, p. 5).
10. Council Decision 2004/752/EC, Euratom of 2 November 2004 establishing the European Union Civil Service Tribunal (OJ L 333, 9 November 2004, p. 7).
11. OJ L 203, 4 August 2005, p. 19.
12. OJ L 288, 29 October 2005, p. 51.
13. Communication COM(2006) 346 final of June 2006 from the Commission to the European Parliament, the Council, the European Economic and Social Committee, the Committee of the Regions and the Court of Justice of the European Communities on adaptation of the provisions of Title IV of the treaty establishing the European Community relating to the jurisdiction of the Court of Justice with a view to ensuring more effective judicial protection.
14. Judgment of 28 November 2006, European Parliament v. Council, C-413/04 and C-414/04, Rep. 2006, p. I-11221.
15. Judgment of 23 October 2007, Poland v. Council, C-273/04, not yet reported.
16. Laval un Partneri, C-341/05, pending.
17. The International Transport Workers' Federation et The Finnish Seamen's Union, C-438/05, pending.
18. Skoma-Lux, C-161/06, pending.
19. Order of 6 October 2005, Vajnai, C-328/04, Rep. 2005 p. I-8577.

7. The European Central Bank: enlargement as institutional affirmation and differentiation

Kenneth Dyson

Economic and Monetary Union (EMU) has been the single most important and ambitious policy project in the history of European integration. It represents 'asymmetrical' integration. Monetary policy is unified in the European Central Bank (ECB), which manages the single currency for a group of member states, whilst fiscal policies and economic policies to promote growth and employment remain the responsibility of the member states. The result is a Euro Area within the larger EU and a single monetary policy that sits alongside a variety of fiscal and employment and growth policies that are formally coordinated at the EU level. Hence the Euro Area has been characterized as ECB-centric (Dyson 2000). A recent empirical study shows that members of the key EU committee in economic governance, the Economic and Financial Committee, believe that EMU had enormously strengthened the effectiveness of the ECB and to some extent the Euro Group of Euro Area finance ministers but substantially weakened ECOFIN, the Council of Economic and Finance Ministers (Dyson and Quaglia 2008). A key question is what effects EU enlargement is having on the institutional structures and functioning of this ECB-centric Euro Area? In addressing this question the chapter focuses logically on the ECB in its institutional context.

The enlargement of the EU from 15 to 25 member states in 2004, and then again to 27 in 2007, had little immediate visible effect on institutional change in the ECB. The number of members of the Executive Board (six including the president and vice-president) remained the same and was scheduled to remain so even with Euro Area enlargement to 27. Its General Council, the institutional embodiment of the European System of Central Banks (ESCB), expanded in 2004 from 15 to 25 national central bank (NCB) governors, making it an unwieldy body of 31 members (including the Executive Board members). However, this expansion of the General Council was of little significance because this body had no real executive powers and met infrequently. More significant was the Governing Council of the ECB, the epicentre of monetary policy decision-making in the Eurosystem. This body brings together the six Executive Board members with the (in 2004) 12 NCB governors of the EU member states that had adopted the euro as their currency. The Governing Council and the Executive Board were not changed, because all the new EU member states had a 'derogation' on the euro. They had an obligation to join, like Sweden, another 'outsider', but unlike Britain and Denmark, which had negotiated 'opt-outs' in the Maastricht Treaty of 1993. However, in order to enter the Euro Area, they had to meet the so-called Maastricht convergence criteria, of which the ECB – along with the European Commission – was a guardian.

Hence, in the discharge of its executive responsibilities, the ECB was under no immediate time pressure to change its institutional arrangements and practices. In this respect it differed from the European Commission, the European Court of Justice, the European Council and the Council of Ministers. Instead, the ECB spent 2001–3 in preparing and agreeing an anticipatory institutional reform that would take effect in two stages once NCB governor membership of the Governing Council, and voting rights, exceeded 15. This point would be reached with the next state entering the Euro Area after Slovenia (2007) and Cyprus and Malta (2008), namely Slovakia.

The institutional architecture of the Governing Council reflected the historical legacy of the structures in which Economic and Monetary Union had been negotiated. In effect, there was an historical 'path dependence' from the creation of the Committee of Central Bank Governors in 1964, through the European Monetary Institute (1994–98) – which negotiated the final transition to stage three – to the ECB. Through the Council of the EMI, and earlier through the negotiation of the Statute on the European System of Central Banks (ESCB) and the ECB by the Committee of Central Bank Governors, EU central bankers had designed their own institutional venue. The ECB was in effect negotiated by NCBs, with the German Bundesbank playing the leadership role (Dyson and Featherstone 1999). The NCBs provided the capital of the ECB according to a weighting determined by formula. In designing the institutional architecture, they shared two key strategic interests: to ensure their strong voice in the Governing Council and especially in the monetary policy area and in development of payments and settlement systems where powers were delegated to the ECB; and, through emphasis on the principle of subsidiarity, to ensure that they retained not just a big operational role in implementing ECB monetary policy but also key responsibilities in policy areas like prudential supervision and financial stability.

In effect, the ECB's institutional structures and functioning embodied coexisting principles of authority. The Executive Board claimed a moral authority as the only members of the Governing Council who are appointed at the European level by a treaty procedure, who operate solely in the Euro Area-wide context and for the ECB, and who therefore are best qualified to represent the Eurosystem at the EU and the global levels. The NCBs rested their claims on different principles of political and technocratic legitimacy. They viewed themselves as representing the distinctive nature of the EU as a 'Union of states' and as safeguarding the principle of subsidiarity in the Eurosystem. In addition, they saw themselves as contributing to the efficiency of the ECB by their national role in communicating and giving operational effect to ECB monetary policies. Institutional change was framed and played out within the field of tensions created by these coexisting principles.

This chapter addresses two main questions. What factors have defined the direction, scope, intensity and timing of institutional change in the ECB? How significant has been enlargement?

EU ENLARGEMENT AND EURO AREA ENLARGEMENT

In answering these questions, we must distinguish between EU enlargement and Euro Area enlargement and between changes in the ECB and in the inter-institutional relations of the ECB. EU enlargement has its main direct effects on the broader institutional framework of European economic governance, notably ECOFIN, the Economic and Financial Committee, and the Economic Policy Committee. They are responsible for the Broad Economic Policy Guidelines (BEPGs), for the Stability and Growth Pact, and for the Lisbon process of economic reforms (for details see Wessels and Linsenmann 2002; also Dyson and Quaglia 2008). The ECB has an interest in their capacity for effective, timely decision-making and, moreover, is represented in these venues of EU committee governance. Economic and fiscal policy reforms that raise the longer-term growth potential of the Euro Area (and more widely of the EU as a trading block) enable the ECB to operate a more accommodating monetary policy and avoid hard trade-offs that expose it to political attack. However, though the ECB's interests are engaged, responsibility in these policy areas resides with member-state governments.

More fundamentally, the interests of the ECB in strengthening ECOFIN and its committees (and, as we shall see, the Euro Group) have their limit in the absolute priority that the ECB attaches to the principle of central bank independence. From the outset of debates about EMU the French government, backed by the Italian government, has pursued the idea of European 'economic governance' (Dyson and Featherstone 1999). This idea involves trying to transform the Council into a centre for macro-economic policy coordination to which the ECB would be held account-able. In contrast, the ECB stresses its accountability to the treaty and to European citizens for delivering its treaty mandate of securing price stabil-ity. Its existential interest lies in preventing any treaty change that would alter this mandate. The threat from EU enlargement was that associated treaty reform processes would produce such an outcome.

EU enlargement significantly affected the size and functioning of ECOFIN, making it into a large-scale meeting in which more hetero-geneous interests were represented. ECOFIN became unsuited to genuine deliberation. Its finance ministers and officials were less likely to recognize each other, let alone know each other well, and were much more heterodox. Business revolved increasingly around presentations of national policy positions and a more overt attempt by large and older member states to dominate proceedings (Dyson and Quaglia 2008).

The effects were paradoxical. ECOFIN's authority over policy remained unimpaired, but its attraction as a venue for debate, let alone policy learn-ing, was significantly reduced. Once the old ERM and the preparations for EMU were past, ECOFIN lacked either a binding shared project or the need to work on exchange-rate crises, both of which had worked to forge a sense of solidarity, as deals had to be made under time pressures and in the knowledge that the domestic impacts could be profound. Once its agenda moved on to tax policies, where unanimity prevailed, and to financial ser-vices, where few states shared Britain's interest, it proved more difficult to make progress.

Again, in a similarly paradoxical way, the Euro Group, comprising the finance ministers of the Euro Area, gained in attraction as a smaller, less unwieldy body, with a shared project – making the euro work. However, it lacked a legal basis of authority (hence it was titled 'group', not 'council'). Moreover, with enlargement, the Euro Group's weight within ECOFIN was diminished from (in 2004) 12 out of 15 member states to 12 out of 25 (13 out of 27 in 2007). This diminution was offset by a continuing tendency of the large Euro Area states to dominate discussions on economic and fiscal policies in ECOFIN, with the partial exception of financial services legislation. The main change in the Euro Group was new working methods agreed by the informal ECOFIN in September 2004. There were to be more forward-looking strategic discussions, especially on structural reforms, and the election of a two-year Euro Group presidency (by a simple majority of Euro Group members) instead of a rotating presidency of six months.

These changes were only in part attributable to considerations of future Euro Area enlargement. By 2007 internal debates about possible institutional changes to the Euro Group to accommodate Euro Area enlargement focused on three options: a weakened Euro Group as it expanded, alongside a powerful ECB with superior institutional capacity; more powers delegated to the elected president of the Euro Group and her/his accountability to the group for their exercise; or the establishment of an official directorate of the Euro Group based on France, Germany, Italy and Spain and matched by a more powerful directorate of the ECB. The broad consensus amongst national officials working in the Economic and Financial Committee was that EMU had weakened the effectiveness of ECOFIN and strengthened that of their own committee and of the Euro Group – but most of all the ECB (Dyson and Quaglia 2008).

The main EU-enlargement-related reform was to the working methods of the Economic and Financial Committee, the body that prepares business for ECOFIN and for the Euro Group. It was in response to a widespread view that the work of the committee would lose flexibility and efficiency with EU enlargement. In fact the reform failed to alter this perception. The reform of June 2003 caught the ECB Executive Board in some difficult crossfire. In the interests of retaining its traditional value as a deliberating and working body, two different forms of institutional change took place. First, more Economic and Financial Committee business was transacted in working groups, like the Euro Group Working Party on Ad Hoc Issues and that on Bonds and Bills Markets. However, even there effective debate proved difficult because of their size.

Second, more formal reform to streamline its work involved a dilution of the role of the NCBs in the Economic and Financial Committee so that they would only be represented when issues related to their tasks and expertise were to be discussed. Otherwise, it would meet in 'restricted' composition, with only members from the finance ministries, the European Commission and the ECB attending. Led by the German Bundesbank, the NCBs of the main EU states objected to this diminution of power and influence over domestic policies of their governments, arguing that the ECB could only focus on the aggregate position in the Euro Area whereas they could subject their own governments to detailed critique in this committee, especially of their fiscal policies. This tightening of scope of involvement was symptomatic of what the NCBs saw as a wider trend to their disempowerment both vis-à-vis the ECB Executive Board and at the domestic level from loss of the financial market supervision function to new integrated financial services authorities. Post-EU enlargement, the Executive Board provides the only consistent central banking contribution in this key committee for European economic governance. Hence in the network of inter-institutional relations the NCBs have seen an erosion of their role at the key nodal point, the Economic and Financial Committee. This institutional change is directly attributable to EU enlargement. In consequence, the ECB Executive Board has had a stronger platform to spell out its views on economic and fiscal reforms in the EU.

Euro Area enlargement is a more protracted process that has led the ECB to use the new 'enabling' clause in the Treaty of Nice to anticipate a future internal reform process. However, change has occurred within two broad parameters. First, the ECB has sought to prevent other actors, notably the French and Italian governments, from using enlargement to open up fundamental questions about the institution, especially by creating opportunities to limit its independence. It has endeavoured to ensure that Euro Area enlargement serves the purpose of affirming the distinctive identity of the ECB as an independent, *sui generis* institution that cannot be placed under a legal injunction to coordinate its policies with other EU institutions. This issue became significant and highly contentious during the European Convention and the IGC on the Constitutional Treaty and united the interests of the Executive Board and the NCBs of the Eurosystem (European Central Bank 2003c). The special character of the ECB was underlined by classifying it as one of the 'other Union institutions and advisory bodies' and separate from the 'Union's institutions' like the European Parliament, the European Council, the Council of Ministers, the European Commission and the Court of Justice, which are categorized as the EU's 'institutional framework'. Again, the German Bundesbank acted as the chief defender of the Treaty status quo.

In addition, the ECB sought to keep the agenda of change very limited to reform of voting rules in the Governing Council, as in the 'enabling' clause in the Nice Treaty. Here the NCBs' interests were strongly engaged and led to more contentious debates in the Governing Council than were typical of monetary policy decisions. The NCBs wished to ensure that their power over monetary policy in the Governing Council was not radically diminished by its delegation to a smaller monetary policy committee, in which the Executive Board would have relatively more power. Agenda control occasioned the only formal intervention by the ECB in the negotiations of the IGC on the Constitutional Treaty. In a letter to the President of the EU Council on 26 November 2003, the ECB President – acting on behalf of the Governing Council – opposed the Italian Presidency's recommendation for a significant extension of the simplified amendment procedure for changes to Article 10.2 of the Statute of the ESCB and the ECB. This recommendation would have extended the scope and level of potential changes to the internal governance of the ECB and allowed for amendments without ratification by the member states. The Council Presidency dropped this proposal.

Secondly, anticipatory reform to the Governing Council – agreed in 2003 – produced a shift in the principles underpinning its operations. The Executive Board and the larger NCBs downplayed the significance of this shift by stressing that it applied only to voting rules. However, it had a much greater symbolic importance and potentially wider implication. It also reflected what was happening in the composition of the Executive Board and in the design and operation of key ECB projects like the TARGET payments and settlement system, where France, Germany, Italy and Spain had leading roles. The shift was from strict adherence to 'one member, one vote' and 'equality of members' to 'representativeness'. The result was 'country rankings' and a more overt intra-institutional differentiation. This institutional differentiation was already discernible within the Executive Board. The retirement of the French, German, Italian and Spanish members was followed by their replacement by fellow nationals. Hence from 1998 onwards four out of six Executive Board members were drawn from these states. The fact that they accounted for some 78 per cent of the Euro Area GDP offered a rationale. It was, however, also clear that the governments of the big states were seeking to ensure that they remained, if only symbolically, 'represented' at the core of the ECB. The more overt institutional differentiation with reform of voting rules of the Governing Council did not, however, serve to strengthen the power either of the Executive Board or of a group of big states (or a combination of both) so much as to weaken that of the small states. Though adopting a rotation model, the Governing Council did not become like the Federal Open Markets Committee in the United States, with the president of the Bundesbank *primus inter pares* like the president of the New York Federal Reserve. Even so, small states – led by Finland and the Netherlands – expressed serious reservations about the ECB reform, seeing it as a dangerous precedent for reform of other EU institutions.

THE ECB: A *SUI GENERIS*, MISSIONARY INSTITUTION

The ECB's approach to institutional change in the context of enlargement has been determined by its self-conception, anchored in the treaty, as a unique institution within the EU. This uniqueness resides in its institutional independence in the making and operation of Euro Area monetary policy and the need to avoid any treaty formulations that imply an obligation to coordinate with other EU institutions. The ECB's understanding of macroeconomic coordination is that it functions post hoc and not ex ante. In short, it is the outcome of different actors fulfilling their particular responsibilities: the ECB for price stability, employers and trade unions for wage moderation, competitiveness and employment, and governments for fiscal discipline and economic reforms to increase potential output growth. Ex ante coordination blurs responsibilities and accountability for performance.

The absolute priority to independence in discharging its responsibility for price stability is grounded in an impressive edifice of monetary economic theory that commands wide consensus and that gives a distinct missionary character to the ECB. This distinct missionary character distinguishes the ECB from the European Commission in speaking from a single cognitive script, characterized as the 'sound money and finance' paradigm (Dyson 2000). Its elements include:

- The core belief that money is neutral: that, over the long term, it does not affect growth and employment (which are the consequences of the structure of the economy, especially in product, services, financial and labour markets). Hence the ECB should focus only on price stability; growth and employment are the responsibilities of governments, employers and trade unions. This belief underpins the ECB argument that effective coordination is the outcome of a clear allocation of responsibilities. It also leads the ECB to play a didactic, agenda-setting role in promoting structural reforms by member state governments to strengthen growth and employment.
- The core belief that inflation is a phenomenon of expectations. Hence the main task of the ECB is to acquire and retain credibility as a central bank that will act vigilantly to curb inflationary pressures. Credibility is best achieved by an independent central bank with a robust anti-inflationary strategy. Disciplined communication of a coherent message about 'vigilance' assumes a central importance.
- The core belief that inflation is a monetary phenomenon and that longer-term developments in money and credit signal inflationary risks and should prompt remedial action. Hence the 'monetary' pillar continues to be given a major role in ECB monetary policy strategy, against which the 'economics' pillar is cross-checked. In holding to this belief the ECB parted company with much work in contemporary monetary economics. It did, however, acknowledge its intellectual debt to the German Bundesbank.
- The core belief that elections provide an incentive for politicians to use fiscal or monetary policy, or both, to pursue expansionary policies irrespective of the economic business cycle, with the result that they generate destabilizing 'boom and bust'. The political business cycle argues for an independent central bank, flanked by clear and

strict fiscal policy rules. An independent ECB offers the condition for 'time-consistent' decision-making in monetary policy.

- The core belief that in a monetary union without a supporting framework of political union the ECB must take special precaution to ensure that monetary policy is distanced from national political or economic pressures. Hence the ECB places great importance on a disciplined communication policy that stresses only Euro Area-wide considerations. The result is no published minutes that might reveal divergent positions in the Governing Council. Accountability focuses on the President of the ECB. Hence the ECB avoids open dialogue amongst Governing Council members that reveals different views about the macro-economy and appropriate monetary policy positions.

Though the independence of the ECB can be said to represent a universal trend since the 1980s, the Maastricht Treaty provides it with an 'extreme' version. The rationale is to be found in the particular problems of a new central bank in establishing credibility and the pronounced difficulty and dangers of trying to do so in the context of a set of assertive national governments with different policy preferences. The ECB enjoys more than just institutional, personnel and financial independence, as well as 'instrument' independence in deciding on the use of the official interest rate. It has 'goal' independence in that it decides how price stability is defined. The initial ECB decision to define price stability as an increase in the Harmonized Index of Consumer Prices of 'below 2%' over the medium term pointed, in an asymmetric fashion, in a tough anti-inflation direction.

In reviewing its monetary policy strategy in 2002–3, the ECB was at pains to stress that Eurosystem experience and the prospects of Euro Area enlargement were not leading it to a 'revision' but to a 'confirmation' and 'clarification'. The central elements were a more precise formulation of the target as 'below but close to 2% over the medium term' and a shift from reference to a 'first' monetary pillar and a 'second' economic pillar to a process of 'cross-checking' results from both pillars, the first medium- to long-term, the second short- to medium-term in orientation (European Central Bank 2003b). In particular, the greater likelihood of higher inflation rates in transition economies that were catching up in real terms with the EU GDP average, linked to the so-called 'Balassa–Samuelson effect', was not seen as requiring either a revision of the inflation convergence criterion or a more accommodating definition of price stability (Dyson 2006, p. 104). Similarly, the volatile capital flows associated with transition economies were judged not to justify any abridgement of the criterion on exchange rates. In short, change in ECB monetary policy strategy in May 2003 was framed around an affirmation of its core beliefs. Euro Area enlargement was solely a matter of new entrants adjusting to the ECB, not of the ECB adjusting its monetary policy strategy to the particularities of post-2004 entrants.

Underpinning this attitude to Euro Area enlargement was a pronounced 'dual' conditionality (Dyson 2006). 'Formal' conditionality meant sustainable compliance with the Maastricht convergence criteria by the applicants:

- an inflation rate that does not exceed by more than 1.5 per cent that of the three best-performing member states;
- participation in the Exchange Rate Mechanism (ERM II) for at least two years 'without severe tensions' and without devaluation;
- an average nominal long-term interest rate that does not exceed by more than 2 per cent that of the three best-performing member states in terms of price stability;
- a 3 per cent ratio of the government budget deficit to GDP (or in certain exceptional circumstances close to this reference value);
- a 60 per cent ratio of government debt to GDP (unless sufficiently diminishing and approaching the reference value at a satisfactory pace).

These tough conditionality criteria are in turn framed by 'informal' conditionality. The ECB is more than just a formal guardian of compliance. It expects euro entrants to 'talk its talk', to have internalized the cognitive script of 'stability-oriented' policies and the body of theory and discourse that underpins them. This cognitive script is in its basics that of international central banking and monetary economics, with a particular variation to reflect the distinctive conditions of 'monetary policy without a state' in the Euro Area. It means that the ECB is a 'missionary' institution, at once intellectually disciplined and tightly consensual. It preaches reforms elsewhere, especially in member states, rather than to its own institutional changes to accommodate enlargement. Its internal institutional changes have been confined to voting rules in the Governing Council. The ECB is, in short, a masterful exponent of the arts of agenda management.

The ECB, along with the NCBs, practised export of institutional changes through its Accession Master Plan of 2003, which covered a wide range of cooperation activities to prepare accession state NCBs for smooth integration into the ESCB and ultimately the Eurosystem. Between 1999 and the end of 2002 more than 300 central banking cooperation activities were conducted in such fields as accounting standards, capital account liberalization, confidentiality, economic policy analysis, ERM II membership, euro banknotes and counterfeiting monitoring, foreign exchange, information technology, legal convergence (including tough, detailed ECB opinions on draft national legislation on central bank independence), monetary policy issues, payment and settlement systems, statistics (including an action plan) and supervision. They were designed to ensure minimum standards and efficient integration into the ESCB on EU entry. Along with the ECB, the central banks of Austria, Finland and Germany were notably active in accession preparations, each hosting the first annual Eurosystem seminars on the accession process.

REFORMING THE GOVERNING COUNCIL: INTERNAL DIFFERENTIATION AND THE AVOIDANCE OF TRANSFORMATIONAL CHANGE

The reform of the Governing Council offers an example both of the ECB mastery of the arts of agenda management and of the complex and subtle tactical manoeuvring between the Executive Board and the NCBs. It was designed to accommodate a potentially long, uncertain sequencing of Euro Area enlargements and in the process ensure 'timely and efficient' decision-making. The ECB's key shared strategic objective was to keep the issue to itself and away from 'politicking' in the European Council that could jeopardize the credibility of the new central bank.

Within the context of this shared objective, the strategic interest of the NCBs was to prevent a mobilization of interest behind more radical reforms of the kind proposed by most monetary economists to reduce the number problem in the Governing Council (cf. Baldwin *et al.* 2001; Giavazzi 2003). The German Bundesbank in particular had a serious problem of role identity after losing its monetary policy leadership role in 1999. This problem of disempowerment had been exacerbated by the domestic reforms to its governing structures and to create the Federal Financial Supervisory Authority (BaFin) (Dyson 2003, p. 220). It was acutely sensitive to further disempowerment, as was then threatened in the reform of the Economic and Financial Committee (see above) and in ECOFIN proposals to strengthen EU-level banking regulation and supervision through extending the 'comitology' procedures in place in securities markets rather than through building on the Banking Supervision Committee of the ESCB (chaired by the Bundesbank).

More generally, the NCBs distrusted the centralizing inclinations of the Executive Board along the lines of the US model and the longer-term implications of the drift of intellectual talent away from them to the new monetary policy centre. They were keen to keep two main types of transformational institutional change off the agenda:

- A revised composition of the Governing Council. The small NCBs sought to prevent an extension of 'weighted' voting to monetary policy according to NCBs' shares in the subscribed capital of the ECB and in transferred foreign reserves to the ECB. This provision already existed in Article 10.3 of the Statute of the ESCB and the ECB for decisions about such matters as the capital of the ECB, transfer of foreign reserves to the ECB or allocation of net profits and losses of the ECB. The small NCBs had a particular interest in preventing the extension of this precedent. They also wished to avoid a 'double' majority system, in which a simple majority (the current rule under Article 10.2) would suffice only if it represented a set percentage of one or more Euro Area indicators (like population, GDP size, relative size of financial sector). Later this last proposal was to be supported by the European Parliament.
- A redistribution of powers and tasks between the Executive Board and the Governing Council. A case could readily be made that best practice in international central banking from an efficiency point of view favours delegation of monetary policy to an independent committee of no more than 8–11 members (compared to 18 in the Governing Council in 2004) (Baldwin 2001; Baldwin *et al.* 2001). The search for consensus in a large Governing Council of diverse economies with different policy preferences, and of different monetary transmission rates, and allowing for the typical conflicts between inflation 'doves' and 'hawks', is believed to create a bias towards the status quo or, at best, to very slow policy responses (Giavazzi 2003). The US Federal Reserve's Open Markets Committee comprises 11 members with the right to vote, of which seven votes are reserved for members of the Fed's board of governors. Later the European Parliament was to recommend that operational monetary policy decisions be taken by an enlarged Executive Board of nine members 'adequately representing the Euro Area economy'. Such representation might well bypass the NCBs.

This strategic objective was achieved through a new but restrictive 'enabling' Article 10.6 to the statute (introduced by the Treaty of Nice) enabling either the ECB or the European Commission (following consultations with the other and the European Parliament) to recommend institutional change to the voting rules (in particular, 'one member, one vote') as laid down in Article 10.2. The formulation contained danger. Faced by the IGC's expectation of early action, and anxious about being outflanked, the ECB moved quickly to pre-empt potential Commission initiative.

However, grounds for ECB worry were reduced by the formal limitation of institutional change to Article 10.2. Any proposals could not prejudice the right of all members of the Governing Council, governors of NCBs and the members of the Executive Board, under Article 10.1, to be present at its meetings and participate in discussions. Hence the European Commission had little incentive to engage strongly.

In addition to this constraint on reform, a key reason for the ECB welcoming the new 'enabling' clause was that it was possible to agree and ratify Treaty change *before* EU enlargement. This temporal sequencing – first ECB reform, then EU enlargement – meant that the new member states could not veto ECB proposals. The risks of veto by new member states were higher, the more that the reform disproportionately disadvantaged small states. Accounting for just over 4 per cent of EU GDP, the ten new member states in 2004 were all economically small.

The key feature of the ECB reform was the introduction of institutional differentiation into the working of the Governing Council through a rotation model based on 'country ranking' (ECB 2003a). The principle of equality in the form of 'one member, one vote' was abridged by the new principle of 'representativeness'. 'One member, one vote' was still important in justifying the ruling out of any reform proposals for 'weighted' voting or 'double majority' voting in the Governing Council. However, the rotation model qualified its significance. The 'one member, one vote' principle would only apply to those voting. Though they would continue to be present in Governing Council meetings and able to participate in discussions, NCB governors would hold the voting right with different frequencies over time depending on whether they came from 'large' or 'small' states. The reform would cap the number of votes in the Governing Council at 21, still very large in international comparison. Its main purpose was not, however, to reduce the Governing Council to a size commensurate with efficient, timely monetary policy decision-making but rather to prevent the equality principle giving more power over decisions to small states as the Euro Area enlarged.

The country ranking hid a complex tactical manoeuvring amongst NCBs. Country ranking was to be based on a composite indicator consisting of two components, with a 5/6 weighting to the former and a 1/6 to the latter:

- the share of a member state in the aggregate GDP of the Euro Area at market prices, based on the argument that the ECB's impact is greater in member states with larger economies;
- the share of a member state in the total aggregated balance sheet of the monetary financial institutions in the Euro Area.

This combination of economic and financial components served to protect the interests of current NCBs during Euro Area enlargement, especially states that were tiny, like Luxembourg, but had a large financial system. As the European Commission noted in its opinion of 19 February 2003, with support from the European Parliament in its more critical resolution of 13 March, the inclusion of a measure of population in the indicator would produce a country ranking that was more 'neutral' and less biased in favour of existing states. In particular, Poland was disadvantaged by this choice of indicators. Spain was in group one; Poland was not.

The rotation system would operate in two stages. In the first stage (16–21 NCBs in the Governing Council), there would be two groups. The five large states (notionally Britain, France, Germany, Italy and Spain) would all continue voting till 18 members; thereafter, four out of five would vote in rotation (80 per cent voting frequency). The second group would have an earlier and sharper fall in the voting rights of members: from 10 out of 11 with 16 members to 11 out of 16 with 21 members (69 per cent voting frequency).

Stage two (22–27 members) would have three groups. The large state grouping of five would remain the same, and it would retain its 80 per cent voting frequency, with four out of five voting in rotation. Crucially, the other existing Euro Area members (including Luxembourg) would form group two on the basis of the combined size of their economies and financial systems. Their voting rights would drop from 8 out of 11 with 22 members (73 per cent voting frequency) to 8 out of 14 with 27 members (57 per cent voting frequency). The third group would comprise small post-enlargement states. Their voting rights would decline from three out of six with 22 members (50 per cent voting frequency) to three out of eight with 27 members (38 per cent voting frequency).

Because of the uncertainty surrounding the temporal sequencing of Euro Area enlargement (such as, for instance, whether and when there is British, Danish or Swedish entry), the precise implementing provisions, including the time interval between the rotation of voting rights, is left to be decided by the Governing Council on the basis of a two-thirds majority of all its members, with or without a voting right. In short, considerable flexibility is built into the implementation process.

The NCBs of the existing Euro Area member states were the main beneficiaries of this reform, if mainly in the negative sense that they kept more radical reforms off the agenda. However, it was reform around a lowest common denominator that satisfied no particular interest inside the ECB. Though constrained from making their views known, members of the Executive Board would have favoured a more centralizing reform with delegation from the Governing Council to an enlarged Executive Board.

This solution would have been consistent with a less parochial decision-making system and a more active and decisive global engagement of the ECB. Large NCBs were by no means happy with the result, even though it established institutional differentiation. The terms of this internal differentiation were of more symbolic than material value. Members of the German Bundesbank, and leading German politicians, were critical of an outcome that did not involve a permanent right to vote of its president, as for the New York Fed in the US system. In terms of voting rights (with a total of 15 votes for governors), the large NCBs would see their vote fall from five to four (with 19 governors). Even if one adds the practice of the four big states members being 'represented' on the Executive Board, the French–German–Italian–Spanish presence amounts to a maximum of eight out of 21 votes. Hence their leadership remains vulnerable to veto by smaller NCBs. Prominent figures in the Bundesbank and in German politics viewed the outcome as a further threat to the primacy of 'sound money' ideas at a time when this primacy was being tested by the troubles of the Stability and Growth Pact.

THE EXECUTIVE BOARD AND INSTITUTIONAL CHANGE: A STRATEGY OF CHANGE BY STEALTH

In this context of a veto role by NCBs, both large and small, and of constraints on its statutory authority, the Executive Board has pursued two strategies of institutional change. Firstly, the ECB has sought to compensate for its relatively small size in relation to the staffing levels of the NCBs by strengthening its technocratic legitimacy. In particular, it has built up an intellectual capacity around its Directorate-General Economics and Directorate-General Research that cannot be rivalled or surpassed by the NCBs (they had respectively 149 and 50 staff in 2002). Along with other Directorates-General, like International and European Relations and General Payment Systems and Market Infrastructure, they have concentrated on attracting the 'brightest and the best' at the expense of the NCBs. The ECB developed the highest ratio between economists and researchers, on the one hand, and other staff, on the other, with only the Finnish and the Dutch central banks in the same league in quality research performance (Eijffinger 2003). Full-time ECB staff numbers rose from 732 at the end of 1999 to 1343 in 2006, with 93 short-term contracts in 2006 to foster an ESCB-wide team spirit across the NCBs of the EU. Short-term contracts were used extensively (123 in 2004) to help draw NCBs from pre-accession states into ESCB working practices. However, this attraction of the 'brightest and the best' has irritated existing Euro Area NCBs, for instance the

Austrian central bank in relation to expertise on East Central Europe and the Bundesbank with respect to economic expertise, and contributed further to a decline in their morale.

Secondly, the ECB has pursued a strategy of 'task expansion'. In particular, it has exploited its statutory entitlement under Articles 3 and 22 of the Statute of the ESCB and of the ECB 'to promote the smooth operation of payment systems' (in contrast to its limited role in prudential supervision under Article 25). The TARGET system offers an integrated payment and settlement system designed to ensure the smooth functioning of the euro money market and efficient implementation of the single monetary policy. NCBs and banks in the new EU member states were able to connect to TARGET either directly or via national settlement systems of existing members like that of the German Bundesbank (as with the Slovenian NCB). By 2006 the ECB was developing proposals to use TARGET2 as a platform for settlement services for securities transactions in central bank money (TARGET2-Securities). In developing and operating TARGET2 it has promoted a lead role for the NCBs of France, Germany and Italy as the main sources of users; they are joined in this role by the Spanish central bank in TARGET2-Securities.

Neither of these ECB strategies for centralization has been much influenced by EU or Euro Area enlargement. They would have taken place independently in the interests of what the Executive Board defines as greater efficiency. They follow a technocratic rationale for institutional change that is informed by the strategic interests of the Executive Board. Given the severe limitations posed by the veto power of NCBs, and their unwillingness to seek out allies for radical reform in other EU institutions for fear of compromising the cherished principle of central bank independence (and hence ECB credibility), the Executive Board pursued a strategy of institutional change by stealth – that is, through sustained, indirect pressure (Dyson and Featherstone 1999, p. 40). They could not credibly make direct threats against the NCBs or circumvent them, for instance in banking supervision.

In banking supervision, responsibility remained national: the ESCB provided coordination. However, a range of national supervisory systems emerged rather than convergence around a single model. In Ireland and the Netherlands the NCB compensated for lost monetary policy by centralizing responsibility for banking supervision. Germany operated a dual system with supervisory decisions by BaFin and operational work by the Bundesbank. Other states followed the UK system of divorcing banking supervision from the central bank into a single financial services authority. The ECB was caught in the frustrating position of lacking support from either the NCBs or the big EU states for centralizing banking supervision.

Hence post-2004 the ESCB's Banking Supervision Committee was over-shadowed by the new EU Committee of European Banking Supervisors (CEBS). No less frustratingly, CEBS was based in London (a symbolic defeat for the Frankfurt-based ECB and the Bundesbank).

More directly related to enlargement was the issue of the ECB's sub-scribed capital and ceiling on foreign reserve assets. Here the Executive Board had a direct interest in an upward adjustment to avoid, under previous rules, being forced after ESCB enlargement to repay a significant amount of its paid-up capital and retransfer foreign reserve assets to current members of the ESCB. These losses would have occurred at a time when enlargement increased the ECB's activities and hence costs. The losses would be the consequence of a reduction of the weightings of the Eurosystem ECBs (which paid their subscribed shares in full) and a new weighting to the accession NCBs (which as Euro Area outsiders paid only 5 per cent of their subscribed shares). On the recommendation of the ECB, ECOFIN agreed a new paragraph under Article 49 of the Statute of the ESCB and the ECB. This paragraph provided for an increase in the ECB's subscribed capital and in the ceiling on initial transfers of foreign reserves by NCBs on accession by the new member states. This change was easy to reach in the Governing Council because it did no more than affirm the position of the ECB.

Ultimately, as US experience showed, radical reforms to the ECB are most likely to arise not through Euro Area enlargement or through the Executive Board's strategy of stealth. They are likely to be precipitated by economic crisis. By 2007 the ECB lacked an experience of crisis that cast serious doubt on either its operational effectiveness or its mandate.

CONCLUSION

The effects of EU enlargement in 2004 on the European Central Bank reflect its *sui generis* institutional character. This *sui generis* character has narrowly circumscribed the direction, scope, intensity and timing of institutional change consequent on enlargement (confining formal treaty change to voting modalities agreed prior to EU enlargement). Treaty provisions endow it with an 'extreme' form of independence; strategic options for institutional change are constrained by the insistence that no abridgement, however minor, shall take place to this principle. No EU policy area is as 'Commission-centric' as the Euro Area is 'ECB-centric' (Dyson 2000). The ECB also combines aspects of a 'missionary' institution with a 'technocratic' bureaucracy. It is distinctively defined by its function (central banking and the secrecy and mystique that attach to it), its tightly focused mandate (price stability), its cognitive coherence, drive and identity (grounded in a formidable edifice of monetary economics), and the linguistic coherence of working only in English. This self-confidence combines, seemingly paradoxically, with the insecurity of a young institution that is making monetary policy for a currency union that is not a state. In addition, the ECB does not work primarily through legal instruments, especially in its main function of monetary policy: they rose from 19 in 2001 to 30 in 2006. Not least, the ECB is the prime embodiment of differentiated integration (Dyson and Sepos forthcoming). EU enlargement and Euro Area enlargement are temporally distinct, so that EU enlargements in 2004 and 2007 meant change neither to numbers nor to people in the ECB Governing Council. The number of states with a derogation and with opt-outs means that Euro Area enlargement is an ongoing process for the ECB, characterized by considerable uncertainty about temporal sequencing and pace.

This context of temporal uncertainty about Euro Area enlargement with its *sui generis* character, especially 'extreme' independence, missionary role and technocratic character, conditions ECB strategy towards institutional change. ECB strategy combines a tough, disciplined approach to Euro Area enlargement (stressing institutional affirmation of core beliefs and practices, their 'export' to insider and pre-accession states, and the socialization of these states into its values, norms and practices) with a model of reform (still to be implemented) that internalizes differentiation in voting rules and keeps more fundamental intra- and inter-institutional reforms off the EU agenda. The ECB's agenda-setting power over institutional reforms has proved formidable.

In the background is a complex and subtle manoeuvring for power between the Executive Board, which seeks out increased power over policies through a strategy of stealth via sustained, indirect pressure, and weakened national central banks, which – with 15 out of 21 votes (2008) in the Governing Council – can act as veto players on Executive Board ambitions, not just in monetary policy but also in key areas like banking supervision.

Perhaps most significantly of all, the early years of the Euro Area – and of EU enlargement in 2004 and 2007 – were characterized by the 'political economy of good times'. Though there were problems like the aftermath of the Asian and Russian crises, the oil price shock and terrorist attacks, they were not 'first-order' economic shocks. By 2007 the Euro Area lacked the kind of economic crisis that had served as the catalyst for radical centralizing reforms in United States central banking in the 1930s. Enlargement itself has not proved to be a catalyst for transformative institutional change. Crisis will offer future opportunities for radical reforms, but its nature, timing and effects cannot be predicted. Moreover, it is unclear whether it will derive from new member states or from 'older' member states or whether it will involve contagion from an extra-EU crisis. The lack of clear responsibilities in European banking supervision is a potential Achilles heel. Another is whether a large Governing Council can deliver decisive ECB monetary policy decisions in a crisis.

NOTE

This chapter incorporates the result of empirical field research carried out under the EU FP6 integrated project INTUNE on communities of experts in the EU.

REFERENCES

Baldwin, R. (2001), *Preparing the ECB for Enlargement*, CEPR Discussion Paper No. 6, Brussels: Centre for European Policy Research.

Baldwin, R., Berglof, E., Giavazzi, F. and Widgren, M. (2001), *Nice Try: Should the Treaty of Nice Be Ratified?*, Washington, DC: Brookings Institution.

Dyson, K. (2000), *The Politics of the Euro Zone: Stability or Breakdown?*, Oxford: Oxford University Press.

Dyson, K. (2003), 'Economic Policies: From Pace-Setter to Beleaguered Player', in K. Dyson and K. Goetz (eds), *Germany, Europe and the Politics of Constraint*, Proceedings of the British Academy 119, Oxford: Oxford University Press.

Dyson, K. (2006), 'Euro Entry as Defining and Negotiating Fit: Conditionality, Contagion and Domestic Politics', in K. Dyson (ed.), *Enlarging the Euro Area: External Empowerment and Domestic Transformation in East Central Europe*, Oxford: Oxford University Press, pp. 7–44.

Dyson, K. and Featherstone, F. (1999), *The Road to Maastricht: Negotiating Economic and Monetary Union*, Oxford: Oxford University Press.

Dyson, K. and Quaglia, L. (2008), 'Committee Governance in Economic and Monetary Union: Policy Experts and their Images of Europe', in *Communities of Experts in the European Union: Final Report*, EU INTUNE, Department of Politicy, University of Exeter.

Dyson, K. and Sepos, A. (forthcoming), *Whose Europe? The Politics of Differentiated Integration*, Palgrave.

Eijffinger, S. (2003), 'The Federal Design of a Central Bank in a Monetary Union: The Case of the European System of Central Banks', *International Journal of Finance and Economics*, **8**, 1–16.

European Central Bank (2003a), 'The Adjustment of Voting Modalities in the Governing Council', *Monthly Bulletin*, May, 73–83.

European Central Bank (2003b), 'The Outcome of the ECB's Evaluation of its Monetary Policy Strategy', *Monthly Bulletin*, June, 79–88.

European Central Bank (2003c), 'The Draft Treaty Establishing a Constitution for Europe', Opinion, OJ C 229, 25 September: 7, www.ecb.int.

Giavazzi, F. (2003), 'A Funny Way to Manage Europe's Money', *Financial Times*, 23 March.

Wessels, W. and Linsenmann, I. (2002), 'EMU's Impact on National Institutions: Fusion towards a "Gouvernance Economique" or Fragmentation?', in K. Dyson (ed.), *European States and the Euro: Europeanization, Variation and Convergence*, Oxford: Oxford University Press, pp. 53–77.

8. The European Economic and Social Committee after enlargement

Nieves Pérez-Solórzano Borragán and Stijn Smismans

The European Economic and Social Committee (EESC) was created by the Rome Treaty as an advisory committee to the European Commission and the Council of Ministers. It was thought at the time that decision-making in the socio-economic areas delegated to the EEC would profit from the advice of a committee composed of the main sectoral interests in these areas, such as management, labour, craft, and agricultural organizations. The institutional set-up of the EESC has not been substantially changed since, but the Committee has had to compete increasingly with other fora of consultation which have often proved more efficient access channels for the interest groups concerned, such as specialized advisory committees in specific sectors, the European social dialogue procedure or – simply – direct lobbying of the main Community institutions. By the end of the 1990s, the EESC attempted (again[1]) to reinvent itself, this time by stressing its role as representative of organized civil society in a European Union ever more in search of legitimacy (Smismans 2000, 2004, pp. 123–82). It is in this institutional context that one should place the EESC's adjustment to the EU's eastward enlargement since 2004.[2] Like all EU institutions the EESC had to integrate a high number of new members from countries with a considerably different political, socio-economic and cultural background. Yet the main changes that have occurred in the functioning and role of the Committee over the last few years are not necessarily due to the accession of 'new' member states (NMS). Over the last decade the EESC has also sought to overcome its marginalization within the institutional framework of the EU by redefining its role and trying to change its working methods. The aim of this chapter is more specifically to identify the effects of enlargement on the EESC, but as our analysis below will show it is not always easy or possible to disentangle institutional change related to enlargement from institutional change related to the broader EESC's objective of redefining its role.

This chapter will first examine the formal adaptation of the EESC to enlargement through new legal provisions. Secondly, we will look at how enlargement has changed the composition of the EESC and its role as 'representative of civil society'. Thirdly, beyond the formal procedural changes and the different composition of the EESC we will assess whether enlargement has influenced the daily internal functioning of the Committee; and finally, whether it has affected the Committee's policy priorities.

FORMAL ADAPTATION

The legal provisions regarding the EESC in the EC Treaty have hardly changed to adjust the Committee to enlargement. The Nice Treaty only introduced into Article 258(1) an explicit maximum number of 350 EESC members. Currently, the Committee is composed of 344 members, respecting the division of seats among the member states as set out in Declaration 20 attached to the Nice Treaty, namely the 'Declaration on the Enlargement of the European Union'.

The Committee itself has changed its Rules of Procedure several times over the last few years. However, enlargement was only a minor reason for these changes. The main change occurred prior to enlargement, namely in 2002, with the drafting of entirely new rules of procedure (EESC 2002), and was the result of the EESC's attempt to redefine its role. Minor amendments have followed to adjust to enlargement and have been added as complements to the Rules of 2002.[3]

In December 2003, the EESC also adopted a Members' Statute of the European Economic and Social Committee.[4] The idea for such a document emerged in the context of the EESC's reflection exercise on its role and functioning which had been under way since the late 1990s. There is a strong heterogeneity amongst EESC members, with some being very active and others hardly realizing what their role as an EESC member is supposed to be. Setting out a clearer statute of EESC members was thought to improve the functioning of the Committee. Enlargement provided a particularly strong additional incentive for this initiative, as the statute would be helpful for the large group of new EESC members. The document clarifies the rights and duties of EESC members. It is worth noting that, in addition to the normal advisory role, it is required that 'within the framework of the inter-institutional legislative process, of which the Committee is an integral part, members shall help to foster a European awareness among organised civil society and to advance the democratic, efficient operation of the institutions within a coherent transparent framework of economic and social progress'. Moreover, 'members shall – as far as possible and within the framework of the Committee's remit – take appropriate action and measures to follow up the opinions adopted and to improve relations between the public, organised civil society and the European institutions' (Art. 4). EESC members thus not only have an advisory role to the EU institutions, but they should play a role as interface between the latter and civil society as well. Fostering European awareness and supporting the development of a European civil society is seen as particularly relevant in relation to the NMS, where intermediary organizations are often weakly organized, poorly resourced and badly informed about the EU (Pérez-Solórzano Borragán 2004).

Enlargement also further strengthened concerns about how EESC members are compensated for their work. EESC members are mainly paid by the organizations they represent. For their work in the EESC they receive only a daily travel allowance and compensation of travel costs. The EESC has argued that it can only fulfil the tasks assigned to it if its members are properly remunerated. In other words, if one wants EESC members to spend considerable time on their Committee work, they should be compensated for it. The issue has become more salient with enlargement, given that EESC members from the NMS are likely to belong to associations with fewer resources. The new Members' Statute of 2003, therefore, states that the 'members and their alternates shall be entitled to the allowances provided for under Article 258 of the EC Treaty,[5] in order to enable them to carry out their various tasks and duties with an independence and status comparable with those of the members of the other European institutions'. It recalls that, 'in view of the Committee's widening remit and role, practical and realistic assessments shall be carried out on a regular basis in order to draw up a proposal for fairer allowances'. However, to date a real upgrading of the allowances of the EESC members, which is the exclusive competence of the Council, has not yet taken place. Formal legal adjustments of the EESC to enlargement have thus remained limited.

COMPOSITION AND REPRESENTATIVE ROLE

Composition per Member State

Like nearly all EU institutions, the EESC has to reflect the diversity of the member states, so each member state has a number of EESC seats allocated to it which is roughly proportional to its population. Yet traditionally the allocation of seats among the member states in the EESC is considerably more favourable to the smaller countries than the distribution of seats in the European Parliament. This may be due to a desire to give the smaller member states a balanced representation of civil society organizations in

Table 8.1   Composition of the EESC by member state

Member state	Members	Member state	Members
Germany	24	Bulgaria	12
UK	24	Austria	12
France	24	Slovakia	9
Italy	24	Denmark	9
Spain	21	Finland	9
Poland	21	Ireland	9
Romania	15	Lithuania	9
Netherlands	12	Latvia	7
Greece	12	Slovenia	7
Czech Republic	12	Estonia	7
Belgium	12	Cyprus	6
Hungary	12	Luxembourg	6
Portugal	12	Malta	5
Sweden	12	**Total**	**344**

the EESC. This reasoning has been maintained in the context of enlargement. As a consequence, since many NMS are smaller countries, the increase in the number of seats in the EESC following enlargement is more noticeable than in other institutions. Prior to enlargement the EESC had 222 members. Today it has 344 members, of which 122 come from the NMS. This is an increase of more than 50 per cent. It also means that, unlike in other EU institutions, NMS representatives have simply been added on to those from the 'old' member states, with the latter not losing any seats.

The current division of seats among the member states, in accordance with the 'Declaration on the Enlargement of the European Union' attached to the Nice Treaty, is shown in Table 8.1.

Composition per Group

The EESC is structured in three groups. Whilst EESC members are not obliged to join a group,[6] it is very exceptional that they do not. Group I represents national employers' organizations, while Group II represents national trade unions. Group III is composed of various other national socio-economic categories and civil society organizations. In Group III there are such diverse interests as agricultural organizations, organizations representing small and medium-sized enterprises (SMEs), the liberal professions, consumer organizations, environmental organizations, representatives of the academic world, persons representing the social economy, and organizations representing persons with a disability. Group III established an internal division in subcategories,[7] namely (1) consumer and environmental interests, (2) social economy, (3) SMEs, the liberal professions and crafts, and (4) agriculture. Group III emerged as a group of socio-economic categories outside the traditional sector of industrial production. Thus one can find, for instance, SMEs in group III despite their also being employers. The borderline between the three groups is not always easy to draw. So, for instance, there are representatives of the agricultural sector in both Groups I and III. In general, Group III accepts those organizations that are not clearly part of Group I or II. The size of the three groups in the Committee has traditionally been more or less equal, although Group I has often been somewhat smaller than the other two groups, which was compensated for by the fact that Group III also includes certain employer interests.

The way in which the EESC is composed has over the last few years been an issue of debate, since the Committee – in an attempt to revitalize itself – has been stressing its role as a representative forum of civil society organizations, thus contributing to the legitimacy of European policy-making (see Smismans 2000, 2004). The Nice Treaty has partially taken into account this attempt of the EESC to redefine its role, introducing into the definition of the composition of the EESC in the treaty the concept of 'organized civil society' and adding 'consumers' as an additional category to be represented in the Committee alongside the already mentioned categories of 'producers, farmers, carriers, workers, dealers, craftsmen, professional occupations and representatives of the general public'. However, the appointment procedure for EESC members has not changed, namely by Council decision on the proposal made by each member state. Within each country, different procedures apply, which include appointment of socio-economic organizations by the central government, by certain governmental departments or by national socio-economic councils. The Council rubber-stamps the proposals made by the member states (Smismans 2004, p. 127). For their part, member states have no legal obligation[8] to send representatives to all of the three Committee groups, but it is extremely rare that they do not.

Given the increasing tendency of the EESC to stress its representative role, it is relevant to look at whether enlargement has changed the type of interest groups represented. As Table 8.2 shows, enlargement has not changed substantially the balance among the three Committee groups. The NMS respect the tradition to send representatives to all of the three groups. As Tables 8.2 and 8.3 show, each NMS sends fairly equal numbers of representatives to each group. However, compared to the old member states, the NMS have sent slightly fewer trade union representatives. As a

Table 8.2   New member states' representatives per group

Country	Group I	Group II	Group III	Total
Bulgaria	5	4	3	12
Cyprus	2	2	2	6
Czech Republic	4	4	4	12
Estonia	2	2	3	7
Hungary	4	4	4	12
Latvia	3	2	2	7
Lithuania	4	3	2	9
Malta	2	2	1	5
Poland	7	7	7	21
Romania	5	5	5	15
Slovakia	3	3	3	9
Slovenia	2	3	2	7
Total	**43**	**41**	**38**	**121**

Table 8.3   Distribution of members per group

	Group I	Group II	Group III
Total EU27	112	120	109
NMS	43	41	38
EU15	69	79	71
Percentage NMS	38.39%	34.16%	34.86%

result, the 'traditional' situation within the Committee, in which Group II was slightly larger, has been altered. Yet the change is so minimal that it is unlikely to change the functioning and orientation of the EESC's work.

A closer look at the composition of Group III offers an interesting internal dynamic. The traditional pattern observed in the 'old' member states is that of more or less equal representation amongst the farmers, the consumer and environmental and the social economy categories, with the SMEs, crafts and the professions being less represented (see Table 8.4). Yet the arrival of the 'new' representatives has slightly altered this balance, with a higher number of representatives belonging to the social economy category (19 compared to seven in the farmers' category and eight in consumers and the environment).

While enlargement does not seem to change substantially the balance between the three groups in the Committee, this does not imply that it has

Table 8.4   Membership of Group III by category

	Farmers	Consumers and the environment	SMEs, crafts and the professions	Social economy
NMS	7	8	1	19
Percentage of category	30.43%	34.7%	10%	54.28%
Old MS	16	15	9	16
Percentage of category	69.5%	65.21%	90%	45.71%
Total	23	23	10	35
Percentage of Group III	21.10%	21.10%	9.17%	32.11%

not affected its representative nature. As the literature on interest representation in the NMS shows (Howard 2002; Pérez-Solórzano Borragán 2004, 2006), civil society in these countries is still weak compared with the position and status of intermediary organizations in the old member states. The defining features of this weak civil society are low levels of organizational membership, low levels of participation in associational life, low levels of trust in organized civil society organizations and limited de facto consultative procedures (Coman 2006; Pérez-Solórzano Borragán 2006, p. 135). Typically, corporatist tripartite arrangements with a strong state and weak dependent social partners constitute the environment for socio-economic interest intermediation in the NMS. Trade unions have moved from a monistic system controlled by the communist party to a situation of excessive pluralism in which they seem more concerned about competing with each other than understanding their role. This has been accompanied by a strong decline in unionization (see Ost 2000; Pilat 2006). In their turn, employers' organizations tend to represent mainly the interests of the big enterprises, with a focus on lobbying rather than engaging in bipartite dialogue with trade unions, and often lack the authorization of their affiliates to undertake binding commitments. According to the EESC itself, 'social partners and other elements of civil society need to strengthen their dialogue with each other and present a common position to their national governments' (EESC 2003a). In the case of Romania, for instance, the EESC expressed concern that social dialogue is often absent both at plant level and above, and that employers' organizations and bodies representing workers are frequently established on a relatively insecure footing. While the presence of NGOs has become one of the factors measuring the health of civil society in the NMS, the jury is still out on what role they are meant to fulfil and what resources they should count on (Pérez-Solórzano Borragán 2006, p. 137). The EESC itself has identified the shortage of financial, human and material resources as limiting the ability of

Romanian NGOs to engage in formal talks with the Romanian government (EESC 2003b, p. 35) and limiting the ability of Latvian civil society organizations to take part in pre-accession consultations with the EESC (EESC 2003c, p. 80).

In view of this fuzzy domestic environment, questions regarding the representativeness and professionalization of EESC members from the NMS are relevant. Obviously these questions could be formulated regarding EESC members from the old MS. However, most often they send representatives of large well-established associations, particularly employers' organizations and trade unions. Not surprisingly, for the same reason, EESC members are often re-appointed to their roles in the Committee. Some signs of a different pattern seem to appear in relation to EESC members from the NMS regarding representativeness, professionalization and permanence in post. For some of them, for instance, it is unclear whether they have an association behind them: in Group III, the Slovak representation includes a representative of a Slovak liberal think-tank or the Slovak Foreign Policy Association, while the Romanian representation includes a representative of 'Academia de Advocacy', who incidentally does not belong to any of the categories in the group. The comparatively high turnover of NMS representatives in the Committee may be another indication of domestic organizational weakness. NMS representatives were first appointed to the EESC in 2004. This happened halfway through the normal EESC four-year appointment period. In 2006 there was thus the normal four-yearly renewal of the EESC. Although this was only two years after the first EESC members from the NMS had been appointed, a considerable number of them were replaced. Moreover, occasionally some NMS even had to replace some of their EESC members in between the normal nomination procedure. The most extreme case is that of Slovakia, which in the first two years replaced seven out of its eight members, followed by the Czech Republic, which replaced eight out of its 12 members, and Lithuania five out of nine. In terms of groups, the most numerous changes took place in Group III, where 15 out of the 38 NMS representatives were replaced during this period. Such a group variation is not surprising given that, despite common general weaknesses amongst organized interest groups in the NMS, employers' organizations and trade unions enjoy a minimum level of membership and resources, while the situation amongst the civil society associations in Group III is less stable. Higher turnover not only affects the representativeness of the EESC; it also limits the ability of NMS representatives to build and sustain their expertise on the Committee, since those who have acquired an understanding of the workings of the institution leave and new individuals need to start from scratch. As we will argue below, the absence of sufficient expertise about the Committee amongst NMS representatives has an impact on their ability to engage actively in its activities and, crucially, to perform more senior functions.

THE FUNCTIONING OF THE EESC

Beyond the formal changes to legal texts and the composition of the EESC, has enlargement affected the actual functioning of the Committee? In this section we will assess the impact of enlargement on the traditionally consensual approach to adopting opinions in the EESC, on the engagement of NMS representatives in the functioning of the Committee, and the effect of greater linguistic diversity.

Plenary Sessions and the Search for Consensus

Legally the opinions of the EESC can be adopted by simple majority. However, the Committee seeks to find large majorities on its opinions, as it is generally believed that opinions are more likely to be influential if agreed upon by most EESC members. Research by Van der Voort reflects this principle: of all the EESC opinions submitted between 1978 and 1990, 72.6 per cent were adopted with unanimity, and only 9.2 per cent were adopted with a dissent of more than ten votes against (Van der Voort 1997, p. 17). Three years after the big-bang enlargement, representatives from the old MS tend to argue that it has now become more difficult to find consensus. Representatives from the new MS are regarded by their more experienced colleagues as lacking a tradition for consensual decision-making and showing a rather different deliberative culture (or lack thereof). Interestingly enough, representatives from the NMS have already argued that consensus within the Committee should not be reached at any price, on the ground that there is a variety of views within the EESC and that 'trying to reach consensus in all cases leads to the watering down of opinions and producing recommendations of little substance' (Mendza-Drozd et al. 2004).[9] However, our analysis of the Committee's opinions and the kind of majority with which they were adopted between January 2005 and December 2006[10] shows that decision-making in the EESC remains highly consensual. The number of opinions adopted by unanimity has indeed decreased considerably, namely 32.94 per cent against the 72.6 per cent in the period analysed by Van der Voort. However, the fact that a handful of EESC members out of 344 vote against an advisory opinion does not seem of high relevance compared to the fact that nearly always a 'near consensus' is reached. In fact, only 8.16 per cent of the opinions in this period post-enlargement were adopted with a dissent of 15 or more votes.[11]

Yet adopting opinions through 'near consensus' does not imply that the entire process of arriving at that opinion is consensual itself, in the sense of being agreed upon after all relevant actors have engaged in debate. The fact that representatives from the NMS are perceived by their 'old' peers as having a different 'debate culture' appears to reflect the limited participation and engagement of the former in the functioning of the EESC, rather than their being particularly confrontational. We argue that this situation reflects the steep part of the learning curve that NMS representatives need to complete. This ongoing 'learning process' is not made any easier by the high turnover identified earlier and by some of the domestic difficulties regarding expertise and resources.

The physical increase in EESC members has also made the decision-making process less smooth, regardless of the degree of new members' participation and the consensual outcome. This is particularly evident in debates within the plenary. Even before enlargement, the distribution of tasks between preparatory work in the study groups and specialized sections and the debate and voting in the plenary was far from efficient, with too many amendments being brought to plenary. This problem has been amplified by enlargement, and a group of NMS representatives suggested the following change:

> We wish to propose that you consider withdrawing from discussion in Plenary sessions those opinions to which five amendments have been tabled (or whatever figure is agreed, excluding stylistic issues). Once withdrawn, the opinion would go back to the section which has put it forward. In observing the voting of amendments, we believe that many sensible and noteworthy amendments are rejected in the Plenary because of time considerations and the difficulty to consider them seriously in such a large assembly. We believe there is no sense in considering opinions to which many amendments are presented before all the EESC. The Plenary should also serve to discuss substantive, and not editorial or stylistic issues.
>
> (Mendza-Drozd *et al.* 2004)

The Rules of Procedure have not been amended to accommodate these suggestions.

'New' Members' Involvement

NMS representatives are not yet performing leading functions in the Committee such as EESC president, or group president.[12] Only one of the section presidents comes from the NMS (namely, Transport, Energy,

Infrastructure and the Information Society), and only four out 18 vice-presidents of sections are NMS representatives.[13] NMS representatives are present in the Bureau of the Committee, since this body aims to include a representative per country in addition to the functions of presidents of groups and sections. A useful proxy to assess the actual involvement of the NMS representatives in the work of the Committee is the number of cases in which they perform the role of rapporteurs. For the 343 opinions adopted between January 2005 and December 2006, we found only 27 instances where the rapporteur came from an NMS. This shows clear under-representation compared to their number of seats in the EESC. Although Hungary is fairly active, with nine rapporteurs (compared to old MS with the same number of EESC representatives, like Belgium providing only four rapporteurs, Austria eight, Greece nine, Sweden 15, Portugal 18 and the Netherlands 21), all the others clearly 'under-deliver'; Lithuania and Estonia had no rapporteurs at all; Cyprus, Slovakia and Slovenia had only one, and Poland had only five (compared to Spain delivering 44 rapporteurs with the same number of EESC representatives).

The question is to what extent the under-representation of the NMS in the main functions in the EESC is due to a lack of interest or a felt need on the part of these members to first go through a longer learning process before taking up such functions, or whether current procedures and established practices tend to disadvantage new members. There seems to be a willingness from some NMS representatives to be more actively involved. Some have complained that current procedural practice tends to privilege 'experienced' old member state representatives to the exclusion of representatives from the NMS. In the letter mentioned above, the group of NMS representatives identify a number of suggestions to widen participation. To a great extent these reflect suggestions for Committee reform already voiced in previous studies debated by the Committee over the last decade, such as the need to focus the work of the EESC on issues on which it has particular expertise (implying that the EESC should also be able to decide not to give an opinion when asked for it) and the need to produce less vague opinions, which are often the outcome of a dogmatic search for consensus. However, some proposals clearly express the particular concerns of the NMS:

> We have grave doubts about the way the same individuals [fulfil] many functions in the Committee (chairman of a section, vice chairman of another section, member of the Bureau of yet another one) . . . we consider it worth giving consideration to the possibility of involving some other members as well . . . this approach would allow us to include different points of view and competencies than has been the case to date, which would no doubt influence the quality of the EESC's work . . . even if there are no barriers to being a candidate to a post,

we note that there are hardly any incentives to do so. The same arguments speak in favour of widening the membership of study groups. We must admit that we are very surprised to find the same names in different study groups, although the topics concerned are entirely different. . . . If we were to estimate the membership of the EESC on the basis of the participation in study groups, one would come to the conclusion that the EESC has 50, and not 300 members.

(Mendza-Drozd *et al.* 2004)

It is difficult, though, to see how incentives for a more balanced distribution of tasks among EESC members could be proceduralized. The Rules of Procedures aim already at balanced representation from MS in sections and study groups, although at the study group level the maximum ceiling of 18 members tends to privilege expertise.[14] Setting a limit on the number of tasks an individual can fulfil (other than the current limit on the number of sections one can belong to) may be an option, but it may hamper the input of the EESC's most dynamic members.

Language

The Committee's language regime is defined in the 2003 Members' Statute (Article 5, paragraph 3):

> The Community's official languages shall have equal status within the Committee, respecting the cultural diversity of the peoples of Europe. The choice of languages for the various areas of work shall be based on objective considerations of efficiency, taking into account the national languages of the participants and their proficiency in other official languages, and shall be made openly and under the responsibility of the meeting president, in accordance with the political guidelines drawn up by the Bureau.

The practice of such a principle with 23 official languages has triggered difficulties for the internal organization of the Committee, which has made some practical choices. Thus the 2006 Implementing Provisions establish that the bureau of each section shall determine the languages into which the minutes must be translated (Rule 41, paragraph A), while study groups may work in four languages according to the study group's composition (Rule 43, paragraph I).

These, however, do not address the practical difficulties faced by new members owing to the absence of adequate translation provision. Thus a number of NMS representatives have complained about the absence of interpreters during the sessions of each section: 'Excuses justifying the lack of interpretation because of the large number of new members and languages cannot be put forward in perpetuity. Since highly specialised vocabulary and terminology is used during the discussion of opinions, it is not simply a question of knowledge of languages but an important problem that requires rapid and effective resolution.' Complaints are voiced on this issue equally with regard to the Secretariat, which is said to send documents for meetings too late. In particular there are 'concerns on correspondence regarding linguistic amendments, which seem to disappear once they are mailed to the sections (there is no feed-back as to their inclusion)' (Mendza-Drozd *et al.* 2004).

The linguistic issue needs to be addressed urgently if the EESC is to ensure the active and smooth engagement of all its members.

ACTIVITIES OF THE EESC

To assess the impact of enlargement on the EESC's activities we will assess the type of opinions produced by the Committee and any possible change in its policy agenda and priorities since the 2004 enlargement.

Types of Consultations

EESC opinions can result from compulsory consultation by the main Community institutions (provided in the treaties), by voluntary consultation by these institutions, or from a Committee's own initiative. Between 1978 and 1990, most opinions resulted from optional consultation (49 per cent), followed by compulsory consultation (36 per cent), whereas own-initiative opinions made up 15 per cent of all opinions (Van der Voort 1997, p. 91). In the post-1992 period it is possible to detect an increase in the own-initiative opinions (both in absolute numbers and in percentage vis-à-vis the total number of EESC opinions). Particularly since the end of the 1990s, the EESC has used the own-initiative opinion as an instrument to play a more proactive role, in conjunction with other instruments such as organizing hearings or sending questionnaires in an active search to identify those issues on which it can provide particular added value (Smismans 2004, p. 141). The right of own initiative allows the EESC to deliver opinions at an early stage of the decision-making process, which may bring to the attention of the Commission or the Council a particular issue on which Community action might be desirable, or it may influence the Commission while still drafting its proposal. In July 2001 the EESC also adopted the so-called 'exploratory opinion', which has since become an established (although modest) practice (Smismans 2004, p. 169). The idea of 'exploratory opinions' has been developed by the Committee to intervene earlier in the policy-making process – with the aim of increasing its influence – 'exploring' the problems and needs on particular issues before

Community initiative is taken. Such 'exploratory opinions' could be 'own-initiative opinions', but the EESC's main aim is to persuade the Commission (via informal mechanisms) to ask for such an 'exploratory opinion' on issues on which the Commission envisages taking action.

With more own-initiative opinions and exploratory opinions the EESC has tried to increase its visibility and influence. Such an approach also reflects the Committee's conscious attempt to redefine its role, independently from the effects of enlargement. However, for the EESC, enlargement and the situation in the NMS is one of the areas in which it can provide added value, and thus a subject on which to adopt own initiatives and exploratory opinions.

Between January 2005 and December 2006 there were 89 own-initiative and exploratory opinions, which constitutes 25.94 per cent of the opinions adopted. We can thus see a further increase in the use of the instruments with which the EESC can set its own agenda and seeks to influence that of other institutions. Interestingly enough, these instruments are particularly used within the areas of industrial change and external relations, both directly related to the interests of the NMS, as we will argue below.

On the other hand, some representatives of the NMS complained that with regard to own-initiative opinions they 'feel the EESC should be more open and flexible to the initiatives put forward by the representatives of the new member states, and the issues they put forward should also be reflected in the work of the EESC' (Mendza-Drozd *et al.* 2004). This brings us to another issue, namely whether NMS representatives have different policy priorities and, if so, whether this has affected the work of the EESC.

Issues of Interest to New Member States

One might expect that the arrival of one-third of new EESC members from countries with a considerably different socio-economic situation and politico-cultural background may influence the nature of the issues and policy areas that are considered priorities for the Committee. Intuitively, one could expect the NMS to be most interested in areas such as structural funds, neighbourhood policy and agriculture.

However, how can we assess whether NMS members give priority to certain policy areas rather than others? One measure of analysis could be an individual's section preference. The Committee is structured in six sections related to groups of policy areas, namely Agriculture, Rural Development and the Environment (NAT), Economic and Monetary Union and Economic and Social Cohesion (ECO), Employment, Social Affairs and Citizenship (SOC), External Relations (REX), the Single Market, Production and Consumption (INT), and Transport, Energy,

Table 8.5   NMS representatives per section

Country	ECO	INT	SMO	TEN	SOC	NAT	SDO	REX	CCMI
Bulgaria	6	5	2	4	2	4	1	3	4
Cyprus	3	3	1	3	3	2	0	3	0
Czech Republic	2	4	2	2	6	3	2	6	7
Estonia	3	3	1	0	4	1	0	6	1
Hungary	5	3	1	5	5	2	1	4	4
Lithuania	4	4	1	7	2	2	0	4	2
Latvia	3	3	0	2	3	2	0	3	1
Malta	1	4	1	1	3	1	0	3	2
Poland	10	8	3	6	8	4	2	5	7
Romania	7	4	1	5	6	3	3	5	3
Slovenia	4	5	1	2	3	3	2	4	1
Slovakia	5	3	1	6	1	1	1	6	4
Total	**53**	**49**	**15**	**43**	**46**	**28**	**12**	**52**	**36**

Table 8.6   EESC members per section

	ECO	INT	SMO	TEN	SOC	NAT	SDO	REX	CCMI
Total	127	128	33	114	130	88	33	129	96
NMS	53	49	15	42	46	28	12	52	36
EU15	74	79	18	72	84	60	21	77	60
Percentage NMS	41.73%	38.28%	45.45%	37.71%	35.38%	31.81%	36.36%	40.31%	37.50%

Infrastructure and the Information Society (TEN). In addition, EESC members can choose to be active in the Consultative Commission on Industrial Change, which has a particular status within the Committee (see below), or in two 'observatories' (the Single Market Observatory, SMO, and the Sustainable Development Observatory, SDO), which conduct surveys, provide information and contribute to EESC opinions. According to the Rules of Procedure, every Committee member is a member of one or two sections,[15] and the Bureau will assign members to sections as far as possible respecting the expressed preferences of the members. The NMS representatives belong to the sections shown in Table 8.5. In total numbers the EESC members appear to be most interested in ECO, REX and INT. It is worth comparing this to the total numbers and participation of representatives of old member states in each section. As Table 8.6 shows, the NMS are 'over-represented' in all sections compared to their total number of

EESC seats. This is due to the fact that sections aim at including a repre-sentative from each country, which implies that the Bureau will allow EESC members from smaller countries, which most of the NMS are, to be active in more than two sections. Compared to representatives from the old member states, they seem relatively more interested in the SMO, ECO and REX. If we take both the total numbers and the relative numbers compared to the old member states, the NMS appear most attracted by ECO and REX, which is not surprising given that ECO includes cohesion policy, par-ticularly relevant to them, and that in REX they have valuable experience as newcomers towards new candidate and associate countries. However, expressing interest in certain policy areas by giving preference to a section does not necessarily translate into active engagement. If we use again the proxy of number of rapporteurs, the NMS were most active in SOC (11 cases), followed by ECO (5) and CCMI (5) but, crucially, with only one rapporteur in REX.

It is difficult to identify how these preferences or relative preferences for certain policy areas may have influenced the work and priorities of the EESC. Given that most Committee activities result from consultations by other institutions, the autonomy of the Committee to set its own agenda is limited. Own-initiative and exploratory opinions constitute an exception. Interestingly enough, these instruments are proportionally[16] much more used in two policy areas, namely external relations (REX) and industrial change (CCMI). In the area of external relations, 63.62 per cent of the opinions are own-initiative or exploratory, and in industrial change 85.71 per cent. These two areas have attracted increasing attention in the EESC over the last decade, and this is clearly related to enlargement. It is there-fore important to examine these two areas in more detail.

External Relations

The EESC has always played a role in 'external relations' by adopting advi-sory opinions in relation to EU initiatives towards third countries. Moreover, in addition to preparing advisory opinions on external relations, it has engaged increasingly in 'horizontal' actions, independently from its advisory role, building up networks with and supporting initiatives for civil society organizations in third countries. The EESC has developed such actions in the context of the Lomé Convention and the Euro-Mediterranean Partnership and with associate and applicant countries.[17] In the light of enlargement to the countries of Central and Eastern Europe, the EESC considered developing interactions with civil society organiza-tions in these countries to be a priority. An enlargement steering commit-tee was set up to coordinate the EESC's activities in this area.

The 'horizontal role' of the EESC has been explicitly recognized by the other EU institutions in the context of enlargement. In the context of the association agreements, the EESC was asked to set up Joint Consultative Committees (JCCs). On the basis of the association agreement between a future EU member state and the EU, the EESC, in agreement with the country concerned, would create a joint body of civil society representatives, composed of an equal number of EESC members and civil society representatives from the candidate country. Meetings would normally take place twice a year. Most JCCs were created in the late 1990s, with the exception of Malta, Cyprus and Latvia, which did not set up a JCC but established more informal contact groups. The Committee's initiatives were aimed at helping civil society organizations operate efficiently at the national level, providing know-how and supporting their participation in European activities. Such initiatives include the organization of training seminars, fact-finding missions to the candidate countries, hearings with civil society and discussions with European Commission delegations. The EESC also sought to build adequate administrative capacity to promote and enhance stakeholder participation in policy-making in the NMS. It equally encouraged the creation of national economic and social committees. The experience with these 'horizontal activities' fed back into the EESC's advisory role, enabling it to produce better-informed opinions on each country's pre-accession and accession process.[18]

The EESC's enlargement initiatives have enhanced its relations with the European Commission and the European Parliament. The Commission has recognized the impact of the EESC's opinions on enlargement in a number of areas. Collaboration with the European Commission's Technical Assistance Information Exchange Office (TAIEX) has also been actively pursued, with REX members attending conferences and seminars as experts on the implementation of particular aspects of the acquis, and the REX Section's secretariat has been involved in the fact-finding visits and EU visitors' programme (EUVP) (EESC 2004, p. 4). The EESC has equally strengthened its links with the European Parliament through talks with the Parliament's Foreign Affairs Committee, and its leading figures on enlargement (EESC 2003b, p. 15).

Whether the EESC initiatives had any impact at the national level remains difficult to assess. A 2002 study undertaken on behalf of the Committee, for instance, shows that the national economic and social committees that the Committee has helped to create operate often informally rather than as strongly institutionalized advisory bodies to their government, and questions remain as to their representativeness (Drauss 2002, p. 169). On the other hand, the horizontal activities have at least had the advantage of partially preparing and socializing civil society representatives of the NMS into the functioning of the EU and the EESC in particular. Thus, many JCC members from the NMS were later appointed to the EESC (EESC 2004, p. 2). After accession the importance of the 'horizontal activities' has not diminished. Given the remaining domestic difficulties of civil society, as described earlier, the EESC is aware that regular adjustments will be needed (EESC 2003d). EESC representatives from NMS have even asked to prioritize focusing resources on new members rather than engaging in civil society building in too many third countries. As expressed by a group of NMS representatives:

> We believe greater resources should be dedicated to meetings of EESC members from various countries in order to exchange experience and working methods, even if this takes place at the cost of visits to countries lying outside the EU. While we understand the importance of such study visits, we believe that the experience and opinions of EESC members themselves remain critical.
>
> (Mendza-Drozd *et al.* 2004)

On the other hand, the EESC members from NMS may be best placed to give advice on issues related to neighbouring countries. They have expertise regarding the adaptation to the acquis, while their geopolitical and socio-economic priorities are shaped by the state of affairs east of their borders. It is therefore not surprising that the contact group for Eastern Neighbours within the section on External Relations is composed mainly of representatives from the NMS: nine out of the 12 members belong to the NMS.

The Consultative Commission on Industrial Change

The Consultative Commission on Industrial Change (CCIC) was incorporated into the EESC structure in 2002.[19] In its Communication of 27 September 2000, drawn up in close consultation with the EESC, the Commission proposed the creation of a specific structure within the Committee that not only would permit the retention of valuable expertise built up during the ECSC years and the continuation of structured dialogue in the areas of coal and steel, but would be expanded gradually, ultimately to cover all issues relating to industrial change.[20]

The enlargement experience and the prospect of the crucial challenges of industrial change faced by many NMS explain the need for such a consultative structure to be maintained. The Committee's Plenary Assembly of 24 October 2002 created the CCIC. It is composed of 45 EESC members and 45 external delegates proposed by European organizations in sectors of industrial change. Interestingly enough, the number of delegates in the CCIC does not correspond to the countries' population but relates to the challenges of industrial change the countries are facing. As indicated above, several NMS are well represented in it. The CCIC is one of these areas in which the EESC has started to play a more proactive role, adopting a high number of own initiatives.

CONCLUSION: 'BUSINESS AS USUAL', BUT . . .

At a first sight, enlargement does not seem to have particularly influenced the functioning and role of the EESC. Formally, hardly any legal provisions have been changed to adapt the EESC to enlargement, except for increasing the number of Committee members. New procedural arrangements were adopted prior to enlargement and were mainly due to the Committee's intention to reshape its own role, independently of the enlargement challenge. However, occasionally the prospect of enlargement contributed to some procedural changes. In particular, enlargement contributed to the formalization of the status of EESC members via a statute for EESC members that clarifies to the new members the tasks to be undertaken. Neither did enlargement substantially change the representative nature of the EESC, since NMS send representatives to all three Committee groups, respecting the balance between them. However, under this surface of balanced representation, enlargement may well increase criticism about whom the EESC representatives actually represent. The question is particularly relevant the more the EESC claims a position for itself in the EU institutional set-up as a 'bridge' with civil society and thus contributing to the legitimacy of European policy-making. Blaming national appointment procedures for this is a simplistic conclusion, since the 'representativeness problem' is not least due to the weak organizational features of civil society in the NMS. The EESC, though, has been well aware of this, and even prior to enlargement set itself the task of contributing to strengthening civil society in the NMS. From this perspective, enlargement has influenced policy priorities within the EESC for quite some time. While the EESC has limited control over its own agenda, since it mainly depends on consultation by the other Community institutions, enlargement has contributed to the EESC being proactive in two particular policy fields, support to civil society in candidate and new member states, and increased attention and own initiatives in the sector of industrial change, both of which are crucial for the new arrivals. The Consultative Commission on Industrial Change's refocusing on broader aspects of industrial change has been triggered by enlargement, and the EESC has made it a central area of own initiatives. It is therefore arguable that the main effect of enlargement on the EESC has not been on the Committee's internal functioning but in providing the opportunity for the EESC to be proactive in some new policy areas where it can develop more 'horizontal initiatives', independently from the requests for opinions it receives from other institutions. While this search for proactive horizontal actions is not new and responds to the Committee's wider repositioning within the EU institutional structure, enlargement opened up a larger field of opportunities.

Regarding its internal functioning, enlargement has not substantially altered the traditional dynamics of decision-making in the Committee. The internal procedures have remained mostly unchanged, although the increase in members and working languages has put additional pressure to solve well-known weaknesses such as the too loosely structured debate in the plenary, the timely delivery of documents or the development of expertise. Most importantly, decision-making is still very consensual at least in terms of the consensual outcome. Yet this does not reveal the real picture of the day-to-day working of the Committee, where NMS representatives do not seem to find or to seek the opportunities to be active contributors and whose presence amongst the most influential Committee roles is still under-represented. For their part, the EU15 representatives may have to adapt to a much more heterogeneous Committee membership in terms of policy priorities and also political and deliberative cultures. It is here where the timing variable becomes a relevant explanatory device: the EESC, like all other EU institutions, is completing a learning curve, which is accompanied by a time lag. Once this curve is completed, the question to ask will be whether the EESC remains a largely consensual body or whether the full integration of the new members will require proper procedural change for business to run as smoothly as usual.

NOTES

1. In earlier attempts, for instance, the EESC had failed to become the central institution for European social dialogue, as specific procedures for this developed outside the EESC from the 1970s onwards.
2. The expression 'enlargement' will refer to the expansion of the EU's membership from 15 to 27 members in 2004 and 2007 respectively.
3. In 2003 (OJ L 258 of 10 October 2003), 2004 (OJ L 310 of 7 October 2004), and 2006, including further Implementing Provisions of the Rules of Procedure (CESE 1060/2006 FR/GW/vh).
4. Internal document CESE 1611/2003 FR/HA/ET/vh, 6 January 2004.
5. The article states simply that 'The Council, acting by a qualified majority, shall determine the allowances of members of the Committee.'
6. Rule 27 para. 12–13.
7. According to Rule 28, members of the EESC may, on a voluntary basis, form categories. Only Group III has formed such categories, although Rule 28 allows for a category to be made up of members of the different groups (for instance, there are members for farmers, SMEs and social economy categories in Group I). Belonging to these categories is voluntary, so some members of Group III do not belong to any.

8. According to the Court of Justice, 'having regard to the limited number of seats, it is not possible for all the components of each category of economic and social activity to be represented by nationals of each of the Member States'. ECJ Case 297/87, *Confederazione italiana dirigenti di azienda (CIDA) and other v. Council* [1988] ECR 3549, para 19; and Case T-382/94, *Confederazione Generale dell' Industria Italiana (Confindustria) and Aldo Romoli v. Council* [1996] ECR II-00519, para. 41.

9. The letter was addressed to Ms Anne-Marie Sigmund on 7 December 2004. It was drafted by four Polish and two Czech representatives, and subsequently signed by several other representatives from the NMS.

10. The choice of period is not accidental. Following Best and Settembri (Chapter 10 in this volume), we decided that a reliable proxy for post-enlargement normality in the EESC would be the year after enlargement had taken place and thus accounting for institutional adjustments.

11. For our data to be comparable with that of Van de Voort we have used the criterion of 15 or more votes against as the measure of dissent, given that EESC membership has increased by 50 per cent.

12. The under-representation of the NMS is also reflected in the composition of the permanent secretariat of the EESC. Although we are talking here about EU officials, without a representative function, it is worth noting that enlargement has not (yet) led to a considerable increase of administrative staff from the NMS in the EESC. The EESC relies on a permanent secretariat to support the work of its members and a joint translation and technical service it shares with the Committee of the Regions. Among the 110 administrators exclusively attached to the EESC, and with the exception of the translation service, there are only six administrators from the NMS. None of them is head of unit or working in the group secretariats or the secretariats of the Presidency and the Secretary-General.

13. Three quaestors are appointed by the plenary assembly on a proposal from the Bureau to monitor and ensure the proper implementation of the Members' Statute. One of them is from an NMS.

14. Rule 17 of the 2006 Implementing Provisions of the Rules of Procedure includes the expectation that members appointed to a study group should have a real interest in the subject, be able to attend meetings and possess relevant expertise.

15. The Bureau may allow a member to belong to more than two sections where justified by the need to ensure fair representation of the member states. Given the fact that most NMS are smaller states, an EESC member of an NMS generally acts in at least two sections, and sometimes in three or even four.

16. Namely, compared to the total number of opinions in that area. If one takes total numbers, each section has adopted fairly the same amount of own-initiative and exploratory opinions, namely around 12 in the two-year period analysed.

17. As a result, annual summits of economic and social councils and similar institutions have been held.

18. For more details see the REX-Europe website, http://www.eesc.europa.eu/sections/rex/europe/index_en.asp?id=5010rexen.

19. A Consultative Committee was set up with the European Coal and Steel Community. It was composed of representatives from producers, workers, consumers and dealers in this field, in order to assist the High Authority. With the expiry of the ECSC Treaty in 2002, and to avoid losing the experience of the Consultative Committee, it was decided it should be continued within the EESC.

20. Communication from the Commission, to the Council, the European Parliament, the conomic and Social Committee, the ECSC Consultative Committee and the Committee of the Regions – 'The future of structured dialogue after the expiry of the ECSC Treaty', COM (2000) 588 final, 27 September 2000.

REFERENCES

Coman, R. (2006), 'Towards Regulating Lobbying in Romania: A Multi-faceted Coin', *Perspectives on European Politics and Society*, **7** (2), 155–69.

Drauss, F. (2002), *La société civile organisée en Pologne, République tchèque, Slovaquie et Hongrie*, Luxembourg: Office des publications officielles des Communautés européennes.

European Economic and Social Committee (EESC) (2002), *Rules of Procedure*, OJ L 268 of 4 October 2002.

EESC (2003a), *Opinion of the Economic and Social Committee on the 'Financial Assistance for Pre-accession – Phare, ISPA and Sapard'*, OJ C 2003/C 61/1761.

EESC (2003b), *The New Shape of Enlargement*, Luxembourg: Office for Official Publications of the European Communities.

EESC (2003c), *Opinion of the Economic and Social Committee on 'Latvia and Lithuania on the Road to Accession'*, OJ C 2003/C 61/1661.

EESC (2003d), *Opinion of the European Economic and Social Committee on the 'Economic and Social Consequences of Enlargement in the Candidate Countries'*, OJ C 2003/C 85/18.

EESC (2004), Directorate B – *Consultative Work Section for External Relations (2004), Activities of the REX Section October 2002 – September 2004*, DI CESE 106/2004.

EESC (2006a), *Rules of Procedure of the Economic and Social Committee*, CESE 110372006 rev.2 FR/GW/ht, 5 December.

EESC (2006b), *Implementing Provisions of the Rules of Procedure of the European Economic and Social Committee Adopted by the Bureau on 12 September 2006*, CESE 1060/2006 FR/GW/vh, 12 September.

Howard, M.M. (2002), *The Weakness of Civil Society in Postcommunist Europe*, Cambridge: Cambridge University Press.

Mendza-Drozd, M., Kamieniecki, K., Czajkowski, T., Mulewicz, J., Stulik, D., Plechata, I., *et al.* (2004), Letter to Ms Anne-Marie Sigmund, 7 December, Warsaw.

Ost, D. (2000), 'Illusory Corporatism in Eastern Europe: Neoliberal Tripartism and Postcommunist Class Identities', *Politics and Society*, **28** (4), 503–30.

Pérez-Solórzano Borragán, N. (2004), 'EU Accession and Interest Politics in Central and Eastern Europe', *Perspectives on European Politics and Society*, **5** (2), 243–72.

Pérez-Solórzano Borragán, N. (2006), 'Postcommunist Interest Politics: A Research Agenda', *Perspectives on European Politics and Society*, **7** (2), 134–54.

Pilat, N. (2006), 'Trade Unions and the Amendment of the Labour Code in Romania', *Perspectives on European Politics and Society*, **7** (2), 185–203.

Smismans, S. (2000), 'The European Economic and Social Committee: Towards Deliberative Democracy via a Functional Assembly', *European Integration online Papers (EIoP)*, **4** (12).

Smismans, S. (2004), *Law, Legitimacy and European Governance: Functional Participation in Social Regulation*, Oxford: Oxford University Press.

Van der Voort, W.J. (1997), 'In Search of a Role: The Economic and Social Committee in European Decision Making', Ph.D. thesis, Utrecht.

9. The Committee of the Regions: multi-level governance after enlargement

Simona Piattoni

INTRODUCTION

The 2004/2007 enlargement of the European Union was expected by many to amount to a veritable 'big bang' for the institutional structure of the Union. The sheer number of new member states, the consequent increase in Union population (but decrease in per capita GDP), the augmented diversity of the languages spoken, the lack of familiarity of many of these new member states with the trappings of democratic politics and international relations – all these factors induced many commentators to anticipate that this round of enlargement would be like no other before it. Certain formal institutional changes were carried out in advance of enlargement in order to prepare the Union for the arrival of the new member states (Dinan 2003; Steunenberg 2001). However, since institutions are governed not just by formal and codified rules of decision but also by informal relations and norms of appropriateness (March and Olsen 1989; Christiansen and Piattoni 2003), enlargement was nevertheless expected to have an impact, above all, on the institutional performance of the Union.

This chapter explores whether the 2004/2007 enlargement has changed the inner workings of the Committee of the Regions (CoR) and its inter-relation with the other EU institutions. While only 'consultative', the CoR is nevertheless an institution 'of some importance' (Warleigh 1997) because it is the main channel through which regional and local authorities make themselves heard in EU policy-making (Hooghe 1995; Hooghe and Marks 1996; Marks *et al*. 1996). It is also an important vehicle for the socialization of representatives of the regional and local authorities of the new member states. And it is one of the main antennae for capturing the voice of the regional and local civil societies – and, ultimately, of the citizens – of the European Union.[1] Although it is not central to all decision-making processes, the CoR is nevertheless fully engaged in the flow of information and debates about all those EU policies that involve regional and local authorities and societies, from cohesion to environment, from youth to transportation, from energy to enlargement. Within these processes, it is generally acknowledged that the CoR contributes the 'view from below' and, as such, it is considered an important element of the complex, multi-level political architecture of the EU.[2]

THE COMMITTEE OF THE REGIONS WITHIN EU MULTI-LEVEL GOVERNANCE

The Committee of the Regions was established in 1992 by the Treaty on European Union (TEU), under the pressure of the Commission and the main inter-regional associations,[3] amidst divergent hopes and expectations. One aim was to give voice to those 'regional societies' of Europe that, according to some (Keating 1988, 1998), were excessively marginalized within the Community architecture. According to this view, the institutionalization of the European Union was distinguishing too starkly between the 'national' and 'regional' levels, thus effectively discriminating against those 'sub-state nations' that, once the carriers of legitimate hopes of sovereign rule, had given in to historical developments that had confined them within the boundaries of larger nation states (Lipset and Rokkan 1967; Tilly 1975).

A second aim was to provide the European Commission with expert advice in those policy fields in which local and regional institutions had supposedly special knowledge, being more aware of the problems that EU policies aimed to address. Large umbrella organizations of European regions and local authorities – the Assembly of European Regions, AER, and the Council of European Municipalities and Regions, CEMR, in particular – had for some time campaigned for a greater say in EU policy-making (Warleigh 1997).[4] They had obtained, in 1988, the creation of a consultative committee, consisting of regional and local representatives selected by the European Commission. This initial consultative committee was created at a time when the Commission was trying to inject new energy into the integration process, but lacked an official channel for regular and official consultation with sub-national authorities. The TEU then officially acknowledged the need for a committee of this kind and set out the basic rules concerning its composition and organization.

Since its inception, however, the CoR was caught between two, potentially conflicting, visions: on the one hand, it was seen as a *representative chamber* of regional interests and minority nationalisms; on the other, it was seen as a *consultative committee* of regional and local experts.

Although clearly a committee of regional and local *authorities*, the CoR was also meant to channel the more differentiated interests of regional and local *civil societies*.

Established in 1994 amid high, albeit mixed, expectations, the CoR has since then tried to define its mission, its scope of action, and its place within the institutional architecture of the Union. The complexity of the CoR's set-up and role created multiple internal rifts – structural cleavages for some, simple conflict lines for others[5] – of an institutional (regional v. local), national (equal to the number of national delegations within the CoR), political (left v. right), economic (urban v. rural), cultural (executive v. deliberative) and 'geographical' (north v. south, subsuming in turn a host of other institutional factors) nature. Considering the potential for such internal divisions, the CoR has shown a perhaps surprising capacity to institutionalize itself, churning out increasing numbers of opinions and establishing working relations with the other European institutions and finding a middle ground between the two visions and the many cleavages (Warleigh 1999).

Scholars are divided in their assessment of the work of the CoR: some see its focus on the more menial task of providing expert opinions on legislative proposals as a potential debasement of its own function (Jeffery 2002); others see it as a smart move leading to its own institutionalization within EU multi-level governance (Warleigh 1999). Those who take a more 'constitutional' view of CoR (Van der Knapp 1994; Christiansen 1995, 1996; Jeffery 1995, 1997, 2000) normally stress the internal divisions that prevent it from speaking with a single voice for Europe's 'third level'. Those who take what one could call a 'governance' view of the CoR (Hooghe 1995; Keating and Hooghe 1996; Loughlin 1997; Warleigh 1997, 1999) emphasize its increased centrality in a number of decision-making processes. The historical record provides both camps with sufficient evidence to uphold these (perhaps only apparently competing) views.

THE INSTITUTIONALIZATION OF THE COMMITTEE OF THE REGIONS

The CoR's initial institutional set-up was suggestive of a weak institution. A consultative body with no essential role in EU decision-making, it was initially supposed to produce opinions at the request of the Council and the Commission; these institutions, in turn, did not even have to report whether or not they had taken them into account. The Committee had no control over its own budget and shared most support facilities with the much older EESC. Its members were nominated by the Council, from lists provided by the member states, following widely divergent procedures and from widely differentiated regional, local and intermediate tiers of government. The elected nature of CoR members was initially only suggested, not mandatory, and there was even consideration (by the UK government) of appointing national ministers as members of the CoR (Warleigh 1999). All of this testifies to the rather difficult beginnings of this minor European institution, but at the same time provides the background to its remarkable process of institutionalization.

The progressive institutionalization of the CoR was determined not only by how the other EU institutions related to it (Tömmel 1998), but also by the way in which the Committee itself tried to define its own role within the institutional architecture of the EU. After a first phase in which it pushed for a 'constitutional agenda', the CoR leadership then concentrated more on contributing technically sound opinions and on playing a more collaborative game with the Commission, the Council and the Parliament.

The first CoR presidents and first vice-presidents were high-level political figures from some of the 'stronger' regions and municipalities in Europe. During the first term (1994–8), Jacques Blanc, the right-wing president of the region Languedoc-Roussillon and president of AER, was president, while Pasqual Maragall i Mira, the leftist mayor of the city of Barcelona and president of the CEMR, was first vice-president, thus reflecting the high expectations that both regions and municipalities had on the representative role of the CoR. They agreed to exchange roles after two years, a practice which began as an informal agreement but was later inserted into the official Rules of Procedure and has been retained until today.

This political agreement, just like the successive one sealed by Manfred Dammeyer (Germany, PES), President of the Nordrhein-Westfalen parliament, and Jos Chabert (Belgium, EPP), President of the city-region of Brussels – who acted as president and first vice-president of the CoR during the 1998–2002 term – reflects the skilful balancing act between several potentially disruptive cleavages (regional v. local, right v. left, north v. south) that the CoR has had to perform since its inception. The third (2002–6) couplet was composed of Albert Bore (UK, PES), Mayor of Birmingham, and Peter Straub (Germany, EPP), President of the Baden-Württemberg parliament, and the fourth one (2006–10) is formed by Michel Delabarre (France, PES), President of the region Nord-Pas de Calais, and Luc Van de Brande (Belgium, PPE), Minister-President of Flanders.

Under the leadership of figures of such political weight, the CoR began issuing opinions which have been highly political, relating to issues outside its mandatory remit. Before long, though, the CoR decided to de-emphasize somewhat its political agenda and concentrated rather more on its own institutionalization: it articulated its internal structure and operating procedures better, focused on the provision of requested opinions rather than on the elaboration of own-initiative opinions on political issues that were marginal to its remit, and sought a better working relation with the other institutions, first and foremost the Commission and the Parliament. Nevertheless, the CoR does not shy away from occasionally reasserting its political agenda whenever appropriate, as it did for example in the context of the Constitutional Convention, and whenever an important point with regard to the desirable competences of the CoR can plausibly be made. In this regard, it is noteworthy how the CoR released own opinions on several issues related to the CAP and the Financial Perspectives that were discussed in 2005.

As a consequence of the 1995 enlargement, the number and remit of CoR 'commissions' – the sectoral committees in which the substantive work on opinions is being done – were changed by the Treaty of Amsterdam (1996). For example, while initially there had been eight permanent commissions and four sub-commissions, permitting each member state to nominate a president and a vice-president, later on the number of permanent commissions was reduced to nine to ensure a more effective handling of the opinions. Eventually this complex organizational set-up was further simplified, and by 2007 the CoR had only six commissions. This process of 'streamlining' was also encouraged by the signing of a 'memorandum of agreement' between the Commission and the CoR, periodically renewed since its first signing in 1995. While initially the CoR was frequently 'out of sync' with the working schedule of the Commission, often failing to provide important mandatory opinions, since 1995 the working relations between the Commission and the CoR have improved enormously, and the CoR started to churn out opinions on the most important issues in its remit.[6]

Since then, and despite the declining interest in the CoR on the part of the most powerful regions in Europe, the CoR has managed to attain many of its most coveted political goals. Of the four 'constitutional objectives' present in the CoR's political agenda since the beginning – making the CoR into a federal chamber; securing regional-level access to the Council; limiting membership in the CoR only to democratically elected representatives of regional and local governments; and incorporating the subsidiarity principle in the treaty, thus granting the CoR a right of appeal to the European Court of Justice for breaches of subsidiarity and making the CoR into its institutional defender – the first was dropped almost immediately after the Maastricht Treaty was agreed (together with another proposal to set up two distinct chambers, one for regional and one for local representatives) and the second was obtained in the Amsterdam Treaty (1996) (though it applied only to Germany, Austria and Belgium).

The principle that CoR members should hold a *representative mandate*, the third goal, was enshrined in the Treaty of Nice (2003), but its formulation – 'The Committee of the Regions shall consist of representatives of regional and local bodies who either hold a regional or local electoral mandate or are politically accountable to an assembly elected by universal suffrage' (Art. 263) – is ambiguous and might be circumvented (CoR 2004). What is more interesting, however, is that, with the Lisbon Treaty, the CoR was granted the right to refer to the ECJ breaches of the *subsidiarity principle*, thus moving one step closer to being a full-fledged European institution (the fourth goal).[7] Although the Lisbon Treaty significantly expands on the meaning of 'subsidiarity' to include specifically also the regional level, the Committee has still not been transformed into the 'institutional guardian' of subsidiarity, as it can refer cases to the Court only ex post and does not need to be consulted ex ante. Nevertheless, a precautionary approach to subsidiarity may lead the Commission (or the Council) to obtain a 'preventive clearance' from the CoR and, therefore, to use the Committee as a sort of 'early warning' system (Christiansen and Lintner 2005) on the issue of subsidiarity. Moreover, as national and regional parliaments may also refer cases to the ECJ on the issue of subsidiarity, it is suggested that having the backing of an opinion of the CoR, however obtained, might strongly strengthen their case (CoR 2005).

The above overview of the CoR's institutionalization process reveals that the CoR has indeed made remarkable progress and that it has managed to entrench itself in the EU multi-level governance system. In particular, the CoR has banked on its distinctive configuration to carve for itself the role of enlargement 'facilitator'. Indeed, we may argue that the CoR has learnt to cope with enlargement faster than any other European institutions, as it started to operate in 1994, right before the 1995 enlargement to Austria, Finland and Sweden. To conclude this discussion about progressive institutionalization, one might want to consider whether the 2004/2007 round of enlargement might have had a pre-emptive impact on the CoR, as suggested by Jeffery (2002): the prospect of enlargement might have thwarted a possible common action by the regions of the EU15 at Amsterdam and/or Nice to press for a further expansion of the powers of the CoR. As it happened, enlargement seems to have made little impact, and the first signs are that the members from the new member states have been smoothly integrated into the CoR system. The next section will analyse whether this is really the case.

THE IMPACT OF THE 2004/2007 ENLARGEMENT ON THE COR

An obvious point of departure when charting the potential impact of enlargement on the CoR is the observation that its membership increased instantly to accommodate the members of the 12 new member states. Brunazzo and Domorenok (2007), relying in part on Scherpereel (2005), illustrate some relevant formal quantitative and qualitative changes. CoR grew by 122 members (+55.0 per cent) between 1995 and 2007, from 222 (EU15) to 344 (EU27), thus approaching the upper limit of 350 members set by the Treaty of Nice (Art. 263).[8]

The internal distribution of CoR's members also changed, as the municipal and community representatives increased relative to the regional and provincial ones. While there were 35.1 per cent of municipal/community and 64.9 per cent of regional/provincial representatives in the EU15 CoR, there are now 47.1 per cent of municipal/community and 52.9 per cent of regional/provincial representatives in the EU27 CoR (Brunazzo and Domorenok 2007, Table 1). This change is due not only to the smaller average size of the new member states – which implies a greater likelihood of states without the need for a regional level of government – but also to their tendency for having more centralized state structures. Hungary, for example, sends to the CoR only representatives of associations of local governments and no regional representatives, while Cyprus, Estonia, Latvia, Lithuania, Malta and Slovenia do not have any regional authorities (CoR 2004).

Thus, it is plausible to argue that enlargement deepened the institutional (regional v. local) cleavage (Christiansen and Lintner 2005; Brunazzo and Domorenok 2007). This cleavage may, in turn, subsume an urban v. rural cleavage, because a relatively higher number of the representatives from the new member states come from rural sub-national authorities. This is, at the same time, also an expression of the deepening of the national cleavage, as the powers and competencies of the sub-national tiers are determined nationally. As a partial corrective to this institutional disequilibrium, most member states appoint CoR representatives taking into account not only the domestic institutional balance between region/province and city/community (where that applies) but also geographical coverage and the representation of 'special regions' where they exist (for example, in the cases of special regions in Belgium, Finland, Italy or Portugal).[9] The political cleavage has probably also deepened following the increased prominence of political groups in forging opinions, but it might also have become less clear cut, given the inflow of a wide array of parties from the east that do not always fit easily with the existing political groups (Scherpereel 2005, p. 21;

Brunazzo and Domorenok 2007, p. 10). Other cleavages, too, have been redefined. For example, the north/south cleavage has been replaced by either a west/east one or by shifting alliances between northern, southern or eastern sub-national authorities, depending on the distributive character of the issues at stake.

Furthermore, new cleavages are beginning to emerge between representatives from small and large member states and from old and new member states. Both these cleavages would require an analysis of the role played by national delegations within the CoR. The representatives of the eight larger member states (including Poland and Romania) make up half of the total membership (50.5 per cent), while the representatives of the 19 smaller member states make up the other half (49.5 per cent). Larger member states, with a greater contingent of CoR representatives, give more support to their sub-national representatives, thus enhancing their capacity to play a leading role in the Committee's core structures, the Secretariat and the commissions. This is then reflected by the lesser involvement of the representatives from the smaller, mostly newer member states in the process of drafting CoR opinions.

Representatives from the old member states can play a more incisive role not only because they are relatively more numerous, but also because they are often more experienced, having served as CoR representatives (or alternates) for a much longer period of time and being supported by better-resourced national delegations. According to Brunazzo and Domorenok (2007, Table 5), new representatives are under-represented in the structures which matter for the functioning of the CoR: the commissions and the Bureau. For example, in 2007 no commission chair was held by a representative from the new member states (although they did hold four out of six vice-chairs). In total, the new member states hold only 14 out of 60 positions (a mere 23.3 per cent instead of the 35.0 per cent that would be proportionate). What is most remarkable, though, is that so far even the 2004 new representatives have not acted as rapporteurs of important dossiers, thus giving the impression of being still somewhat marginal to the Committee's internal decision-making processes. Indeed, according to Scherpereel (2007, p. 36), 'of the eighty-four opinions discussed in the CoR plenary between May 2004 and November 2005, only three had been prepared by rapporteurs from new member-states'.

New member states' representatives are relatively more present in the coordinating structures (Presidency and Bureau) of the political groups. However, their presence is unevenly distributed, a consequence of the somewhat different structures of party systems in these countries (Brunazzo and Domorenok 2007, Table 6; Scherpereel 2007, Table 5). The political groups are increasingly central to CoR activities, as they represent the obvious link to the European Parliament, through which they can exert a greater impact on EU decision-making. However, because political groups use just one or two working languages (mostly English and French), newer members are at a disadvantage within them. The overall impression, therefore, is that the new members are not yet fully integrated in the workings of the Committee, despite the efforts made by the Committee to involve representatives from the prospective member states as observers before accession took place.

The regional representatives from the old member states include such 'heavyweights' as Bavaria, Scotland, Catalonia and Lombardy – regions which often play their own independent game outside the CoR. Most members of the so-called 'REGLEG group' are drawn from among their ranks. This group, consisting of representatives of regions with 'legislative powers', was established in the wake of the IGC which led to the Treaty of Amsterdam and made its first official impact by securing the addition of a declaration to the Treaty of Nice. Their status was officially acknowledged by the Council in the Declaration of Laeken, and they managed to select five of the six regional representatives that participated in the Constitutional Convention. The Treaty of Nice and the Constitutional Treaty bear traces of their input, as they both refer to the possession of a political mandate or accountability to an elected regional assembly as a criterion for being a member of the CoR. Clearly, the arrival of 122 new CoR members since 2004 has not helped the REGLEG agenda, and indeed enlargement might see this group of regions set even further apart from the remainder of regional, provincial, municipal or community representatives. A new cleavage is thus forming within the CoR, not just between regions/provinces and municipalities/communities, but also between regions endowed with legislative powers and the rest, which may weaken the role and effectiveness of the CoR.

In order to test the actual impact of these qualitative changes, one can examine the decisions taken by the Committee's plenary by distinguishing between majority decisions and unanimous decisions. Unanimous decisions are considered to carry more weight in the Union than majority decisions. In other words, it is normally assumed that the CoR's chances of having an impact on EU policy-making are greater if it is seen to 'speak with one voice'. The share of majority and unanimous decisions did not change over the first three terms of the CoR (1994–8, 1998–2002, 2002–6). However, if calculations are made distinguishing between the pre-enlargement and the post-enlargement decisions within the third term, then we can see that the share of majority decisions shot up (from 26.5 per cent to 47.1 per cent) after the new enlargement representatives took office (Brunazzo and Domorenok 2007, Table 8).

Does that mean that the new members of the CoR have not yet been completely socialized to the formal rules and informal norms prevailing in the Committee? We know from interviews with senior CoR staff that the representatives from the new member states do not contribute frequently to the discussion in the commissions or in the plenary. However, they then, unexpectedly, vote against the tabled amendment or opinion. Yet the percentage of current CoR members who once were observers is remarkably high (on average 83.2 per cent) (Scherpereel 2007, Table 1). This would suggest that this pattern is not a question of being unfamiliar with the formal rules, but that the new representatives are in fact not fully socialized into the CoR's informal code of behaviour.

The CoR made its first contacts with sub-national authorities in applicant countries in 1997 through an ad hoc liaison group; later the CoR's RELEX Commission took over the responsibility for activities related to enlargement. These activities consisted mainly of conferences, which were held in the candidate countries and co-organized by the CoR and associations of local and/or regional authorities. Their purpose was to create the opportunity for reciprocal acquaintance and exchange of opinions. After these conferences, a delegation of ten representatives from the candidate country would be invited to attend a CoR plenary, where they would intensify contacts with the liaison group, offer input to rapporteurs and generally network with other Brussels-based lobbies and organizations (Scherpereel 2007, pp. 27–8). Three candidate countries – Cyprus, the Czech Republic and Poland – established Joint Consultative Committees (JCCs) composed of eight members from the candidate country and eight members from the CoR each. Since 2003 a number of observers from the candidate countries equal to the eventual number of official members started to attend regularly plenary and commission meetings; many of these observers, having already been socialized to the workings of the CoR, would later be selected to become the official CoR members (Scherpereel 2007, Table 1).

Apart from the CoR, sub-national associations from the prospective member states had joined the most important transnational associations, such as the AER, the CEMR, the Conference of Maritime and Peripheral Regions (CMPR) and Eurocities, before accession. Many of them were also involved in INTERREG programmes or in thematic networks created by the Commission (Scherpereel 2007, p. 30). Knowledge about the EU system of multi-level governance had been disseminated through a number of channels well in advance of actual accession. Some regions, cities and sub-national associations from Central and East European countries also took the initiative of opening offices in Brussels (Scherpereel 2007, Table 2), probably out of 'institutional emulation' of the West European experience. Political assertiveness, though, does not always coincide with administrative capacity, and it is this latter that, at the end of the day, is of greatest interest for the Commission. The Czech Republic, Hungary, Poland and Slovakia created democratically elected regional authorities, but in three of these countries (the Czech Republic, Hungary and Slovakia) these are too small to qualify as so-called NUTS II-level regions – the administrative level at which structural funds are managed. These countries, then, had to create administrative NUTS II-level regions as associations of NUTS III-level regions in order to make use of pre-accession and structural funding. Poland, instead, created democratically elected regions at the NUTS II level with representatives that could then be involved in the management of the pre-accession and structural funds. Other enlargement countries such as Estonia, Latvia, Lithuania and Slovenia can be considered in their entirety as NUTS II regions (Scherpereel 2007, pp. 39–40). In general, it is fair to say that regional authorities in the new member states have had to climb a steep learning curve.

THE 'REVERSE EFFECT' OF ENLARGEMENT ON THE NEW MEMBER STATES

In exploring the potential changes brought about by enlargement, we should not ignore the impact that EU membership has exerted on the new member states and, in this way, also back on to the EU itself. The most significant change that occurred in the enlargement countries with respect to multi-level governance has certainly been the creation of a 'second', and sometimes also a 'third', level of elected government (Scherpereel 2007). The socialist communist countries of Central and Eastern Europe had been extremely centralized. Therefore the creation of democratically elected municipal governments and, in some cases, also of provincial or regional governments was welcomed as a much-needed and long-awaited injection of democracy and decentralization into these systems. While the provisions contained in the accession agreements and the prospect of receiving EU structural funds certainly played an important role in conditioning such decisions, it is nevertheless plausible to argue that some degree of decentralization and democratization would have occurred anyway (Hughes *et al.* 2004).

The impression one gathers from accounts of decentralization processes in the accession countries is that the European Commission took advantage of the leverage afforded by the accession agreements and the Copenhagen criteria in order to push for the creation of a regional (NUTS II level) tier. Even though, formally, the European Commission could not enforce any particular decentralization model, it nevertheless insisted on the creation of (administrative or legislative) regions for the implementation of structural policies. The pressure began to mount in earnest even before accession, when the prospective enlargement countries were receiving the pre-accession funds through PHARE, ISPA and SAPARD – pressure which can in part be explained by the experience of Commission officials with the management of the structural funds prior to enlargement (Brusis 2003; Keating 2003).[10]

Such pressure touched a raw nerve in the countries of Central and Eastern Europe which had only recently regained sovereignty from Soviet rule and were unwilling to relinquish it again to the European Union. For many of these countries, the unitary state structure was not merely a legacy of communism, but also the format that had allowed many of them to finally 'escape from the grasp of the dynastic empires' after the First World War and to equip themselves with a 'streamlined administration' considered at the time as the 'epitome of modern statehood' (Batt 2002, p. 5). Consequently, while these countries resisted the Commission's attempts to re-shape their internal territorial divisions, several new member states implemented rather far-reaching administrative and constitutional reforms in order to sustain the process of democratization. In considering the impact that the arrival of the new member states and their representatives had on the CoR, it is therefore important to look at the detail of the changing territorial politics in these countries, in order to examine the kind of actors and new dynamics that such domestic processes have on the European level.

Poland, for example, had undergone rather significant territorial restructuring under communist rule that had rearranged and broken up the historical 17 voivodships. In the 1990s, it reverted back to the original units and created democratically elected governments at the municipal (*gminas*), county (*poviats*) and regional (*voivodships*) levels. However, while legislative and managing functions at all these levels were carried out by elected assemblies, management boards and their elected marshals, control functions were performed by centrally appointed voivods at the regional level. Significant confusion of competencies ensued and, as a result, civil society failed to orient itself towards the regional level. 'The lack of coordination between the national and subnational actors and levels of government as a result of the unclear allocation of competencies constitutes a serious problem for the planning and implementation of the EU structural policy in Poland' (Czernielewska *et al.* 2004, p. 471). According to these scholars, problems were further compounded by a lack of social capital, party politics domination, and diffuse clientelism at the local and regional levels (ibid., p. 492). The upshot of the half-hearted Polish reform has been that the Commission itself toned down its initial enthusiasm for regional involvement and reverted to a close collaboration with central government. 'Given the background of underdeveloped regional identities, the weakness of the new institutional structures and their financial dependence on the central state lead to the strengthening of the central administration in the regional policy-making and public funds redistribution' (ibid., p. 487).

The case of the Czech Republic tells us a similar story of a democracy-inspired thrust towards regionalization followed by an efficiency-driven retrenchment towards centralized management of the funds. The Czech case, however, also shows that, once initiated, reforms are not easily undone (Baun and Marek 2006; Marek and Baun 2002). Again, the same mix of confusing signals – stressing first territorial reform and then administrative efficiency, two potentially converging but also potentially diverging objectives – was sent by the Commission in the case of the Czech Republic.[11] In 1997, 14 self-governing regions (*kraje*) were created, each with its democratically elected assembly, despite strong domestic opposition on the part of Prime Minister, Václav Klaus's Civic Democratic Party (ODS). These 'regions' came into effect in 2000, but gained a certain degree of administrative independence from the centre only in 2003 (Baun and Marek 2006, pp. 412–13). The *kraje* were, however, too small to satisfy the NUTS II-level criteria and, therefore, eight NUTS II-level 'cohesion regions' were created. 'Each of the eight cohesion regions would have their own Regional Council, consisting of representatives from each of the regional [i.e. *kraje*] assemblies within a particular NUTS II region. The Regional Councils would also serve as regional managing authorities and would be responsible for preparing the Regional Operational Programmes (ROPs) necessary for receiving structural funds assistance' (Baun and Marek 2006: 413). The amalgamation of the 14 *kraje* into the eight cohesion regions created problems of consistency in the management of the funds, putting some *kraje* at a disadvantage vis-à-vis others. This territorial and administrative restructuring was further emasculated by the failure of the Commission and the Czech government to involve these new structures in the implementation of the pre-accession aid programmes. Eventually, in July 2002, preference went to implementing one centrally managed Joint Regional Operational Programme (JROP) and six Sectoral Operational Programmes (SOPs). The disappointment of the regional leaders, coupled with the electoral success of the governing party (ODC) at the regional level, contributed to strengthening the regionalist agenda and prompted a joint action of the Association of Czech Regions (AKÇR) and the Committee of the Regions in Brussels in favour of the concession of wider competencies and money to the Czech regions. The tug-of-war between the Czech Ministry for Regional Development (MRD) and the regions over the preparation of either one central JROP or several distinct ROPs arose again at the beginning of 2005 in view of the 2007–13 programming period, but at this time the regions obtained the power to prepare and manage individual ROPs with the central assistance of the MRD, which remains the national negotiator for the entire Czech 'envelope'.

Hungary appears to be a more straightforward case of genuine decentralization, which nevertheless suffers from the same shortcomings as the other countries. Since 1870, Hungary had had both a municipal and a county level governed by popularly elected councils – authorities which were nevertheless more an expression of the control of a unitary central state over its periphery than of self-rule. The situation did not change under communist rule. In particular, the province remained 'the locus for the articulation of local interests, the formulation of policy-making and the redistribution of public resources throughout this period' (Pálné Kovács *et al.* 2004, p. 432). The directly elected county assembly was the main forum of interest representation and intermediation at the sub-national level of government, the elected bodies in the villages and towns being subordinated to the county councils. From the 1970s onwards, regions began to appear as instruments of centralized economic planning and, with the Association Agreement of 1991 and the adoption of the Copenhagen Criteria in 1993, they became also the Commission's instruments for structural action. Yet ten years later, the last Monitoring Report on Hungary's preparation for membership still highlighted the 'weaknesses of the institutional infrastructure at the subnational level of government, emphasizing in particular the dominance of political parties in centre–periphery relations, phenomena of corruption and the lack of cooperation among public bodies to overcome these problems' (ibid., p. 436). Indeed, these three symptoms – dominance of party politics, corruption and insufficient inter-institutional and state–society cooperation – have been highlighted as characteristic of the 'Latin' mode of regionalization that correlates with the historical experience of authoritarianism (Goetz 2001). Since 1990, however, a number of reforms have tried to re-establish the autonomy of local governments in Hungary and to delegate to them real responsibilities, particularly at the municipal level. Finally, the Act on Regional Development and Physical Planning of 1996 (and its amendment in 1999) completed the creation of a three-tier system of county, regional and national government, which granted municipal associations the right to participate in the county councils (Pálné Kovács *et al.* 2004, p. 437). As in the Czech Republic, seven planning regions/regional development councils were created at NUTS II level 'as the main locus for coordination of the activities of de-concentrated government departments' (ibid., p. 437), with the 19 county councils representing the first meso-level of government at

NUTS III level. As a consequence, the same mismatch between the level at which economic interests historically congeal (the county) and that at which decisions concerning structural policies are made (the region) occurs in Hungary as we have witnessed in the Czech Republic. It is easy for party-directed clientelist networks to find a breeding ground in the cracks of such a system. Eventually, the Hungarian central state took advantage of this situation to manage centrally the preparation of the National Development Plan and the Regional Operational Programmes. 'Thus, ironically, the EU Commission's push towards regionalization, as a means of enhancing democratization and participation at the regional level of government, seems to have led to the re-centralization of the policy process' (ibid., p. 442).

Altogether similar stories could be recounted also in the case of Slovakia, Bulgaria (Brusis 2003) and Romania (Papadimitrious and Phinnemore 2004). For the other enlargement countries – Cyprus, Estonia, Latvia, Lithuania, Malta, Slovenia – regionalization was never an issue, given their size (Scherpereel 2007). Coming back from this overview of the 'reverse effect' EU membership had on the territorial politics of the new member states to our analysis of the CoR, we can reassess the implications that these developments have had for the functioning of the CoR. The weak regionalization in the new member states meant that the regional and local representatives sent from these countries to Brussels had only fledgling democratic credentials, strong party political connotations and personalistic ties to their home constituencies.

CONCLUSION

It is exceedingly hard to disentangle the EU's internal developments from developments set in motion by enlargement, as this process started to cast its shadow on the institutional dynamics of the EU from as early as the Maastricht Treaty. Since then, the political life of the EU has been characterized by, first, the anticipation and, then, the processing of the anticipated or actual consequences of enlargement. As we have seen, enlargement certainly added a particular momentum to the multi-level nature of EU decision-making, representing 'an enormous injection of economic, political, legal and cultural diversity' (Zielonka 2007, p. 188). The most balanced answer to the timing and the causality of such effects is that enlargement has both induced novel changes, which would have not occurred otherwise, and strengthened existing dynamics, which were already at work.

It would seem reasonable to conclude that the CoR experienced some changes as a result of enlargement, but that these are not of such magnitude as to fundamentally alter the functioning of the Committee or to derail it from its own institutionalization path. Some questions of the timing and the causality remain to be explored in the future. In particular, it would be interesting to investigate further not only why the CoR decided to champion the early integration of the sub-national representatives from the future enlargement countries in its own workings by granting them the status of observers and holding some Bureau meetings in enlargement countries, but also whether this progressive strategy actually had an impact on the work and the standing of the CoR. In this regard, we have to remember that enlargement and neighbourhood policies, as well as Trans-European Networks (TENs) and immigration, have become areas on which the Commission and the Council *must* seek the CoR's opinion. The EU's external borders are, after all, the place where specific regions find themselves on the front line of a number of problems, be they cohesion, immigration, transport or trans-border cooperation.[12]

In addition to the changes that took place directly at the institutional level, as a consequence of the increase in members and representatives (first-order changes), other changes took place because the environment in which these institutions work changed and prompted adaptation in the inter-institutional dynamic (second-order changes). Enlargement might have brought about systemic changes – a certain 'Euro-fatigue' and perhaps even an integration backlash – which weakened certain institutions, in particular the European Commission, and generally slowed down the integration process. The Constitutional Treaty ratification setback revealed both the difficulty and the need to re-focus and gain new momentum. As in the past, the Commission has sought allies among those actors – regional and local authorities – that may be considered as legitimate interlocutors, even though they are perhaps regarded as marginal to the institutional architecture of the Union.

The CoR, far from shunning this responsibility, has taken this opportunity and has offered its assistance by making cross-border cooperation and dialogue with the regions of the new member states into one of its primary commitments. The twinning programme also saw the direct involvement of several EU15 regions in close collaboration with newly formed NUTS II regions and other sub-national authorities in the future enlargement countries in an effort to 'teach' them the 'nuts and bolts' of cohesion policy (Papadimitrious and Phinnemore 2004). This involvement was part of a skilful strategy on the part of the CoR to demonstrate that, when it comes to translating visionary goals into daily practice, sub-national authorities are precious allies. The CoR's strategy has been to project itself as a forum in which problems are debated concretely by the representatives of those levels of governments which need to get things done.[13] As a result of close cooperation between regions and the European Commission, for example in the context of the 'Territorial Dialogues' that since 2006 have been part of the Lisbon Process, the working relationship between Commission and CoR has significantly tightened.[14]

In conclusion, if the CoR has become a 'platform for action' rather than an actor in its own right (Christiansen and Lintner 2005), then this may be the strongest indicator of its institutionalization within the EU system of multi-level governance. The CoR's current situation, therefore, is the result of the direct impact of enlargement as well as the reflection of its new role in the inter-institutional relations of the enlarged European Union.

NOTES

1.   In the preface to Schöbel (1997), Pasqual Maragall i Mira, then President of the CoR, emphasized the notions of 'proximity', 'grass-roots concerns' and 'bottom-up approach to the building of Europe' as aptly describing the role of the CoR in the Community's architecture (Schöbel 1997, p. 5). Dietrich Pause, then Secretary-General of the CoR, saw CoR's role as that of making Europe 'topical, tangible and accessible to the "man in the street"' (Schöbel 1997, p. 6)
2.   The literature on multi-level governance is by now extremely wide, encompassing several dimensions of this same concept (cf. Piattoni 2005). The main references are: Hooghe (1996); Marks, Hooghe and Blank (1996); Marks and Hooghe (1997, 2003, 2004); Hooghe and Marks (2001); and Bache and Flinders (2004).
3.   Among these, the Assembly of European Regions (AER) and the Council of European Municipalities and Regions (CEMR) were the most vocal. These organizations, which have a larger membership than just the regions and municipalities belonging to the Community member states, spearheaded the creation of a consultative body made up of regional and local representatives in order to institutionalize the input from regional and local societies.
4.   While CEMR was founded in 1951 by a handful of mayors under the auspices of the Council of Europe, AER was created in 1985 under the direct auspices of the European Commission.
5.   Inaugurated by Van der Knaap (1994) and Christiansen (1995, 1996), the 'cleavage reading' of the CoR has become a mantra for CoR studies (see Warleigh 1999; Hönnige and Kaiser 2003; Piattoni 2002; Brunazzo and Domorenok 2007; Scherpereel 2007).
6.   Still, the CoR monitors, and occasionally provides opinions on, issues which lie outside its mandatory remit, such as the CAP or the EU budget, that can be plausibly argued to be relevant also for the regional and local levels of government. This proves that it is rather difficult to circumscribe the remit of governmental tiers that, in many EU countries, have general competencies and thus cannot be immediately compared with functional interests like employers' and workers' associations.
7.   Article 8 of the Protocol on the Application of the Principles of Subsidiarity and Proportionality states that: 'In accordance with the rules laid down in the said Article, the Committee of the Regions may also bring such actions against European legislative acts for the adoption of which the Constitution provides that it be consulted.'
8.   The distribution of representatives by country is as follows: France, Germany, Italy, UK 24; Poland, Spain 21; Romania 15; Austria, Belgium, Bulgaria, Czech Republic, Greece, Hungary, Netherlands, Portugal, Sweden 12; Denmark, Finland, Ireland, Lithuania, Slovakia 9; Estonia, Latvia, Slovenia 7; Cyprus, Luxembourg 6; Malta 5.

9. Some member states also pay special attention to gender distribution: Denmark, Estonia, Finland, Ireland, Latvia, Malta, the Netherlands and the UK have introduced a special provision to this effect in their selection mechanism (CoR 2004).
10. 'Many of the Commission actors involved in the technical aspects of enlargement in PHARE (*Pologne–Hongrie Assistance à la Restructuration des Economies*), and the Commission's "country teams", had been influenced by the ongoing debates within the Commission over the reform of structural and cohesion policy in the early 1990s' when the Commission tried to impose a common format on the territorial organization of the member states in view of a more efficient use of the structural funds (Hughes *et al.* 2004, pp. 530–31). In the event, 'intergovernmentalism prevailed', and the procedures for structural funds remained highly differentiated from country to country (a development that has led some observers to refer to the changes introduced in 1993 as a 'counter-reform'). 'There is evidence to suggest that Commission officials, who had been frustrated by the 1993 reform, were motivated to use enlargement conditionality to pursue their particular agenda for the implementation of regional policy in the candidate countries' (ibid., pp. 31–2). Eventually, in the absence of sufficient regional administrative capacities, the Commission had to shift focus and revert to interacting mainly with central governments.
11. 'In the pre-accession period, at least, the Commission played a rather ambiguous role in this debate, promoting the partnership concept in principle, yet discouraging its application in practice by emphasizing the need for expediency in pre-accession preparations and efficiency in the use of EU funds' (Baun and Marek 2006, p. 416).
12. An important expansion of the CoR's remit is entailed by Art. III-388 of the Reform Treaty: 'Where the Economic and Social Committee is consulted, the Committee of the Regions shall be informed by the European Parliament, the Council or the Commission of the request for an opinion. Where it considers that specific regional interests are involved, the Committee of the Regions may issue an opinion on the matter. It may also issue an opinion on its own initiative.'
13. Personal interviews with senior CoR officials, 13 February 2006.
14. In 2005, in order to revitalize the Lisbon Agenda, a Lisbon Monitoring Platform involving Local and Regional Authorities (LRAs) was set up in order to prepare National Reform Programmes (NRPs). This platform explicitly acknowledges the unique and fundamental contribution that regions and cities can give to the implementation of the Lisbon Strategy. It was launched at the first Territorial Dialogue in March 2006, when some of the 65 regions involved in helping to implement the Lisbon objectives reported on the progress made. The second Territorial Dialogue meeting was held in February 2007 and was based on the active involvement of 100 regions.

REFERENCES

Bache, I. and Flinders, M. (eds) (2004), *Multi-Level Governance*, Oxford: Oxford University Press.

Batt, J. (2002), 'Introduction: Region, State and Identity in Central and Eastern Europe', *Regional and Federal Studies*, **12** (2), 1–14.

Baun, M. and Marek, D. (2006), 'Regional Policy and Decentralization in the Czech Republic', *Regional and Federal Studies*, **16** (4), 409–28.

Brunazzo, M. and Domorenok, E. (2007), 'The Enlargement of the Committee of the Regions: Evaluating the Entrance of New Members in a Representative Institution', EU-CONSENT online paper, http://www.eu-consent.net/library/deliverables/D17_Team9_Brunazzo-Domorenok.pdf.

Brusis, M. (2002), 'Between EU Requirements, National Traditions and Competitive Policies: Re-creating Regions in the Accession Countries of Central and Eastern Europe', *Governance*, **15** (4), 531–59.

Brusis, M. (2003), 'Regionalisation in the Czech and Slovak Republics: Comparing the Influence of the European Union' in M. Keating and J. Hughes (eds), *The Regional Challenge in Central and Eastern Europe: Territorial Restructuring and European Integration*, Brussls: P.I.E Peter Lang, pp. 89–105.

Christiansen, T. (1995), 'Second Thoughts – The Committee of the Regions after its First Year', in R. Dehousse and T. Christiansen (eds), What Model for the Committee of the Regions? Past Experience and Future Perspectives, *EUI Working Paper EUF*, **95** (2), 34–64.

Christiansen, T. (1996), 'Second Thoughts on Europe's "Third Level": The European Union's Committee of the Regions', *Publius: The Journal of Federalism*, **26** (1), 93–114.

Christiansen, T. and Lintner, P. (2005), 'The Committee of the Regions after 10 Years: Lessons from the Past and Challenges for the Future', *Eipascope*, **1**, 7–13.

Christiansen, T. and Piattoni, S. (eds) (2003), *Informal Governance in the European Union*, Cheltenham, UK and Northampton, MA, USA: Edward Elgar.

Committee of the Regions (CoR) (2004), *The Selection Process of CoR Members: Procedures in the Member States*, CoR Studies I 1/2004, Brussels: Committee of the Regions.

Committee of the Regions (2005), 'CoR Impact Assessment Report 2004', submitted for approval by the Secretary-General to the 86th CoR Bureau Meeting, R7EdR 62/2005 Item 10.

Czernielewska, M., Paraskevopoulos, C. and Szlachta, J. (2004), 'The Regionalization Process in Poland: An Example of "Shallow" Europeanization?', *Regional and Federal Studies*, **14** (3), 461–95.

Dinan, D. (2003), 'Governance and Institutions: Anticipating the Impact of Enlargement', *Journal of Common Market Studies*, **41**, Annual Review, 27–43.

Goetz, K.H. (2001), 'Making Sense of Post-Communist Central Administration: Modernization, Europeanization, or Latinization?' *Journal of European Public Policy*, **8** (6), 1032–51.

Hönnige, C. and Kaiser, A. (2003), 'Opening the Black Box: Decision-Making in the Committee of the Regions', *Regional and Federal Studies*, **13** (2), 1–29.

Hooghe, L. (1995), 'Sub-national Mobilization in the European Union', *West European Politics*, **18** (3), 175–98.

Hooghe, L. (ed.) (1996), *Cohesion Policy and European Integration: Building Multi-level Governance*, Oxford: Clarendon Press.

Hooghe, L. and Marks, G. (1996), ' "Europe with the Regions": Channels of Regional Representation in the European Union', *Publius: The Journal of Federalism*, **26** (1), 73–91.

Hooghe, L. and Marks, G. (2001), *Multi-level Governance and European Integration*, Lanham, MD: Rowman & Littlefield.

Hughes, J., Sasse, G. and Gordon, C. (2004), 'Conditionality and Compliance in EU's Eastward Enlargement: Regional Policy and the Reform of Sub-national Governments', *Journal of Common Market Studies*, **42** (3), 523–51.

Jeffery, C. (1995), 'Whither the Committee of the Regions? Reflections on the Committee's "Opinion of the Revision of the Treaty on European Union" ', *Regional and Federal Studies*, **5** (2), 247–57.

Jeffery, C. (1997), *Sub-national Authorities and European Integration: Moving Beyond the Nation-State*, Birmingham: University of Birmingham Press.

Jeffery, C. (2000), 'Sub-national Mobilization and European Integration: Does It Make Any Difference?', *Journal of Common Market Studies*, **38** (1), 1–23.

Jeffery, C. (2002), 'The Europe of the Regions from Maastricht to Nice', *Queen's Papers on Europeanisation*, **7**.

Keating, M. (1988), *State and Regional Nationalism: Territorial Politics and the European State*, Hemel Hempstead, UK: Harvester Wheatsheaf.

Keating, M. (1998), *The New Regionalism in Western Europe: Territorial Restructuring and Political Change*, Cheltenham, UK and Lyme, USA: Edward Elgar.

Keating, M. (2003), 'Regionalization in Central and Eastern Europe, The Diffusion of a Western Model?', in M. Keating and J. Hughes (eds), *The Regional Challenge in Central and Eastern Europe: Territorial Restructuring and European Integration*, Brussels: P.I.E. Peter Lang, pp. 51–67.

Keating, M. and Hooghe, L. (1996), 'By-passing the Nation State? Regions and the EU Policy Process', in J. Richardson (ed.), *European Union: Power and Policy-Making*, London, Routledge, pp. 216–29.

Lipset, S.M. and Rokkan, S. (eds) (1967), *Party Systems and Voter Alignments: Cross-national Perspectives*, New York: Free Press.

Loughlin, J. (1997), 'Representing Regions in Europe: The Committee of the Regions', in C. Jeffery (ed.), *The Regional Dimension of the European Union*, London: Frank Cass.

March, J. and Olsen, J.P. (1989), *Rediscovering Institutions: The Organizational Basis of Politics*, New York: Free Press.

Marek, D. and Baun, M. (2002), 'The EU as Regional Actor: The Case of the Czech Republic', *Journal of Common Market Studies*, **40** (5), 859–919.

Marks, G. and Hooghe L. (1997), 'The Making of a Polity: The Struggle over European Integration', *European Integration Online Papers*, **1** (4).

Marks, G. and Hooghe, L. (2003), 'Unravelling the Central State, but How? Types of Multi-level Governance', *American Political Science Review*, **97** (2), 233–43.

Marks, G. and Hooghe, L. (2004), 'Contrasting Visions of Multi-level Governance', in I. Bache and M. Flinders (eds), *Multi-level Governance: Inter-disciplinary Perspectives*, Oxford: Oxford University Press, pp. 15–30.

Marks, G., Nielsen, F., Ray, L. and Salk, J. (1996), 'Competencies, Cracks and Conflicts: Regional Mobilization in the European Union', *Comparative Political Studies*, **29** (2), 164–92.

Pálné Kovács, I., Paraskevopoulos, C., Horváth, G. (2004), 'Institutional "Legacies" in the Shaping of Regional Governance in Hungary', *Regional and Federal Studies*, **14** (3), 430–60.

Papadimitrious, D. and Phinnemore, D. (2004), 'Europeanization, Conditionality and Domestic Change: The Twinning Exercise and Administrative Reform in Romania', *Journal of Common Market Studies*, **42** (3), 619–39.

Piattoni, S. (2002), 'Il Comitato delle Regioni', in S. Fabbrini (ed.), *L'Unione europea: Le istituzioni e gli attori di un sistema sopranazionale*, Roma: Laterza, pp. 227–48.

Piattoni, S. (2005), 'La governance multi-livello: sfide analitiche, empiriche, normative', *Rivista Italiana di Scienza Politica*, **35** (3), 417–45.

Scherpereel, J.A. (2005), 'Absorbing the Shock: Enlargement's Effects on the Committee of the Regions', Paper presented at the 9th biennial conference of the European Union Studies Association, Austin, TX, March–April.

Scherpereel, J.A. (2007), 'Sub-national Authorities in the EU's Post-socialist States: Joining the Multi-level Polity?', *Journal of European Integration*, **29** (1), 23–46.

Schöbel, N. (1997), *The Committee of the Regions: A Preliminary Review of the Committee's Work during its First Two Years of Operation*, Tübingen: European Centre for Research on Federalism (ECRF).

Steunenberg, B. (2001), 'Enlargement and Institutional Reform in the European Union: Separate or Connected Issues?', *Constitutional Political Economy*, **12**, 351–70.

Tilly, C. (ed.) (1975), *The Formation of National States in Western Europe*, Princeton, NJ: Princeton University Press.

Tömmel, I. (1998), 'Transformation of Governance: The European Commission's Strategy for a "Europe of the Regions" ', *Regional and Federal Studies*, **8** (2).

Van der Knaap, P. (1994), 'The Committee of the Regions: The Outset of a "Europe of the Regions"?', *Regional Politics and Society*, **4** (2) (Summer), 86–100.

Warleigh, A. (1997), 'A Committee of No Importance? Assessing the Relevance of the Committee of the Regions', *Politics*, **17** (2), 101–7.

Warleigh, A. (1999), *The Committee of the Regions: Institutionalising Multi-level Governance?*, London: Kogan Page.

Zielonka, J. (2007), 'Plurilateral Governance in the Enlarged European Union', *Journal of Common Market Studies*, **45** (1), 187–209.

10. Legislative output after enlargement: similar number, shifting nature

Edward Best and Pierpaolo Settembri

The most visible aspect of the work of the European institutions is the production of legislation. At least superficially, it can also seem to be the most easily measurable and thereby objectively comparable over time. Efforts to measure change in the legislative output of the post-enlargement EU have led to a remarkable number of studies and to the collection of a large amount of new information (e.g. Dehousse *et al.* 2006; Sedelmeier and Young 2006; Hagemann and De Clerck-Sachsse 2007).

A common message in these studies has been one of overall continuity between pre- and post-enlargement Europe: there appears to be more or less the same level of output as before. Dehousse *et al.* (2006) thus maintain that enlargement has not blocked the European machine and that, in certain respects, decision-making even became more expeditious after 2004. Hagemann and De Clerck-Sachsse (2007, pp. 34, 36) report that, in terms of the total amount of legislation passed per year, the Council 'seems to have almost fully "recovered" from the significant increase in the number of actors' and that, concerning voting behaviour, 'official disagreement . . . has not been found to increase'.

Yet such accounts do not address fully some underlying qualitative questions. Are there any observable trends regarding the nature and content of the acts adopted? For example, is there a significant drop in the production of Community legislation as compared to other forms of Community action or purely intergovernmental acts? In general, are the acts adopted by the EU25 as important as those adopted in the EU15 in terms of their novelty and salience? Does their nature tend to strengthen or to weaken further deepening of the integration process?

This chapter therefore looks beyond global figures. It sets out to evaluate the evolution of the Union's legislative output in terms of the nature of the acts adopted as well as of the decision-making process, and to assess the possible influence of enlargement in bringing about these shifts.

On the one hand, this means asking whether enlargement could have contributed to changes in the quality of the legislative process. Could a similar level of efficiency in decision-making have been maintained in the new conditions of the EU25 at the cost of a reduction in other desirable aspects of European policy-making – for example, real political input from within the institutions, or the degree of transparency?

On the other hand, it means trying to assess to what extent enlargement, as a result of the particular interests of the new member states, may have affected legislative activity in terms of a shift in the balance of thinking within the Union over substantive policy preferences and/or over choices of policy instruments. Have the new member states seemed to fit into pre-existing patterns, or can one observe some more fundamental shift?

The first section presents the analytical framework. The following sections present the findings, looking at general trends in the nature of the output and in the quality of the process, followed by evidence from specific policy areas.

ANALYTICAL APPROACH

The present analysis is based upon quantitative data and two case studies. The quantitative data are drawn from the same dataset used in Chapter 3, described in greater detail in the Appendix:[1] the dataset contrasts two comparable periods of decision-making before and after the 2004 enlargement, the Greek and Italian presidencies in 2003, and the British and Austrian presidencies in the second half of 2005 and the first half of 2006.

The decision-making *output* is assessed in terms of a number of qualitative variables which have not been addressed by existing studies:

- *Type of act.* A distinction is proposed between (1) 'Community legislation', in the strict sense of an act adopted by the Council, or by the Parliament jointly with the Council, following a Commission proposal on the basis of a treaty article;[2] (2) 'other Community acts', which are similar to Community legislation except for the fact that they are not adopted directly on the basis of a treaty article; and (3) 'intergovernmental acts', which are not based on a Commission proposal and concern, in most of the cases, acts in the area of the Common Foreign and Security Policy (CFSP).
- *Salience.* Can acts produced by the EU be ranked according to their salience? We propose here a distinction between 'major', 'ordinary' or 'minor' acts on the basis of the importance apparently attached

by the institutions and of the characteristics of the act itself. Five properties are proposed. Has the Commission introduced the bill by oral procedure? Has the Council at least once discussed the act as a 'B point'?[3] Have any other committees of the Parliament, in addition to the Committee responsible, adopted at least one opinion on the proposal? Is the act based on a treaty article (as opposed to secondary legislation)? Is the act 'innovative', in the sense that it represents something more than a mere adjustment or update of existing norms? Acts that score positively on all five or four of these questions are considered as important (major acts). Those which score positively on three or two questions are considered of average importance (ordinary acts). All the other pieces are considered of marginal importance (minor acts).

- *Length.* It is assumed, following Huber and Shipan (2002), that the length of legislation is a proxy for a principal's effort to constrain the actions of the agent. Enlargement entails a multiplication of policy goals and an amplification of preferences divergence among decision-makers. Longer legislation in the EU25 is thus assumed to be generally proof that more interests need to be accommodated and that this is achieved through more tortuous and particularistic legislation.

The dataset also considers certain aspects of the *process* by which acts are adopted. If it is the case that the institutions have managed to maintain the same level of 'efficiency' in producing output, this could have been achieved at the expense of other qualities of decision-making, namely the degree of political input, and the transparency of the procedure.

- *Political input.* Three measures are proposed, one per institution: the number of real discussions and the quality of representation in the Council, as indicated in Chapter 3; the percentage of Commission proposals adopted by the 'oral procedure' in the College, i.e. that receive explicit endorsement at the highest political level; and the average number of opinions adopted by EP committees on each proposal before adoption of Parliament's legislative resolution, together with some more general trends on the parliamentary activities.
- *Transparency.* Three indicators are used. The first one concerns the proportion of acts that are partially removed from the traditional decision-making process by deferring portions of their content to the operation of comitology procedures, which are governed by much weaker transparency rules than the traditional legislative process. The second measure estimates, before and after enlargement, the

percentage of legislation subject to the highest transparency requirements in terms of publication by the Council of voting results, voting explanations and voting rules applicable.[4] The third measure concerns the percentage of all codecision files that are adopted at first reading, considering that the informal negotiation of agreements at this early stage is relatively less subject to traditional mechanisms of accountability than formal procedures.

The selection of *cases* to perform a meaningful 'before-and-after' comparison is very difficult. It is hard even to find cases in which the same issues were considered in Council before and after 1 May 2004, the only major change being the expansion in the number of member states. Moreover, there was a sort of understanding, or gentleman's agreement, that new member states would not reopen issues that had been agreed before their accession. Although this may not always have been the case in practice, this inevitably weakens any attempt at simple comparisons.

In addition, one has to be careful not to confuse the Council's need to deal with specific issues imported together with the new member states and the ability of the enlarged Union to deal with issues that are not specific to them. Thus, on the one hand, it tells us very little to compare how the Union institutions have acted before and after enlargement in the case of, say, Kaliningrad. On the other hand, even if one can identify particular issues which have required a decision before 1 May 2004 and another decision afterwards, which are not of specific interest to particular member states, and which are not significantly shaped by any other trends, such that the only difference would be in the decision-making procedure, it is not obvious what the comparison would tell one – even if documentation was available to measure all dimensions of the two procedures in practice, which it is not. No documentation is available to measure the number and nature of contacts made in advance of meetings, informal interactions around the meetings, or the number and length of interventions during meetings.

Yet it is only by looking into particular cases that one can try to explore how the specific issues introduced by enlargement – whether in procedure or in substance or both – have been dealt with in practice. The directives on bathing water and extractive industries' waste were selected as two cases of codecision procedures which 'straddled' the enlargement. Although the fact that both concern environment policy limits the extent to which they may provide generalizable conclusions, this was considered to be outweighed by the interest in examining a sector in which enlargement was assumed, not entirely accurately, to have a strong impact.

GLOBAL TRENDS

The Nature of the Output

The numbers of acts adopted in the EU15 and the EU25 are broadly similar. This is in line with findings reported by other studies. However, even if the overall number of acts adopted by the Community seems to have remained fairly constant (they have decreased by 5 per cent), there have been significant shifts in the nature of the output.

First, the proportion of Community legislation out of total Union acts has shifted. Legislation accounted for 56 per cent of output in the pre-enlargement period under consideration, and 49 per cent in the post-enlargement period, with the absolute number of legislative acts dropping by 16.5 per cent from 267 to 223 (see Figure 10.1). The number of intergovernmental acts, on the other hand, increases, with four-fifths of these acts adopted in the area of CFSP in the EU25, as opposed to two-thirds in the EU15.

Second, although the proportion of innovative acts out of total Union acts has remained stable,[5] there has been a pronounced change in the share of important legislative acts. The number of both major and ordinary acts decreases by roughly one-third after enlargement (see Figure 10.2), while 'marginal' acts come to represent a majority (57.1 per cent) of acts adopted in the EU25 (compared to 42.6 per cent in the EU15).

Third, the average length of Community acts has increased. In the EU25, a legislative act is on average 15 per cent longer than in the EU15. The same measure shows even greater rates of increase when it comes to important pieces of legislation (+83 per cent). Interestingly, there is an important difference between files decided under the codecision and consultation procedures (see Figure 10.3). Whereas, regardless of the procedure, legislation tends to be longer as its importance increases, the variation between acts within the same category of salience varies radically depending on the procedure. Under consultation, there is no increase (or a minimal increase, for ordinary acts) in the length of legislation before and after enlargement. Under codecision, on the contrary, the rise is already pronounced for minor and ordinary acts and becomes dramatic for important acts. Figures change also depending on the type of act: for example, directives have, on average, more than doubled their length, whilst regulations are some 9.5 per cent shorter in the EU25.

The same variation is present if one distinguishes between legislation adopted under unanimity or QMV (see Figure 10.4), with the latter showing trends of legislative increase similar to those under the codecision procedure: this causes little surprise, as codecision and QMV are – with few exceptions – applied together.

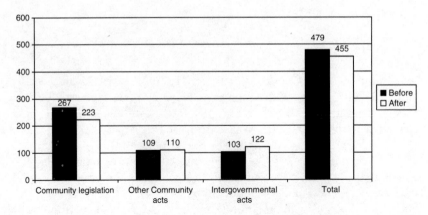

Figure 10.1   Acts adopted at the EU level, by type

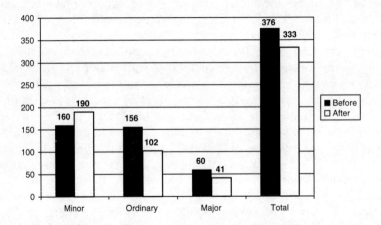

*Figure 10.2   Importance of Community acts adopted before/after
             enlargement*

The data thus suggest that, although the overall number of acts remains roughly similar, the Union is adopting a smaller number of legislative acts and a smaller number of important acts. Those which are adopted, especially under codecision, tend to be longer than before. This increase in length merits further reflection, especially since it seems to go against both the trend to keep measures short because of translation costs and the pursuit of simplification and 'better regulation'. The main factor appears to be the complexity of the issues in a context of increased diversity. In some cases this results in greater flexibility in legislative acts and, in some areas, a shift away from legislation towards non-legislative methods.

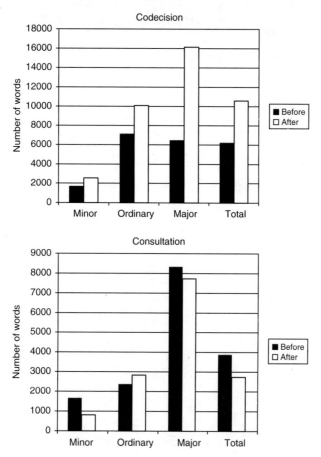

Figure 10.3 *Average length of Community legislation by importance of
act and procedure*

Changes in such respects are not necessarily connected with enlargement, of course. Quite apart from the evolution of the international
context, they also reflect broader shifts in the policy agenda. The number
of new Commission proposals has been shaped by the general concerns of
Better Regulation.[6] To take only two specific cases which are treated in this
volume, there has been a global trend away from 'command-and-control'
approaches in environmental policy since the early 1990s, reflected in the
EU's move to look beyond a strictly legislative approach, as well as a clear
shift more recently in the Commission and many member states to give
environmental considerations a lower priority. Employment policy and
labour law have seen major changes since the early 1990s, away from

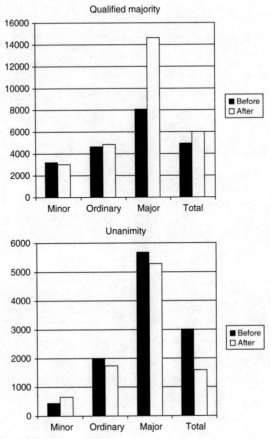

*Figure 10.4   Average length of Community legislation by importance of
act and voting rule*

legislation towards autonomous agreements between social partners
and/or the non-binding forms of policy coordination. Enlargement, and
the concomitant increase in diversity, has accentuated many such trends,
further encouraging flexibility in EU norms but, as argued in Chapter 12,
these developments in the modes of European governance cannot be attributed to the entry of the new member states.

The Quality of the Process

Concerning the *political input* provided by the EU institutions, findings are
consistent in indicating a lower level of intensity of the political input to

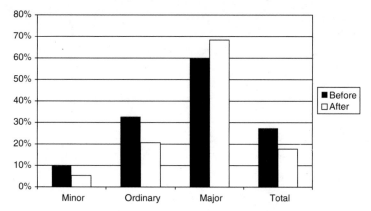

Figure 10.5   Percentage of Community acts containing comitology provisions before/after enlargement, by salience

decision-making. In the case of the Council (see Chapter 3), there has been a drop in the relative number of political discussions and in the level of political representation. The Commission has adopted, since enlargement, only 12.6 per cent of its proposals, by oral procedure (18.9 per cent[7] before enlargement).[8] The Parliament has, on average, adopted in the EU25 one-third fewer opinions per act (0.6 opinions per act in the EU15 compared to 0.89 in the EU15).[9] More generally, additional data made available by the EP website suggest that it is mainly its legislative activity which has 'suffered' since enlargement: whereas the average number of non-legislative acts adopted yearly has remained stable since enlargement (0.36 per deputy, just as before enlargement), the number of adopted legislative acts has decreased by over 22 per cent (from 0.54 to 0.42 per deputy).[10]

Concerning *transparency*, the percentage of acts adopted by the Council which are published in Annex III of the monthly summary of Council acts – thus entailing the disclosure of less information – increases (+4.5 per cent), to the detriment of acts published in Annex I (−21 per cent).[11] Resort to comitology procedures decreases significantly overall under both consultation and codecision: in the EU25, only 17.7 per cent of Community acts contain comitology provisions (as compared to 27.4 per cent in the EU15). However, the percentage increases from 60 per cent to 68.3 per cent in the case of important acts (see Figure 10.5). Neither of these trends, however, can be specifically attributed to enlargement.

As for the evolution of codecision files, data confirm the increasing number of acts (in both absolute and relative terms) adopted at first reading: whereas before enlargement only 29.6 per cent of codecision files

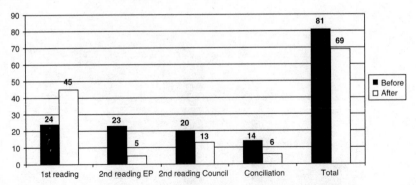

*Figure 10.6   Number of acts adopted under codecision before/after
enlargement, by reading*

were adopted at first reading, they increase to 65.2 per cent in the EU25 (see
Figure 10.6).

This significant increase in the share of codecision files which are concluded at first reading (as well as in pre-negotiation of agreement at the
common position stage) has implications not only for the transparency of
the process but also for the nature and evolution of inter-institutional relations.

These figures, and the possible contribution of enlargement to this trend,
demand some caution. There has been an inter-institutional learning
process since the entry into force of the Amsterdam Treaty (reflected in
the adoption and revision of a Joint Declaration on the Practical
Arrangements for Codecision) regarding the development and consolidation of informal practices required to prepare formal outcomes – the informal tripartite meetings between small negotiating teams from each
institution. The systematic improvement in mutual information at an early
stage has been a fundamental contributing factor in permitting first-
reading agreements. The Parliament, moreover, may at earlier stages have
found it of institutional interest to go to conciliation in order to demonstrate its new powers but now has no need to do so. There have also been
changes in the substantive scope of codecision since enlargement, namely
its extension as of 1 January 2005 to most Community provisions on visas,
asylum, immigration and other policies related to free movement of
persons. Coreper II, responsible for this field, is well known to favour early
agreements. The figures may also have been distorted by some temporary
phenomena – for example, the fact that a significant number of files were
adopted under strong time pressure following belated agreement on the
Financial Perspectives, in order to implement spending in 2007. In

addition, files which began during this parliament (that is, in 2005) and which were not agreed at first reading would go to second reading only in 2007, such that the overall proportion of conclusions at later stages may well be significantly higher for the parliamentary term as a whole.

One could also argue that, since the number of individuals involved in the tripartite meetings has not changed, enlargement does not have any significant practical impact. Yet conversely, and in a broader perspective, the reliance on these small informal negotiating teams to reach deals has been in large measure precisely a response to the increase in numbers, which has made plenary inter-institutional negotiation less and less viable. Here again, the conclusion must be that there has been a mutual reinforcement between enlargement and other trends.

At the same time, as noted above, there has been an increase in the average number of days required to conclude a file under codecision. This must mean that, in a significant number of cases, it is in fact taking more time to reach a compromise between Council and Parliament and to have this compromise ratified. In addition to the basic complexity of the issues (which could be intensified by an increase in underlying diversity as a result of enlargement), one cause of this delay could be unexpected complications in the steps involved: notably the extent to which committee recommenda-tions are taken over or not by plenary and, going back one step, the degree to which proposed inter-institutional packages of compromise amend-ments are taken up or not by committees. It is beyond the scope of this chapter to try to look more systematically at patterns of change within the Parliament. The two examples drawn from environment policy may nonetheless shed some light on this aspect, as well as on the possible con-tribution of enlargement.

The Position of the New Member States

Looking at the voting behaviour of individual Member States, the data confirm a finding already held by other academic works, namely the absence of a cleavage between 'old' and 'new' member states.[12] 'New' member states are neither quieter nor noisier than 'old' ones: during the two presidencies after enlargement covered by this study, both 'old' and 'new' member states have contested[13] on average the adoption of a legisla-tive act subject to QMV 2.3 times. The perfect symmetry continues also when one considers the member states that opposed legislation most fre-quently (Greece and Poland) or the only two that never complained during an entire year (Belgium and Lithuania) (see Figure 10.7). Out of the 14 coalitions of countries opposing legislation detected after enlargement, just one comprises only 'new' member states.[14] Most coalitions (8 out of 14) are

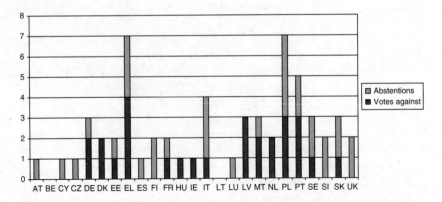

Figure 10.7   Number of votes against and abstentions in the adoption of Community legislation after enlargement

Table 10.1   'Singletons' and coalitions of Member States opposing Community legislation after enlargement, by member state

Coalition size	1 MS	2 MSs	3 MSs	4 MSs	5 MSs	6 MSs	7 MSs
Frequency	14	4	7	1	1	0	1
Of which only EU10 coalitions	5	1					
Of which only EU15 coalitions	9	2	3				
Of which mixed EU15+ EU10 coalitions		1	4	1	1		1

'mixed', i.e. bringing together at least one delegation from both 'new' and 'old' member states (see Table 10.1).[15]

EVIDENCE FROM SPECIFIC POLICY AREAS

The general trends presented above manifest themselves in different ways, depending on the issue/policy area. As already demonstrated in Chapter 3 on the Council, it seems clear that, although there are naturally some issues of specific concern to a significant number of the 10/12, there are relatively few issues on which there is a simple opposition of old and new countries, and there is indeed a preference to avoid going to a vote where this might seem to be the case. Even in the area of social policy, where the assumption has been strongest that enlargement has favoured the UK-led camp (for example over working time), the new member states have split, with only a slight majority joining the 'Anglo-Saxon' camp. Coalitions continue to be issue-based, and generally led by the larger member states, with the incoming members of Council joining these camps (Naurin 2007).

In the case of agriculture, between the EU15 and the EU25, the number of legislative acts adopted has increased, from 35 to 40, but the number of important ones has halved, from ten to five. Legislation is one-third shorter. In the field of environment, the amount of legislation adopted has remained identical (14 legislative acts per period), but the number of important acts has decreased from eight to five. As for the length of legislation, however, the change is the opposite of that in agriculture: legislation in general is more than 50 per cent longer after enlargement, and the fewer salient bills adopted in the EU25 are 150 per cent longer.

Two examples shed light on how the acceding countries fitted into ongoing procedures. Bathing water 'straddled' the enlargement in the sense that the same dossier was discussed in Council both before and after 1 May 2004. In the case of extractive industries' waste, the Commission proposal was presented and Parliament's first reading took place before enlargement, and the Council common position was adopted in 2005. In both cases, the new member states did have specific concerns, but these basically fitted into the existing positions.

Bathing Water

The Commission presented a proposal in October 2002 to replace the 1976 Bathing Water Directive. The main issues concerned the scope, notably recreational waters; parameters, which would be reduced from 19 to two microbiological parameters complemented by visual inspection and pH measurement in fresh waters; the categories of classification of bathing water quality: 'poor', 'good' or 'excellent' in the Commission's proposal ('poor' being waters causing more than 5 per cent risk of contracting gastro-enteritis); flexibility in monitoring frequencies; and provisions for public participation and information. The European Parliament adopted its amendments at first reading in October 2003.

A distinction between coastal waters and inland waters appeared in the Presidency's compromise texts towards the end of the year, proposing less stringent standards for inland waters (on the grounds that the presence of the same level of microbiological contamination represents a higher health risk in salt water than in fresh water). Although important differences remained with regard to the classification issue, it was hoped to find a political agreement in December 2003. The Council meeting, however, failed:

there was no debate; the Commission and Germany made critical statements, and a sour atmosphere prevailed.

The Irish dealt with the file in the last two months of their presidency,
which coincided with the accession of the new member states on 1 May. The
reason, however, was not to try in some way to take advantage of the
enlarged Council. First, the Irish Presidency had had a notably busy
agenda in the first months of the year, pushing ahead with a multitude of
dossiers which could be finished, not only in advance of enlargement but
also before the European Parliament stopped doing business in advance of
the European elections. Second, given the events of December, the Irish
had no interest in having their presidency tainted with a bad-feeling failure
over bathing water. They would only take it forward if there was some reasonable chance of success.

Following talks with those delegations which had had difficulties, the
Presidency indicated in late April 2004 that it intended to reopen negotiations, proposing two options: introduction of a new category of 'satisfactory' (equivalent to 10 per cent risk); or maintaining the original three
categories, but with a specific review foreseen for 2012 to aim at reducing
the health risk to 5 per cent by 2015. At the 11 May meeting of the Working
Party on the Environment, the option of introducing a new category
received more support, and a revised proposal based on that option was
considered on 24 May and 3 June. The draft was discussed three times in
Coreper, and a political agreement was reached in the Council on 28 June
2004.

Enlargement did introduce some substantive changes in the nature of
the issues. Notably, given European geography, it increased the relative
significance of inland waters compared to coastal waters. Hungary was
particularly anxious to avoid the imposition of very high standards.
Slovenia too was reported to have 'contributed actively' to the discussions
in the course of 2003.[16] On the specific issue of defining limit values for the
'satisfactory' classification of inland waters, seven of the eight CEE countries (EE, LV, LT, HU, PL, SI, SK) opposed the Commission's proposal for
lower limits in early June (together with BE, ES, IT, NL, PT, FI).[17] On the
whole, however, the concerns of the acceding countries were seen generally
to mirror those of existing member states.[18] The new member states were
not very active at the higher levels within the Council framework. The only
issue raised in Coreper, by Cyprus and Hungary, was the exact name to be
given to the new category. None of them raised any issues within the
Council.[19] From the Common Position onwards, there was no particular
influence on Council's position resulting from the new member states.

The Council agreed in its Common Position on the new category of
'sufficient', as well as the distinction between inland waters and coastal

waters. Parliament's ENVI Committee proposed deleting both of these in its draft amendments adopted on 21 April, as well as advancing the deadline for the new system. These amendments in particular were seen to leave no flexibility for the Council. A proposed compromise package was drawn up in the working party on 21 April: Parliament would drop these amendments; in exchange Council would offer some changes on public information and participation, perhaps making more explicit the review clause to respond to concerns about the 'sufficient' category. For the rest, the Presidency sent a strong message to Parliament that 'the Council has no flexibility on other issues and would prefer the *status quo* to the adoption of a Directive containing the other elements of its draft second-reading opinion'.[20] The package was not accepted at the informal trialogue on 25 April, and the Committee proceeded with the amendments.

These proposals, however, were not adopted in the plenary vote on 10 May,[21] although the plenary did introduce more stringent standards for the 'sufficient' category. The main reason for this seems to be a selective increase in the extent to which MEPs vote according to national interests rather than group position. It is hard to evaluate to what extent, if any, enlargement has contributed to this. In the case of bathing water, there were only eight roll-call votes on the 55 second-reading amendments considered in plenary. In those cases, group discipline was maintained to a high degree, with one exception – Amendment 42 from the Group of the Greens/European Free Alliance. In this case, the Socialist Group was more or less equally divided. The extent to which national delegations voted as such is more or less the same for 'old' and for 'new' member states (see Table 10.2).

Extractive Industries' Waste

The directive on extractive industries' waste of December 2005 (usually referred to as 'mining waste') has widely been seen as reflecting 'a more industry-friendly approach, attributed largely to the influence of the new member states, with their strong mining sectors and relatively low levels of regulation. Poland and other new member states successfully opposed measures in the extractive industries which would have imposed strict safety requirements on closed mines' (Burson-Marsteller 2006, p. 16). Yet things are not quite so clear if one looks into the case more closely.

The proposal was presented in June 2003. Parliament adopted its first-reading position in March 2004. It proposed broadening the scope, providing for continued obligations of operators after closure of mines, an inventory of closed sites, and the obligation to include safe disposal in waste management plans from the very beginning. Only two amendments proposed by the Committee failed to be adopted.

Table 10.2   *A snapshot of national interests within political groups in the EU25: the division of PES voting over Amendment 42 on bathing water at second reading, 10 May 2005*

'OLD'	For	Against/abstain	'New'*	For	Against/abstain
BE	4	–	LT	2	–
DK	3	–	MT	3	–
IE	1	–	SI	1	–
GR	7	–	SK	3	–
AT	6	–			
FI	3	–			
SE	4	–			
DE	20	1			
FR	24	1			
IT	7	2	PL	5	3
PT	4	3	CZ	1	1
ES	2	20	EE	1	1
NL	–	6	HU	–	6
LU	–	1			
UK	–	17			

Notes:
Not all MEPs voted.
* Cyprus and Latvia have no PES members.

Source: Elaborated from voting record in OJ C92E of 20 April 2006, pp. 42–3.

The Common Position of the Council was adopted in April 2005. This further weakened the proposal in several respects by, *inter alia*, introducing a new category of non-hazardous non-inert waste for which some exemptions would apply, and further weakening definitions of extractive waste facilities and their most dangerous category. The leading actors in the negotiations were 'old' member states, the camp generally preferring a weaker measure led by the UK and Germany, and that generally pressing for strong measures led by Spain, which had suffered the Aznalcóllar accident in 1998. The 'new' member states divided between these two positions. The pro-weakening camp was joined by Poland and the Czech Republic (and others on some issues). On the other side, Spain was joined by Hungary, which had received quantities of waste water containing cyanide and heavy metals from the Baia Mare accident in Romania in 2000. Hungary, together with Austria, indeed abstained in the adoption of the Common Position.

Following adoption of draft amendments by the Environment Committee on 25 May including key amendments proposed at first reading on scope and post-closure obligations, the Presidency proposed a compromise package for the informal trialogue on 5 July.[22] The Committee only partially modified the draft recommendation on 13 July, and maintained most of the amendments which had been considered unacceptable by the Council. The Parliament's press service stressed that the Committee was insisting on:

> an inventory of closed sites to be established by every Member State in the three years following the entry into force of the directive, prioritising the most dangerous sites. The site should if necessary be rehabilitated in the following four years at the expense of the waste producers. This point is of particular importance to the new Member States of Central and Eastern Europe where many mining companies have long flouted safety standards.[23]

At second reading, however, 12.5 of the amendments failed to be adopted. Most of these had been proposed at first reading. None had been accepted (or accepted fully) by the Council in the compromise package. A common perception was that 'the Parliament had caved in to concerns expressed by Central and East European countries by removing a requirement to clean up old and abandoned mining sites'.[24] Since there were no roll-call votes it is not possible to provide objective evidence as to whether the behaviour of MEPs from new member states was the main element involved, far less the precise motivations behind the voting. Even at the Committee stage, there was some manifestation of uncertainty, with 36 votes in favour, five against and 15 abstentions.[25] It seems plausible that those larger countries which were pressing for a 'proportionate' measure may have succeeded in rallying MEPs from new (as well as old) member states to vote against the repeated amendments of most concern. Although Council could not adopt all the amendments, and thus had to go to conciliation, the end-game for the UK Presidency was now much easier.

What do these cases tell us? They confirm the point made in Chapter 3, that the entry of the new member states has on the whole not resulted in major shifts in the balance of positions within the Council. They also support the conclusion of Donnelly and Bigatto (this volume, Chapter 5) that there has been no major change in the political culture of the European Parliament as a result of enlargement: voting according to national interests remains the exception, and Members from new member states indulge in it to much the same degree as those from older member states. And they reinforce the view that the changes taking place in EU legislative procedures are more to do with matters of inter-institutional dynamics rather than of internal Council procedures.

CONCLUSION

The main finding of this chapter is that the Union has proved to be a flexible system, showing an extraordinary capacity of adapting to a new environment with increased membership and, arguably, increased political diversity. After enlargement, the system delivers a comparable amount of acts; on average, it does so faster and without greater political contestation. These results are even more remarkable if one considers that they have been achieved without the broader treaty revision promised after the adoption of the Treaty of Nice.

A closer look at what the EU produces and the way it operates, however, shows that the EU25 is somewhat different from the EU15, more different than most recent accounts would admit. When the rules leave a wide margin for negotiation (i.e. under QMV in the Council and/or when the EP codecides), the system delivers on time and without increased political 'noise'.

Nevertheless, this efficiency of the system seems to have been accompanied by changes in two other dimensions. On the one hand, legislation is shaped, in addition to the inherent complexity of many issues, by an increased variety of interests, and its content is fundamentally altered. Diversity is accommodated through significantly longer acts, and one may wonder whether more detailed legislation is well suited to fostering more integration. On the other hand, the decision-making process becomes more bureaucratized and enjoys less political input. As shown in Chapter 3, the Council discusses legislation less frequently and, when it does, the representation of the member states is less frequently entrusted to ministers. The Commission decides by oral procedure one-third less frequently than before enlargement and, in the EU25, bills benefit from a significantly lower number of opinions voted by the committees of the EP. Finally, resort to comitology provisions removes an increased share of major acts from the traditional decision-making process.

The main driver behind these changes is the codecision procedure: all the trends traced in this work are magnified when Council and Parliament are required to act together. The difference between codecision in the EU15 and the EU25 is apparent on at least two levels. On the one hand, the dynamics of the procedure itself have significantly changed. Since enlargement, deals are increasingly reached at first reading. Although this could be interpreted as an indicator of greater maturity in the relationship between Council and Parliament, the development does not seem to provide the EU system with more efficiency: on the contrary, codecision at 25 is some 22 per cent slower than at 15. First readings, in particular, are now more than 40 per cent slower than before enlargement. On the other hand, the output of codecision is different: after enlargement, Community legislation is almost

30 per cent shorter when adopted under the consultation procedure, but 70 per cent longer if adopted through codecision.

Not only does codecision slow down the process and change the content of the legislative output; it also alters the nature of inter-institutional relations. The high frequency of codecision files concluded at first reading, the fact that emissaries of Council and Parliament get together to broker an agreement from the outset of the procedure, and the practice of adopting package deals amalgamating amendments from both institutions suggest that a new type of procedure is surfacing. It will be left to future research to investigate more closely the consequences of this trend, in at least three respects: the quality of the output it produces, the quality of the process with regard, in particular, to its amenability to public scrutiny, and the evolving role of the Commission.

Determining the specific influence of enlargement in all this, however, is not a simple matter. On the one hand, the evidence suggests that the new member states have on the whole fitted into the existing system without causing fundamental changes in the degree of contestation or the patterns of coalitions in the Council. Nor have they caused any major shift in the patterns of voting behaviour in the Parliament. On the other hand, although both the reduced intensity of political input and the evolution of the codecision procedure can plausibly be linked to the increase in numbers of member states and Members of the European Parliament respectively, the impact of enlargement is probably more a matter of reinforcing existing trends than of introducing radical changes.

This ambiguity, finally, may be seen as a reflection of the real issues involved in thinking about the 'impact' of enlargement and the nature of institutional change. It is not so much a matter of measuring particular differences in the old Union but of looking at the new one, which is inevitably different, in order to understand how the institutional arrangements have evolved to keep the system on track – albeit in a slightly different direction.

NOTES

1. This dataset was first used in Settembri (2007).
2. As an exception, the definition includes also acts adopted under Title IV TEC and Title VI TEU (generally referred to as 'JHA' acts), even if they are not based on a Commission proposal.
3. The Council agenda is divided into two parts: A and B. 'A' items can be approved without discussion. 'B' items are usually discussed and, under certain conditions, can be subject to a vote.
4. It measures, in particular, the percentage of acts published in Annex I of the monthly summary of Council's acts (out of the total). See the Appendix for a distinction between Annex I and Annex III in the monthly summary of Council's acts.

5. Both in the EU25 and the EU15 the number of innovative acts, in the sense of acts which do more than modify existing measures, is slightly more than one-half of the total.

6. Nevertheless, whereas this can be true for specific policy areas, data concerning the overall number of proposals put on the table by the Commission before and after enlargement show that the decrease of adopted Community acts could hardly be attributed to a lower number of initiatives. On average, the Commission proposed some 546 Community acts per year in 2002 and 2003, against 549 in 2005 and 2006 (source: Prelex, accessible at http://ec.europa.eu/prelex/apcnet.cfm).

7. This value might even be downward biased because the databases consulted failed to provide information on the Commission decision mode on roughly one-third of the cases, some of which might have been adopted by oral procedure.

8. The result is quite unsurprising, as one might have easily hypothesized that, given the same time available for meetings, a College of 25 Commissioners coming from 20 countries would have been able to take a lower number of 'oral' decisions than a College of 20 coming from 15. At the same time, however, it should be noted that the 'decongestion' of Commission meetings has been deliberately pursued by the current Commission since (and because of) enlargement, for example by creating several groups of Commissioners and introducing the 'finalization' procedure, allowing decisions to be moved from the oral to the written procedure with the agreement of the heads of cabinet (see also Chapter 4 on the Commission).

9. This finding is consistent with those works that look at the nature of activities within the EP. Maurer (2007, p. 13), for example, submits that after the 2004 enlargement the number of own-initiative and urgency reports (i.e. non-legislative activities) increases significantly and suggests that this is due to the fact that particularly deputies coming from Central and Eastern Europe concentrate on this type of activities. Increased focus on similar functions inevitably causes a diminution in the resources available for legislative activities.

10. In this case, the data before enlargement refer to the parliamentary activities of 2001, 2002 and 2003, whereas for the period after enlargement they refer to 2005 and 2006 (the year of the elections, 2004, has been intentionally excluded). They are taken from a specific section of the EP website, which is accessible at http://www.europarl.europa.eu/sce/server/internet/stats/sce_stats_main_01.jsp.

11. This is not to suggest, obviously, that the Council purposely chooses to publish its acts in the section of the minutes that entails reduced disclosure information. It is only pointed out that, out of the global legislative production of the Council, the portion that is more visible and can be properly analysed is quantitatively much more modest since enlargement.

12. See, for example, Naurin (2007) and Hagemann and De Clerck-Sachsse (2007).

13. By voting against or abstaining.

14. *Regulation (EC) No. 562/2006 of the European Parliament and of the Council of 15 March 2006 establishing a Community Code on the rules governing the movement of persons across borders (Schengen Borders Code)*, on which Hungary voted against and Slovenia abstained.

15. These data do not necessarily coincide with those presented in other accounts of the same phenomena (see, for example, Mattila 2004; Dehousse *et al.* 2006; Hayes-Renshaw *et al* 2007; Hagemann and De Clerck-Sachsse 2007). There might be three explanations for this discrepancy: first of all, we only consider votes on final acts (and not on interim documents). Secondly, the selection of acts covered by this study is not based on the definition of 'legislative act' given by the Council but on the basis of criteria exclusively related to the specific features of each act (as explained in Chapter 3): this means that we include also some acts published in Annex III of the Monthly Summary of Council Acts, provided that they satisfy our definition of 'legislative acts'. Thirdly, we do not count as 'opposing' or 'contesting' those delegations that abstain from the adoption of an act subject to the unanimity rule. As abstentions under the unanimity rule do not prevent the adoption of the act, we have serious reservations on the frequent practice of counting them as equivalent or similar to abstentions under QMV.

16. Doc. 15790/03 of 9 December 2003.
17. Doc. 10082/1/04 REV 1 of 11 June 2004.
18. Doc. 15790/03 of 9 December 2003.
19. Information from Council Secretariat.
20. Doc. 8075/1/05 REV 1 of 21 April 2005.
21. The vote on deleting the 'sufficient' category was actually in favour (320 in favour, with 291 against and 11 abstentions) but was below the threshold of the absolute majority of members required to adopt second-reading amendments. The amendment on suppressing the distinction between coastal and inland waters was defeated by a show of hands. OJ C 92 E of 20 April 2006, p. 31.
22. Council doc. 10682/05 of 29 June 2005.
23. http://www.europarl.europa.eu/news/expert/infopress_page/064-1450-238-08-34-911-20050826IPR01432-26-08-2005-2005-false/default_en.htm
24. *Euractiv*, 'EU strikes agreement on mining waste', 22 November 2005.
25. The possibility of a change in position after enlargement was openly taken into account regarding admissibility of amendments. A point was raised at that meeting under Any Other Business on 'Second reading amendments on common positions currently being considered within the Committee. In reply to a question by Mr Bowis, the Chairman confirmed that he would support a flexible, open approach to amendments tabled on these issues on which Parliament's first reading had taken place in the last Parliament and before enlargement.' Minutes of the meeting on 12 and 13 July of the Committee on the Environment, Public Health and Food Safety. ENVI_PV(2005)0712_1, http://www.europarl.europa.eu/meetdocs/2004_2009/documents/pv/572/572404/572404 en.pdf.

REFERENCES

Burson-Marsteller (2006), 'Big Bang – Smaller Shocks: Enlargement 2004's Impact on EU Policies and Process', http://www.bmbrussels.be/pdf/Enlargement2004. pdf, 17 October 2006.

Dehousse, R., Deloche-Gaudez, F. and Duhamel, O. (2006), *Élargissement: Comment l'Europe s'adapte*, Paris: Presses de Sciences Po.

Hagemann, S. and De Clerck-Sachsse, J. (2007), *Old Rules, New Game: Decision-making in the Council of Ministers after the 2004 Enlargement*, CEPS Special Report, March.

Hayes-Renshaw, F., van Aken, W. and Wallace, H. (2006), 'When and Why the Council of Ministers of the EU Votes Explicitly', *Journal of Common Market Studies*, **44** (1), 161–94.

Huber, J. and Shipan, C. (2002), *Deliberate Discretion? The Institutional Foundations of Bureaucratic Autonomy*, Cambridge: Cambridge University Press.

Mattila, M. (2004), 'Contested Decisions: Empirical Analysis of Voting in the European Union Council of Ministers', *European Journal of Political Research*, **43** (1), 29–50.

Maurer, A. (2007), 'The European Parliament post-1993: Explaining Macroscopic Trends of Inter- and Intrainstitutional Developments', Paper presented at the Biennial Conference of the European Union Studies Association, Montreal, 17 May.

Naurin, D. (2007), 'Network Capital and Cooperation Patterns in the Working Groups of the Council of the EU', *EUI Working Paper*, RSCAS 07/14.

Sedelmeier, U. and Young, A.R. (2006), 'Editorial: Crisis, What Crisis? Continuity and Normality in the European Union in 2005', *Journal of Common Market Studies Annual Review*, **44**, Special Issue, 1–5.

Settembri, P. (2007), 'The Surgery Succeeded. Has the Patient Died? The Impact of Enlargement on the European Union', *Jean Monnet Working Paper*, 04/07. Available at http://jeanmonnetprogram.org/papers/07/070401.html.

11. Implementing committees in the enlarged European Union: business as usual for comitology?

Manuela Alfé, Thomas Christiansen and Sonia Piedrafita

INTRODUCTION

EU legislation is not complete without the implementation of the legislative acts that have been adopted by the Council and the Parliament. Implementation requires, in many cases, actions at the national level, for example when it comes to the transposition of EU directives. However, beyond this decentralized mode of implementation, over time the *centralized* implementation of Community acts has also become essential to the functioning of the EU's administrative system. Centralized implementation involves the delegation of powers to the European Commission to adopt executive measures, and the supervision of the Commission's use of these powers through committees of member state representatives. The term 'comitology' has been coined to describe this system of about 250 implementing committees and their interaction with the European Commission.

Institutionally speaking, comitology has an oddly hybrid nature, combining the intergovernmental dimension of bringing together national representatives, comparable to Council working groups, with the supranational character of the Commission which is chairing the meetings and ultimately adopting the executive measures submitted to the relevant committee. This, together with the high volume of decisions taken in this realm (2500–3000 executive measures are adopted annually),[1] gives comitology a special place within the institutional structure of the EU.

The question addressed here is whether the 'big bang enlargement' of 2004/2007 has had a significant impact on comitology, and whether any observable changes to the comitology system can be related to the arrival of the new member states.

As in the Council of Ministers, there had been an expectation among those involved that, because of the expansion of membership and the different approaches that representatives from the new member states might bring into the deliberations, meetings would take longer and agreement might be more difficult to reach. In contrast to what happened in the Council, however, no explicit provisions were made to reform the system in preparation for EU enlargement. On the other hand, comitology has in any case developed dynamically over the past decade, and there have also been major reforms to the formal arrangements of the system in the years after the 2004 enlargement.

The chapter first recalls some of the fundamental aspects of the comitology system, distinguishing between formal and informal arrangements, and highlighting the major changes which have taken place. The second section looks at the impact of the 2004/2007 enlargement on the comitology system, analysing how the implementing committees have been working and how the new members are adapting. This analysis is based primarily on a set of 94 structured interviews conducted with officials participating in a cross-section of comitology committees, coming from both 'old' and 'new' member states as well as the European Commission. The last section examines the main implications of these changes for the overall system and the most important challenges for the future.

THE EVOLUTION OF COMITOLOGY: FORMAL RULES AND INFORMAL PRACTICES

In order to examine the main features and issues in comitology, it becomes necessary to look into both the formal and the informal arrangements that rule the system. The formal arrangements are based on treaty provisions and are set out in a number of pieces of horizontal legislation, mainly the so-called 'Comitology Decisions' of 1999 and 2006. Beyond these formal arrangements, the informal dimension to comitology has always been very important, as individual committees have found distinct ways of working and interacting with the Commission and the European Parliament. This section will briefly review the main issues in the evolution of the comitology system and the main features of the way implementing committees work in practice.

The genesis of comitology in the 1960s was closely tied to the search for an ad hoc solution to the difficulty of regulating the economic and social life of the Community while relying exclusively on legislation.[2] The need to address changing circumstances quickly and effectively led Community legislators to a course of action that is well known at the domestic level: the delegation of implementing powers to the executive. Faced with increasing difficulties in the legislative process, delegating implementing powers for routine measures to the Commission was an attractive solution, but required a degree of administrative innovation: implementing powers were delegated to the Commission, but each individual legislative act also provided for the supervision of the Commission's use of these powers by committees composed of member state representatives.

Even though it occurred outside the letter of the Rome Treaties, the European Court of Justice was satisfied when comitology was for the first time tested in the Courts: comitology committees did not upset the institutional balance of the Community, as they were only tasked with providing opinions rather than actually taking decisions.[3] And the separation between executive and legislative powers was maintained, as only decisions about non-essential elements of the legislation were delegated to the Commission. According to the ECJ, the rights and duties of the legislator were not infringed through delegation and comitology.

It was on this basis that comitology then developed rapidly through the 1970s and 1980s. What was initially a limited solution to problems concerning the Common Agricultural Policy (CAP) quickly became a success story in many sectors of Community policy-making: before long, many other areas of legislation such as environment policy, consumer protection, transport and energy or single market regulation also involved delegation of powers and the arrival of comitology committees. Indeed, the growth of comitology was such that it became an issue as soon as the treaties were being reformed for the first time with the Single European Act. The subsequent 1987 Decision,[4] laying down the procedures for the exercise of implementing powers conferred on the Commission, provided for the first time a range of systematic procedures which the Commission would have to follow in consulting implementing committees.

With the appearance of the codecision procedure in the Maastricht Treaty, a reform of the comitology system was required, in particular in order to address the European Parliament's (EP) concerns. It took the form of Council Decision 1999/468, a milestone in the evolution of comitology and still the legislative base for the procedures governing the relationship between the Commission and implementing committees.

The 1999 Decision simplified the system, by reducing the number of procedures from seven to four. Under the *advisory procedure*, member states vote by simple majority and deliver a non-binding opinion. The *management procedure* is mainly used for the implementation of agricultural measures and financial support programmes. The Commission may adopt the implementing measure so long as there is no qualified majority against the proposal. In cases where this threshold is met, the matter is to be referred to the Council, which has the option of adopting a different decision. Under the *regulatory procedure*, measures can only be adopted by the

Commission if a qualified majority of member states are in favour. Otherwise, the act has to be forwarded to the Council, which may ultimately adopt the act. This procedure, used for all implementing measures having a 'legislative impact', especially in the field of health and safety of persons, also foresees the possibility of the EP exercising its right of scrutiny in cases where there is a lack of positive opinion within the Committee.

The 1999 Decision also increased the role of the European Parliament by granting it the right to scrutiny on measures implementing acts adopted under codecision and a more general right of information. Additionally, it improved transparency by obliging the Commission to set up a register of comitology committees, to publish a list of committees and, every year, a report on the working of comitology committees. Finally, it provided criteria according to which the EU legislature was expected to choose the comitology procedure appropriate to a given delegation of powers. Following the adoption of the 1999 Decision, the Commission adopted the standard rules of procedure (SRP) for the comitology committees. These cover most aspects of the preparation and conduct of committees, but notably do not mention working languages.

Even though the 1999 Decision represented an important shift in the history of comitology, it did not prevent further inter-institutional tensions.[5] In the light of the limited powers gained under the 1999 Decision, the EP pushed for further parliamentary involvement in control over the Commission's delegated powers – pressure that increased further when it became evident that the Commission had not always respected the EP's prerogatives.[6] In this context, the creation of a European Convention and the drafting of the Constitutional Treaty provided an opportunity to address Parliament's long-standing grievances in the area of comitology.

As long as there were prospects for a fundamental reform of the treaty, neither EP nor Council was concerned with further legislation on comitology. This situation changed, however, when the failed ratification of the Constitutional Treaty appeared to bury parliamentary hopes for an equal status with the member states in controlling of the Commission's delegated powers. At that point, the EP renewed its pressure on Commission and Council via the Lamfalussy process[7] – a tactic that proved to be very effective in getting the member states to negotiate about expanding the powers of the EP. In late 2005, towards the end of the UK Presidency, Coreper set up a Friends of the Presidency Group – a designated working group to prepare the Council response to a Commission proposal for a new comitology decision that had already been submitted to Council in late 2002. With Article 202 being the treaty base of this legislative proposal, a decision on this matter required unanimity in Council – another factor that explains why the reform of this system is fraught with such difficulty. And yet, despite the two years of inactivity after the original proposal had been submitted by the Commission, and even though the initial positions among the member states differed quite considerably from one another, negotiations were intense under the Austrian Presidency and progressed rather swiftly towards the adoption of a new decision in July 2006 (Council Decision 2006/512/EC) that allows Council and EP to ultimately reject implementing measures proposed by the Commission, beside the standard 'control' provided by comitology committees.[8]

As we have seen, the comitology system has developed through a process of progressive standardization and increasing openness with respect to its formal procedures. However, we can also observe, on closer examination, a high degree of informality in its workings, with different practices and traditions present in different sectors. A comprehensive understanding of how comitology has changed in response to the enlargement of the EU therefore requires a look at both the formal and the informal aspects of the system. This creates the challenge of studying not only the way comitology is formally constituted, but also how it is practised. We therefore base our analysis not only on the formal and legislative provisions, but also on the statistics on the working of comitology committees provided by the European Commission and interviews conducted in the framework of an empirical research project on comitology.[9] Statistics have been obtained through reports provided yearly by the Commission on the working of comitology committees,[10] and by analysing documents available on the Comitology Register.[11] The interviews were conducted on a sample of 94 participants in comitology committee meetings, from the 27 member states and from the European Commission. This study covered a number of key sectors – agriculture, environment, health and consumer protection, transport and energy, taxation and customs – which together account for more than the 90 per cent of the total of implementing committees in the EU.

Looking at the informal arrangements, there is a considerable diversity of practices across different sectors and indeed across individual committees. Owing to the historical evolution of the comitology system, much in the actual execution of the work of comitology committees differs according to the diverse traditions and the different needs in different sectors of EU policy-making. Thus, in the area of agriculture, committees are more numerous and meetings much more frequent than in other sectors, reflecting the longer experience with comitology and the greater reliance on delegated powers. It is also in this area that the most extensive provision for interpretation is being made.

Language has, in fact, been a long-standing and sensitive issue in comitology. As already noted, no general statements are made in the standard rules of procedure (SRP) concerning language, and the system on the whole relies on each committee finding a workable arrangement with respect to both simultaneous interpretation during the meetings and the translation of documents before the meeting. The ideal scenario from the perspective of national representatives (and the EP) – namely to have all official languages available – is generally seen as unworkable because of the Commission's limited resources, the costs involved and the additional time that a comprehensive language regime would imply. However, the absence of a formal language regime means that these issues need to be resolved on a case-by-case basis in the context of individual committees.

Interpretation is somewhat less contentious than translation. The Commission's working languages, English and French, are most frequently also used in comitology committee meetings, and interpretation into the other 'big' languages and a few of the 'smaller' ones is generally seen as sufficient. As in other parts of the EU, the secular trend in favour of English as *the* working language is evident also in the world of comitology. Participants in meetings are generally proficient in one or more of these languages and therefore do not insist on interpretation into all languages.

Matters are different with respect to translation: documents submitted to committees tend to be highly technical in nature, and failure to receive these in the native languages of national administrations makes internal coordination within the member states difficult, if not impossible. This, together with the short time span that committee members have between receiving documents and attending the committees (formally at least 14 days but in practice often less), means that they often go into meetings without having fully consulted domestically on Commission proposals. Committee members can demand from the Commission the submission of documents in their own official language, and in cases where such demands have not been met, or documents have arrived late, the ECJ has ruled against the Commission.[12] But there is a general recognition by those working within comitology that such requests cannot be generalized without the entire system slowing down or collapsing altogether. A practical arrangement has therefore developed around the understanding that member state representatives only request their respective language versions when this is actually necessitated because of the specific nature of a particular measure.

As we mentioned above, it is impossible to generalize on the number of times a committee meets in a particular period, and how many such meetings are necessary before the Commission can adopt a proposed measure. On average a Committee meets two to three times per year,[13] but there are significant variations: in the agriculture sector many management committees meet on a weekly or fortnightly basis, while at the other end of the spectrum some committees exist on paper only, without ever meeting.

In part, the uncertainty about the duration of comitology procedures originates in the practice of the Commission of tabling draft implementing measures initially only as agenda items for an 'exchange of views'. Such preliminary discussions are seen to be required in order to allow the Commission to gather sufficient feedback on member state positions before submitting final drafts to the committee 'for a vote'. The preparatory work done in this way, permitting the Commission to fine-tune their proposals before the formal vote in the committee, is part of the reason why there have been so few referrals of implementing measures to the Council (following a negative, or absence of, opinion within the committee). In fact, the Commission has been extraordinarily 'successful' in achieving the necessary majorities at the 'committee stage', with only very few measures every year being submitted to the 'supervisory stage': since 2001, when annual reports on comitology started being published by the Commission, such referrals have amounted to less than 1 per cent of all executive measures adopted by the Commission.[14]

The Commission's ability to 'manage' the delivery of committee opinions in such a manner is also aided by the generally favourable climate that is predominant in the proceedings of comitology committees. While the formal procedure of voting always remains an option, in practice members of the committees try to adopt opinions on as many occasions as possible by consensus. In the same vein, whereas according to the formal arrangements the national representatives' main function is to control the Commission, in practice there is usually a rather cooperative spirit between both so that member states' representatives may be seen as 'assisting' rather than 'checking' the Commission in its implementing functions. Some scholars even regard the comitology committees as arenas for policy deliberation among national and European officials,[15] which others regard them as the fusion place for both the national and the European administrative systems.[16] In any case, it shows that the comitology system, as well as the assessment of the impact of enlargement, can only be explained if we consider both the formal and the informal arrangements.

In general, the implementing committees did not witness any formal adaptation of their procedures with the arrival of the new members. The formal changes introduced by the 2006 Comitology Decision aimed mainly at satisfying the EP's demands for more involvement in comitology, especially in fields governed by codecision. The result has been the introduction of a new comitology procedure, the *regulatory procedure with scrutiny*, that allows Council and EP to ultimately reject implementing measures proposed by the Commission, besides the standard 'control' provided by comitology committees. Pressures for reform in terms of working methods – such as a new bilateral agreement between the EP and the Commission, and modification of the SRP – have likewise been linked to the new procedure rather than enlargement. However, some informal changes have taken place in the practice of comitology and the next section will look into these.

IMPLEMENTATION COMMITTEES IN THE ENLARGED EUROPEAN UNION

The prospect of ten, and eventually 12, new members in the implementing committees was initially seen with some concern. The number of members would almost double; the newcomers could not count on the same procedural expertise; they would bring in a different administrative culture; the debate on the language regime would re-emerge; implementation measures would meet greater opposition from states usually reluctant to accept further regulation; and the traditional channels to reach agreements would not work as before. All this could make the decision-making process very difficult to manage, increasing concerns about the future legitimacy and efficiency of the system. However, the new member states seem to be adapting to the committees' dynamics quite well and, for the time being, their arrival does not seem either to have brought the comitology system to a halt or to be creating pressure for future change.

The following assessment of comitology in practice since enlargement is based on the above-mentioned interviews conducted with officials participating in committees in key sectors, and also on comparing our data with the results of a previous research project by Egeberg, Schaefer and Trondal.[17]

The new member states had been represented as observers in comitology committees for several years before accession. The resulting familiarity with both the nature of the dossiers under discussion and 'the way things are done' in each committee helped to prepare them for full membership, and also facilitated a process of socialization with the norms and attitudes governing the interaction within the committees. This socialization process contributed not only to familiarizing new members with the intricacies of comitology, but also to ensuring that their representatives would not 'rock the boat' once they gained the power of the vote.

Indeed, the perception of many interviewees from the old member states is that the role of the representatives from the new member states has remained similar after full membership to that which they had played as observers, apart from the formal power to vote. They still do not contribute to the debates preceding any vote in committee and are usually seen to play only a marginal role in the decision-making process. This perception is not always shared by the new members themselves, many of whom feel that they are more active than the others perceive them to be. On the one hand, they think their responsibility has increased after full membership and therefore their actual involvement in committee activities. On the other hand, they believe they bring along new data, a fresh perspective and approach to the issues, different state cultures, other national views and a wider spectrum of opinions.

The evolution of the role of the new representatives from observers to full membership has also depended on other specific factors, quite apart from individual experience. On the one hand, increasing active participation seems to depend on the size of the country and its voting power. Most participants responding to our questionnaire agreed that the representatives coming from Poland in particular, and to a lesser extent from Hungary and the Czech Republic, are becoming the most active and participative. On the other hand, representatives from the new member states seem to be most active in those issues where there is a special national interest at stake or in relevant sectors in their respective countries (e.g. in management committees in agriculture).

On the whole, however, the new members are perceived by established members of the committees as being less proactive and influential in the implementing committees than the representatives coming from the old member states. This can be explained not only by the lack of experience and confidence and the need to gain the credentials as 'good members' of the group but also by the fact that they often do not get interpretation facilities. Both factors make participation in the comitology committees uneven. In contrast to the situation for the Council, no new language regime has been developed to accommodate the greater number of official languages. In very few cases have comitology committees seen the addition of a language of the new member states to the interpretation or translation scheme, with rare exceptions, mostly to provide for Polish. Even if most participants can cope with English – which, owing to enlargement, is developing into the dominant language of interaction in comitology – the absence of translated documents or interpretation in native languages does compromise the effective participation of new member states in a number of ways.

First, even if the representative him- or herself is able to manage well in English, circulating draft measures and explanatory documents inside the national administration in advance is made difficult or impossible, which in turn seriously hampers the coordination of national positions and the drafting of instructions for those attending the committees. Second, in the meeting itself, active participation is made more difficult – psychologically or practically – if participants are not able to intervene in their native language. All these language-related issues are likely to have combined to also limit the impact that the representatives of the new member states have had on decision-making in comitology committees, and hence the impact on the system as a whole.

Perhaps surprisingly, the new members rarely complain about the lack of interpretation or translation services, and they usually accept the Commission's justification: translating all draft documents before the meeting into all the languages would not only increase massively the costs of meetings, owing to the provision of interpretation facilities from and into all 23 official languages of the EU; it would also significantly delay the process, since meetings would take much longer to prepare and the time lag between the proposal of implementing measures and their eventual adoption would increase.

In general, the representatives coming from the new member states are perceived as very cooperative with the Commission. Many participants in committee meetings from the old member states believe that the Commission has found a good ally in the newcomers and that this makes it actually more difficult to build up a potential coalition that would be opposed to the Commission's proposals. The new members indeed have usually a more positive perception of the Commission than the representatives from the old member states. When asked how they regard the relations between the Commission and the member states, the new members usually use terms such as 'cooperative', 'open', 'very good', 'respectful', 'friendly', 'easy' and 'constructive', whereas the representatives of the old member states consider these relations 'accommodative' and 'cordial', but also 'imposing', 'controlling', 'dominant', 'hard', 'difficult', and with some 'tensions' and 'mistrust'.

The general view is that the arrival of the new member states has not made much difference to the way in which decisions are taken, nor to the ability of the system to achieve outcomes. The increased number of representatives attending the committees has created some significant challenges. In most cases, however, measures have been taken to adapt working methods in order to avoid a negative impact on the efficiency of the system.

In order to avoid any possible impact on the output of increased membership, the Commission is, for example, providing the member states with more *information* in advance.[18] There is also an increasing *formalization* of the procedures. For instance, in some cases the discussion and the voting sections of the meeting are now clearly separated, while they were more intertwined previously. In other cases, there is no longer any formal *tour de table*, and only those representatives with objections to the Commission's proposal are given the floor. In any case, those present limit their intervention times much more than before, not only as a result of the Commission's pressure but also out of their own initiative, since the sessions have become longer.

If we compare the results of our questionnaire with those of a similar one carried out in 1999, we can also observe that many committees seem to be meeting more often during the year.[19] This fact, together with an increased number of members and committees, raises the bill of comitology, given the higher costs for more participants meeting more frequently. However, this trend is somewhat offset by more effective preparation of those meetings where opinions on draft measures are being adopted: as more (informal) work is being done in between meetings, fewer meetings are now required in order to adopt an opinion on a particular proposal. That also explains why it has been possible in the enlarged EU to adopt a *rising* number of implementing measures.[20] Another way of seeking to control costs has been for the Commission to put pressure on member states to reduce the number of representatives that they send to comitology committee meetings.

Despite the lack of interpretation facilities, implementation measures still have to be translated into all the official languages once they have been agreed in order to become binding in the member states. The time between agreement and publication (after translation) has considerably increased since enlargement, causing some legal gaps and technical difficulties in the national administrations.

The need to accommodate a greater number of specific concerns seems also to have led the Commission to concentrate its negotiating efforts on those delegations which are most directly affected by a particular regulation and those necessary to achieve the qualified majority. Some national representatives interviewed thus considered that the effort to reach consensus has decreased and that proposals are being put to the *vote* more often and earlier, usually as soon as the Commission knows it can count on sufficient support.

Although there seems to be a certain 'symbiosis' in the relationship between the Commission and the new members, the latter also occasionally might seek support from some of the old members. An 'Eastern' coalition has not emerged, except in a few specific issues where the new member states happen to share the same interest, such as agriculture or structural funds. New members usually join existing groupings of countries, whether these are traditional or ad hoc. For them, given the difficulties they may still encounter in being proactive, it is much easier to defend their national interest by going under the 'umbrella' of old member states. Although there are no stable patterns and 'allies' vary depending on national interests in each specific issue, some 'collaborations' are common. For instance, Malta and Cyprus frequently join the traditional 'Mediterranean alliance' (France, Italy, Spain, Greece, Portugal) in the agricultural sector. Finally, some special links and collaborative networks developed during the accession process between certain old and new member states still remain to some extent (e.g. Romania with Spain, Cyprus and Bulgaria with Greece, Poland with Germany, the Baltic states with the Scandinavian states).

Some interviewees, especially from the agriculture committees, agree with the observation that France is progressively losing its traditional leadership; Germany is seen to be making big efforts to take along the new members so as to increase its capacity to influence the process; the UK seems to reinforce its role as the leader of the liberal positions. In general, the larger countries have lost some of their traditional power to broker agreements, and an agreement between France and Germany is no longer as important for proposals to move ahead. Enlargement mainly brought in small countries, and it is now easier for them to build up a coalition and influence the process against some larger member states' interests. Coalitions are thus becoming rather volatile and based on short-term interests.

The increased number of actors and difficulties, the changing influence capacity of the member states and the tendency to short-term coalitions have strengthened the role of the Commission in the decision-making process – something which may be considered necessary in order to provide the process with some sense of direction and common purpose to ensure its effectiveness.

Some features of the participation of the new members in the comitology system also contribute to explaining the limited impact of enlargement on the output. The more supportive attitude of the representatives coming from the new members towards the Commission, their lack of confidence or procedural experience, their level of expertise, the inadequacy of the language regime or the insufficiencies in their national coordination systems all explain the fact that new members are not usually blocking dossiers. Some representatives from old member states even believe that, after enlargement, it is much more difficult to form a coalition against the Commission's proposals.

Therefore, looking at the first few years of comitology in the enlarged EU we cannot observe major variations with respect to substantial outcomes. Additionally, much of the variations in the procedural legitimacy might be due to the recent comitology reform rather than enlargement itself.[21] However, it is worth considering some consequences that the new trends in both the procedures and the participation mechanisms might have for the input legitimacy of the system. The inclusiveness and representativeness of the process could be affected, owing to factors such as the unequal participation of the new members and their limited capacity to influence the decision-making process in comparison with the old members.

Furthermore, the increased formalization and technocratization of the process make debates more technical and less 'politically' interesting and deliberative. Deliberation usually involves a higher degree of consensus and satisfaction with the measures, favouring agreements round the best argument rather than trading-off negotiations. Increasing shifting coalitions and more technical meetings with less room for personal interaction and debates might also reduce the diffuse reciprocity within the committees and the feelings of solidarity and mutual understanding among their members.

Better organization and increased transparency from the Commission may help the member states to hold it accountable but it may also affect the inclusiveness of the process if there is a lower degree of flexibility when it comes to accommodating the different national sensitivities and concerns. Based on our research, we observe that quite often the draft proposal is not substantially amended, especially when the Commission knows that it has the support of the required majority. Complaints from national delegations about the system are indeed related to the insufficiently accommodative and inclusive efforts by the Commission. At the same time, the control that the national representatives may exercise over the Commission, and therefore the accountability of the system, could be undermined because of both the increasing power and 'presidential' style on the part of the Commission, and the incentive to search for prior agreements behind the scenes in view of the limitations of the committee meetings, given the higher incidence of disagreements and diverging preferences among committee members.

CONCLUSIONS

As has been observed several times before, also in other contributions to this volume, it is still too early for final assessment of the impact of enlargement. We have identified in this chapter a number of issues that need to be raised when trying to make such an assessment, and the analysis demonstrates that the majority of changes so far have occurred in the informal dimension to comitology, in the way in which comitology is *practised* rather than *regulated*. The major formal changes to the comitology system that have occurred before and after the 2004 enlargement round – the creation of standard rules of procedure for committees in 2001, the establishment of an online comitology register and the introduction in 2006 of a new regulatory procedure with scrutiny – cannot be directly related to enlargement. These reforms are best explained in terms of the long-standing drive towards achieving greater systematization and transparency in the system, which in turn owes a lot to the pressures from the EP for a greater degree of parliamentary scrutiny over comitology proceedings.

Enlargement has had certain effects chiefly with respect to the informal side, where working practices, operational procedures and generally the 'way of doing things' have somewhat changed. However, change here is uneven and difficult to generalize about beyond the observations we have made above. The ultimate answer to the question we raised at the outset – the question that also governs the overall approach to this book – is that one cannot speak of any transformation of the comitology system in response to the arrival of the ten or 12 new member states. Instead, it is more appropriate to identify processes of mutual adaptation – instances where the comitology system has changed its (informal) arrangements to better accommodate the new participants, but also aspects which imply new obligations and the need to reform for the administrations of the new member states. In other words, there has been a 'give and take' on both sides, and the result is a system that so far has changed remarkably little or, rather, it has changed significantly but in a direction in which it would have changed anyway, even without enlargement as the additional impetus.

However, it may be too soon to conclude on such a 'trouble-free' note for a number of reasons. First, even if we have not identified significant changes that have yet occurred, we have pointed to a number of pressures for *future* change, for example when it comes to the (lack of a) language regime in comitology. Second, there are further changes ahead arising from the treaty reform process which are still ongoing at the time of writing. These expectations for future change may yet alter the image we have of the impact of enlargement, and should therefore be briefly highlighted.

Raising the language issue, for example, allows an interesting comparison with a previous round of enlargement – that of the Mediterranean states joining the EU in the mid-1980s. Here the initial pattern was the same – no new languages were offered to the new arrivals in comitology committees. While initially this was accepted, the tide eventually turned when Spanish representatives demanded after a few years that their language be made available. When this was granted, other member states both old (Italy) and new (Portugal) followed suit. Based on that experience, there is some pressure for reform building up in the current arrangement. Clearly the new member states are dissatisfied with the lack of language resources available to them and, if Poland increased further the pressure for the inclusion of its language, other Central and East European countries could add their voices to the demand for change. The result would be a more costly and cumbersome system, but also one that would make comitology procedures more manageable and indeed more legitimate for the administrations of the new member states.

Indeed, these observations make one wonder whether the comparatively smooth and unproblematic inclusion of members from the new member states in comitology committees is not so much a reflection of successful adaptation but simply a mirror of the incomplete integration of the new member states in the system: given the restrictions of language and time, and the increasing distance between those that negotiate in Brussels and those that are involved in national administrations, meaningful domestic coordination is hardly possible and thus effective participation of representatives from the new member states unlikely. However, as national administrations catch up and develop the required resources, mechanisms and procedures, they could also be expected to become more involved in comitology – a development that might rupture the permissive consensus that we have observed so far.

Beyond these considerations, the comitology system is likely to experience further changes in the near future, owing to the treaty reform process. After the failed ratification of the Constitutional Treaty, a reflection period was followed by the launch of a new IGC which agreed, in October 2007, the Lisbon Treaty. Just as the Constitutional Treaty did, the Lisbon Treaty contains significant new provisions concerning the delegation of powers to the European Commission. This includes the distinction between 'implementing acts' (to be adopted according to the 'traditional' comitology procedures, which would however fall under codecision between Council and Parliament) and the new instrument of 'delegated acts' (to be adopted by the Commission if no objections are received from Council or Parliament). These new treaty provisions would require further secondary legislation (as well as new inter-institutional agreements to facilitate the relations between Commission, Council and Parliament in detail) in order to give them effect. We are therefore looking at the need for yet further reforms, in the shape of either a new comitology decision or indeed a wider regulation of administrative governance in the EU, if and when the treaty is ratified.

Against the background of these potentially quite significant changes in the world of comitology, we might expect opportunities and challenges for the system to also adapt further to administrative life in a Union of 27 or more member states. The formal changes that are yet to come provide an opportunity to also address some of the issues that have arisen, but are not yet resolved, in terms of the practical working arrangements of comitology. Thus, comitology remains an area to watch when it comes to the impact of enlargement. So far, matters have been remarkably quiet on this front, but it may turn out to be just the quiet before the storm.

ACKNOWLEDGEMENTS

Previous drafts of this chapter were presented at EU-CONSENT workshops in Brussels in April 2007 and in Maastricht in June 2007, as well as in the context of the Research Seminar series at ARENA Centre for European Studies at Oslo University in May 2007. We are grateful to the participants of these seminars for their useful comments, and to Johanna Oettel for specific comments on a draft chapter. Thomas Christiansen wishes to acknowledge with gratitude the opportunity to spend time at the ARENA Centre for European Studies during which part of the research and writing for this chapter was undertaken.

NOTES

1. All reference to figures concerning the working of comitology committees can be found in the report prepared yearly by the European Commission: Report of the Commission on the Working of Committees during 2005, COM(2006)446 fin and SEC(2006)1065.
2. For a thorough description of the early developments of comitology, see C.F. Bergström (2005), *Comitology: Delegation of Powers in the European Union and the Committee System*, Oxford: Oxford University Press, pp. 57–73.
3. See Case Law C-25/70 Köster (1970) ECR, p. 1161.
4. Decision 87/373/EEC of the Council.
5. For a comprehensive description of the impact of the 1999 Comitology Decision, see C.F. Bergström (2005), *Comitology: Delegation of Powers in the European Union and the Committee System*, Oxford: Oxford University Press, pp. 264–84, 320–63.
6. In April 2005, on the occasion of a resolution adopted on the basis of its right of scrutiny, the EP asked the Commission to publish a list of all cases in which the Commission did not respect the provisions concerning the transmission of Comitology documents to the EP. See European Parliament resolution on a draft Commission decision amending the Annex to Directive 2002/95/EC of the European Parliament and of the Council on the restriction of the use of certain hazardous substances in electrical and electronic equipment (B6-0218/2005 / P6-TA-PROV(2005)0090).
7. The Lamfalussy process has been used to adopt and implement certain acts in the financial services sector, and it was characterized by a more structured use of comitology and a major role for the European Parliament. See B. Vaccari (2005), 'Le processus Lamfalussy: une réussite pour la comitologie et un exemple de "bonne gouvernance européenne" ', *Revue du droit de l'Union européenne*, **4**, pp. 803–21.
8. See T. Christiansen and B. Vaccari (2006), 'The 2006 Reform of Comitology: Problem Solved or Dispute Postponed?', *EIPASCOPE*, **2006** (3) for a detailed analysis of the 2006 reform.
9. The interviews were conducted on a sample of 94 participants in comitology committee meetings from the 27 member states and from the European Commission over a period of ten weeks in the first half of 2007. Interviewees responded to 25 semi-structured questions contained in a questionnaire. This study covered a number of key sectors – agriculture, environment, health and consumer protection, transport and energy, taxation and customs, and statistics – in which more than 90 per cent of all comitology committees in the EU are active. Our thanks go to the respondents of this survey, as well as to Jerome Boniface, Gijs-Jan Brandsma, Johanna Oettel, Ania Tobur and Beatrice Vaccari for their support in this project. A more detailed presentation of the results of this study, together with contributions on other aspects of comitology, are forthcoming in Thomas Christiansen and Beatrice Vaccari (eds) (2008 forthcoming), *21st Century Comitology: The Role of Implementing Committees in the Wider European Union*, Maastricht: EIPA.
10. See, for instance, Report of the Commission on the working of committees during 2005, COM(2006)446 fin and SEC(2006)1065.
11. The instrument contains a register and repository of documents which relate to the work of comitology committees and are transmitted from the Commission to the European Parliament and covers transmitted documents since 1 January 2003. It can be consulted at the following link: http://www.europa.eu.int/comm/secretariat_general/regcomito/registre.cfm?CL=en.
12. See, for instance, Cases C-465/02 and C-466/02, of 25 October 2005: Germany and Denmark vs. Commission ('Feta case'). For a comprehensive description of the case, see

A. Türk (2000), 'The Role of the Court of Justice', in M. Andenas and A. Türk (eds), *Delegated Legislation and the Role of Committees in the EC*, London: Kluwer Law International, pp. 217–53.

13. According to responses from interviewees and confirmed by a cross-analysis of the documents on the Comitology Register.

14. For instance, in 2005 only 11 implementing measures, out of a total of 2654 adopted by the Commission, were sent back to the Council, mainly for absence of opinion within the Committee.

15. C. Joerges and J. Neyer (1997), 'Transforming Strategic Interaction into Deliberative Problem-Solving: European Comitology in the Foodstuff Sector', *Journal of European Public Policy*, **4** (4).

16. W. Wessels (1998), 'Comitology: Fusion in Action. Politico-Administrative Trends in the EU System', *Journal of European Public Policy*, **5** (2), pp. 209–34.

17. In 1999, Egeberg, Schaefer and Trondal conducted a survey involving some 250 participants in EU committee meetings. Further details about, and the results of, this study, which included members not only of comitology committees but also of Council working groups and of expert advisory groups, is published in M. Egeberg, G.F. Schaefer and J. Trondal (2003), 'The Many Faces of EU Committee Governance', *West European Politics*, **26** (3).

18. If we likewise compare both questionnaires, in 1999 45 per cent of the respondents said they were getting the background information and documentation from the Commission only the day before the meeting or even during the meeting, whereas in 2007 the percentage went down to the 14 per cent and delivery at the meeting itself became rather exceptional.

19. Comparing the results of the 1999 questionnaire (M. Egeberg, G.F. Schaefer and J. Trondal (2003), 'The Many Faces of EU Committee Governance', *West European Politics*, **26** (3) and our 2007 questionnaire, we can observe that the percentage of interviewees responding that they meet one to three times a year has decreased whereas those who say they meet eight or more times a year has increased.

20. According to our empirical research, in 2007 many proposals took only one or two meetings to be adopted. The second one was usually needed for the Commission to incorporate any amendments.

21. Collective decisions may derive legitimacy from both the inputs and the outputs of the system. Input-oriented legitimacy refers to the mechanisms or procedures which link the decisions to the constituents' preferences by means of representation, inclusiveness and accountability. The extent to which the Commission is held accountable, the process is transparent and representative and participation is equal are all elements of this procedural legitimacy. Output-oriented legitimacy refers to the success of the system in carrying out its functions, that is, whether it is effective or not. See F.W. Scharpf (1999), *Governing in Europe: Effective and Democratic?*, Oxford: Oxford University Press. For a discussion of the impact of the 2006 reform on the accountability of the comitology system, see G.J. Brandsma (2007), 'Accountability Deficits in European "Comitology" Decision-Making', *European Integration online Papers* (*EIoP*), **11** (4) and K. St Clair Bradley (2008), 'Halfway House: The 2006 Comitology Reforms and the European Parliament – a view from the Ground Floor', *West European Politics*, **31** (4).

12. Widening, deepening . . . and diversifying: has enlargement shaped new forms of EU governance?

Edward Best

INTRODUCTION

This chapter considers the role played by enlargement in the evolution of new modes of European governance. In other words, it is concerned not with changes in the nature or functioning of the European institutions, nor with the operation or effectiveness of the procedures by which those bodies adopt European instruments. It looks at the ways in which the range of instruments and approaches which are employed within the EU has become broader and more complex, to include a variety of non-legislative methods, and tries to assess the importance of enlargements in shaping these developments.

It asks two questions. On the one hand, looking to the past, what has been the influence of enlargement in the emergence of these new approaches? On the other hand, looking to the future, are there any ways in which the latest enlargements from 15 to 27 member states could lead to a further transformation of such methods? And, if there are indications of such an impact, does this reflect more structural differences which will remain or capacity gaps which may be overcome?

The first section briefly recalls the main ways in which non-legislative approaches have emerged in the European Union. It distinguishes between the various forms of non-binding policy coordination known generically as the open method of coordination (OMC), on the one hand, and the different ways in which new forms of public–private interaction have been explored under the banner of alternative methods of regulation, on the other.

The second section looks at the emergence of policy coordination against the background of the broader changes in policy context in the 1990s, as well as the impact of the 1995 enlargement and the start of preparations for the next waves of accession.

The third addresses alternative methods of regulation. After recalling the basic choices and dynamics involved, it suggests three ways in which enlargement could affect the development of particular arrangements. In this light, it looks at two cases, the European social dialogue and energy efficiency, in which there have been notable examples of self- and co-regulatory activity since the 1990s, and shifts in the pattern of regulatory interaction in recent years.

THE EMERGENCE OF NON-LEGISLATIVE APPROACHES IN THE EU

The Community was born as a community of law. The Rome Treaty laid down rules for achieving a common market supported by a number of common policies, primarily through legislation. It was never the idea to establish a directly applicable body of uniform law in all the fields covered. The creation of the directive provided for some degree of flexibility on the part of the member states in assuring the results which were laid down. Moreover, non-legislative approaches were also contemplated in the original deal. Non-binding instruments (recommendations and opinions) were foreseen from the beginning, while Article 6(1) provided that 'the Member States shall, in close co-operation with the institutions of the Community, co-ordinate their respective economic policies to the extent necessary to attain the objectives of this Treaty'. Yet the key to the Community was the agreement by the founding member states to submit themselves, in limited fields and under certain conditions, to the rule of supranational law.

By the end of the first decade, both the customs union and 'normative supranationalism', as well as core common policies, had been consolidated. Since then, there has been a deepening of hierarchy and the 'supranational' approach in some respects, through the expansion of Community legislative competence, the extension of qualified majority voting, and the increase in powers of the European Parliament. Yet there has also been a proliferation of other methods as the Community, and later the Union, has responded to new ambitions, new pressures and new members.

These may be thought of in terms of a simple matrix bringing together two dimensions of modes of governance (Figure 12.1).[1] On one axis, one has the nature of the relationship between actors, or 'steering mode', ranging from hierarchy backed by sanctions at one extreme, through non-hierarchical negotiation, to persuasion and learning at the other extreme. On the other axis, one has the identity of the actors involved, from purely public, through public and private, to purely private.

STEERING *MODE* *ACTORS*	Hierarchy/ sanctions	Bargaining/ incentives	Persuasion/ learning
Public only	*Supranational* *EU regulation*	*Intergovernmental* *agreements*	*Open method of* *coordination*
Public and private	*C O · R E G U L A T I O N*		
Private only	*European association* *with disciplinary* *powers (e.g. UEFA)*	*Codes of conduct/* *voluntary* *commitments*	*Framework of* *actions*

Figure 12.1   A matrix of methods of EU governance

The dominant mode of governance originally foreseen was hierarchy, even if the respective degrees of obligation, precision and delegation would vary according to the issue.[2] Other forms of cooperation might be used between the same countries but outside the Community framework. The actors involved were mainly public.

There has since been an explicit choice in some cases between Community and intergovernmental approaches – that is, a preference for non-hierarchical negotiation between states completely outside the Community framework. This was clearest in the creation of European Political Cooperation (EPC) in 1970, the formalization of a separate basis for EPC in the Single European Act, and the establishment of the 'second pillar' of Common Foreign and Security Policy (CFSP) at Maastricht.

Other fields came to be developed *within* the Community through various forms of non-binding policy coordination. The Maastricht Treaty established the system of coordination of national economic policies around the Broad Economic Policy Guidelines, with a system of multilateral surveillance and the possibility for the Council to address recommendations to member states. It also introduced into the Community provisions for cooperation and the exchange of experience in fields such as education, culture and public health, with the explicit exclusion of harmonization. The 1997 Amsterdam Treaty introduced a new chapter on employment policy which drew on the new paradigms of economic policy coordination and the convergence criteria for monetary union. Common 'Employment Guidelines' would be agreed; member states would submit national action plans; the Council would adopt country-specific recommendations, while peer review mechanisms would be implemented to promote mutual learning. The following years saw adoption of a Cardiff Process on structural reform and a Cologne Process of Macroeconomic Dialogue leading to the 2000 Lisbon Strategy and the open method of coordination (OMC). Still softer variants of this approach have been adopted for social inclusion, social protection, research, enterprise policy, information society and education.

Commitments under these forms of coordination are not legally binding. With the exception of the excessive deficit procedure, no sanctions are involved. Governments are expected to follow the guidelines, and then respond to specific Council recommendations, peer pressure through benchmarking, and the demands of their own national stakeholders and publics. The objectives include convergence and the achievement of common targets – with more or less precision according to the case – but the fundamental goal is improved national policy performance in the spirit of mutual learning. Flexibility is seen as a positive characteristic.

The involvement of private actors, notably the social partners, is urged in order to improve legitimacy as well as effectiveness. Yet this kind of policy coordination is primarily a matter of different degrees of commitment between countries – non-hierarchical coordination through competition, with the goals of persuasion and learning.

New forms of interaction between public and private actors – 'alternative methods of regulation' – also began to be systematically developed at European level, reflecting in different ways the dynamic interaction between the credibility of legally binding measures, as 'the shadow of the law', and the credibility of commitments by non-state actors, promising more rapid and flexible solutions on the ground. This set of interactions constitutes the universe of 'co-regulation', as indicated in Figure 12.1.

The first example of 'co-regulation' is usually held to be the New Approach, formulated in a 1985 Council Resolution, which recognized that this harmonization could in many cases be limited to the definition of 'essential requirements' (usually of health and safety). Conformity with these requirements could be shown either by conforming to harmonized standards drawn up by standardization bodies or by other means.

New forms of public–private interaction emerged in social policy, mainly in the form of the European Social Dialogue. The procedure agreed at Maastricht (now Articles 138 and 139 of the EC Treaty) provided that the Commission should consult European social partners[3] before submitting proposals. The social partners could then choose to negotiate between themselves. If the negotiations resulted in an agreement, two options would be available for implementation: by the procedures and practices specific to management and labour and the member states, or by a Council decision on a proposal from the Commission. The European Parliament was given no formal role at all in the whole process, although it has in practice been informed by the Commission at all stages of the procedures. In recent years, there has been a significant evolution towards purely autonomous agreements.

The end of the 1980s saw the first experiments in alternative approaches to regulation in the field of the environment, whereby industry commitments to achieve specified targets were publicly recognised at European level. These took the form of Commission recommendations for the labelling of detergents and cleaning products, and the reduction of chlorofluorocarbons (CFCs) and halons. The Fifth Environmental Action Programme of 1992 then proclaimed a general move from a top-down approach based on legislation to a more 'bottom-up' strategy involving a 'reinforcement of the dialogue with industry and the encouragement, in appropriate circumstances, of voluntary agreements'. Negotiated agreements over the reduction of CO_2 emissions from passenger vehicles were recognized in Commission recommendations with European, Korean and Japanese manufacturers. The Commission also endorsed unilateral commitments concerning detergents and energy efficiency. Communications were adopted by the Commission in 1996 and again in 2002 aiming at formalizing environmental agreements at European level. Although little has come of this latter idea, a new approach building on standardization has begun to be explored in the 2005 Eco-design directive, which foresees application of the criteria agreed in the legislation to specific product groups either through comitology or by conditional recognition of self-regulatory schemes.

The following sections set out to assess the influence of enlargement in the evolution and perspectives of these two broad groups of non-legislative approaches.

ENLARGEMENT AND POLICY COORDINATION

To the extent that the adoption of non-binding policy coordination has reflected an acceptance of greater flexibility in the face of increasing diversity, one can argue that the progressive enlargements have had a major and direct impact, at least with regard to social policy. This growing diversity has not been limited to contrasting preferences of governments in power but has also reflected an increase in the underlying differences in models of the welfare state (Esping-Andersen 1990). Whereas the founding Six could all be characterized as having 'Bismarkian' continental models, the degree of national diversity has grown with each enlargement (Pochet 2005, pp. 44–5). The 1973 enlargement added the Anglo-Saxon/liberal (UK and Ireland) and the Scandinavian/Social Democratic (Denmark). The Mediterranean enlargements brought in a Southern model (or variant of the continental model). The 1995 round reinforced the presence of the Scandinavian model. The 2004 enlargement brought in what can be considered to be a post-socialist 'Eastern European model' (Eurofound 2006) and in all events introduced yet more diversity in labour and welfare institutions (Vaughan-Whitehead 2005).

In this perspective, the impact of the successive enlargements of the EC/EU has been to make it more and more true that 'uniform European social policy is not politically feasible or even desirable . . . [U]niform European solutions would mobilize fierce opposition in countries where they would require major changes in the structures and core functions of existing welfare state institutions' (Scharpf 2002, pp. 651, 666). Even if it is argued that some of these models require reform, it is still generally recognized that 'Europe cannot and should not have a strategy for reforming national labour market and social policies. It is up to each national government to devise its own strategy' (Sapir 2005, p. 7). The member states may try to cooperate, to learn from each other and to promote some general convergence. One could make use of framework directives to provide appropriate counterparts to market regulation. There will not be uniform policies at European level.

In the early 1990s, the Community faced strong pressures to adopt a more developed social policy to match the internal market which was then being legislatively completed – and to deal with mounting unemployment – but confronted serious divergences of opinion between member states about how to proceed. The OMC in employment policy started to emerge from this constellation of pressures immediately after the Maastricht Treaty. The Commission's 1993 White Paper on Growth, Competitiveness and Employment was clear that there could be no simple, Community-wide, answers:

> Pro-active labour market policies will be central to such a strategy. . . . The vast bulk of these measures will be for individual member states to decide upon in responding to their diverse national situations.
>
> However, the Community can and must play an important supporting role by:
>
> • providing a forum where a common broad framework strategy can be agreed, and by
> • underpinning national measures with complementary Community action, whether in the form of financial support through the European Social Fund . . . or through networking and other measures designed to ensure the transfer of good practice and experience.
>
> (CEC 1993a, B.8.9)

Similar conclusions were reached regarding social policy and labour relations. The response to the 1993 Green Paper (CEC 1993b) and 1994 White Paper on European Social Policy (CEC 1994) noted that 'Member States and others were divided in their opinions about the need for further legislative action at European level, particularly as it concerns labour standards'.

In this context, the Essen European Council in December 1994 identified five key areas in which measures should be taken and outlined what was a precursor of OMC:

> the European Council urges the Member States to transpose these recommendations in their individual policies into a multiannual programme having regard to the specific features of their economic and social situation. It requests the Labour and Social Affairs and Economic and Financial Affairs Councils and the Commission to keep close track of employment trends, monitor the relevant policies of the Member States and report annually to the European Council on further progress on the employment market.

The emergence of the OMC was not a consequence of enlargement, even in social policy. Yet it is reasonable to argue that in the field of social and employment policy, at least, there was a special kind of interaction between the evolution of the method and the successive enlargements. The emergence of OMC in this field coincided with both the impact of the 1995 accession of Austria, Finland and Sweden, and the beginning of preparations for eastern enlargement. In addition to increasing the degree of underlying diversity, enlargements have also had a more direct impact on the balance of thinking between the member states as to how to respond to issues of common concern.

The most obvious case had already been that of the UK. As the 'Val Duchesse' process began in 1985, with the aim of promoting dialogue between the European social partners as part of the European Social Space proposed by Delors, the UK led an alternative approach in the 1986 Action Programme for Employment Growth. The UK did not support the 1989 Community Social Charter, in which 11 of the 12 Heads of State or Government explicitly declared that the internal market required labour law intervention at EC level. And the UK was then largely responsible for the blockage of various legislative proposals in the Council between 1989 and 1991.

The 1990s, however, saw a different kind of interaction. The conception of the new employment strategy was very directly influenced by enlargement. The entry of Sweden and Finland had an important impact on 'the balance of forces' in the EU (Jenson and Pochet 2003, p. 7). Sweden played a very active and influential role in the employment debate (Lightfoot

1997; Johansson 1999), notably in the persons of Allan Larsson, who became Director-General for Social Affairs and Employment in the Commission, and Gunnar Lund, Sweden's representative to the 1996–7 Intergovernmental Conference which adopted an employment chapter that, compared to the Maastricht agreements, was seen as being 'a bit more ambitious, largely thanks to the efforts of the Government of Sweden' (Juncker 2002, p. ix). This influence over the design of the compromise approach was then reinforced by the political impact of the changes of government in both France and the UK in 1997 (Schaefer 2004).

Some observers have suggested another kind of interaction between the evolution of new policy modes and enlargement, namely that the new modes of governance which were emerging shaped the new enlargement policy being elaborated with a view to the entry of Central and Eastern European countries, which would require preparations going beyond the traditional Community method (Preston 1995). In this view, the enlargement strategy presented at the December 1997 summit could be seen to include most of the characteristics of the new strategy for coordination of national employment policies agreed at the Extraordinary Summit on Employment in Luxembourg in November 1997: overall EU-wide objectives, national action plans (accession partnerships and national plans for the adoption of the acquis), benchmarks and the exchange of good practice (e.g. through twinning), evaluation by the Commission according to common indicators, and so on (Tulmets 2005). Likewise, in specific sectors, new mechanisms for horizontal learning were created, such as the Pan-European Regulatory Forum (PERF) for pharmaceuticals (Koutalakis 2004), with a view to facilitating implementation of the acquis in the acceding countries.

Yet inasmuch as these approaches were intended to assist eventual implementation of legally binding commitments, however, there is a fundamental difference with OMC processes, which are *not* preparatory mechanisms of this nature. The existence of such commonalities in approach is a reflection of the broader changes affecting European policies in the mid-1990s.

On the one hand, new methods were being sought to put pressure on member states in order to ensure that the internal market legislation which had been adopted would be applied in practice. One of the first formalized modalities of 'naming and shaming' emerged precisely as a means to improve the situation regarding the implementation of legal commitments: the first formal Scoreboard for member states' records in transposing single market directives was also produced in November 1997.

On the other hand, discussion of means to help improve European competitiveness was going beyond traditional legislative approaches. This was partly due to the nature of the issues involved: complex challenges not allowing for uniform solutions and generally not falling under Community legislative competence. It was also shaped by the broader policy discourse of 'new public management' and international trends, notably the OECD's promotion of policy transfer in its 1994 'Jobs Strategy' (Arrowsmith *et al.* 2004). And it was a result of close interaction between the Commission and European industry. Benchmarking as a method to improve the competitiveness of enterprises had been mentioned in the 1993 White Paper and was emphasized in the first report in June 1995 of the Competitiveness Advisory Group set up by the Essen Summit. By October 1996, in parallel with proposals of the European Round Table of Industrialists (ERT 1996) the Commission was urging the adoption of benchmarking to improve 'framework conditions' for industry, in addition to enterprises and sectors (CEC 1996).

OMC emerged as part of a broader policy evolution. This new way of working together could well be seen as being particularly suited to the challenges of increased diversity in the expanding EU. As the high level group on the future of social policy in an enlarged European Union set up by the Commission argued in its 2004 Report:

> The open method of coordination is all the more important in the prospect of enlargement since it is based on catching-up and benchmarking. It can foster convergence on common interest and on some agreed common priorities while respecting national and regional diversities.
>
> (CEC 2004a, p. 35)

However, the OMC was not created in anticipation of any enlargement nor in response to perceived impacts of enlargement. Even in the social field, the OMC would almost certainly have emerged without further enlargement. Indeed, with regard to employment policy, some have argued precisely that the strategy was *not* adapted to take into account the specific concerns of new member states (Celin 2003; De la Rosa 2005; Mailand 2005).

Finally, it would be misleading to think of an 'impact' of enlargement as if this were a variable introduced into an otherwise stable situation from one day to the next. The new member states were brought into the process gradually over a number of years. In 1999, employment policy reviews began to be carried out in the candidate countries by the governments together with the Commission, leading to signature of joint assessment papers (JAP) with all 12 of the incoming countries between 2000 and 2002. Progress reports were submitted on the implementation of the JAP commitments, before the new member states submitted their first national action plans together with the existing member states in 2004. In the case of social inclusion, which got under way in 2001, a joint inclusion memorandum (JIM) was signed with each country in 2003. In other areas in which some form of OMC emerged, there was little time for such actions (the formal OMC in research only really began in 2004), while the lesser formalization in these cases created less pressure to conduct equivalent preliminary procedures.

ENLARGEMENT AND ALTERNATIVE METHODS OF REGULATION

Two basic differences are involved when assessing the relevance of enlargement for alternative methods of regulation as compared to OMC. First, whereas policy coordination emerged in a context of increasing diversity and complexity which was shaped by enlargement, there is no suggestion that the beginning of the exploration of alternative regulation is in any way related to enlargement. Second, it is only in the very largest sense that one can see OMC and legislation as policy options: that is, when the basic rules of the game are being decided in treaty reform. In the absence of EU legislative competence, there is no prospect of moving to binding measures if the results of OMC were to be considered inadequate. 'Alternative regulation', by contrast, rests on a dynamic interaction between the possibility of legally binding measures and the credibility of private commitments.

To sum up what has been called 'horizontal subsidiarity', the EU is expected to legislate only where necessary. Some areas are reserved for legislation more or less by definition – where fundamental rights or risks are involved, or uniformity is essential. Some others may be completely eliminated as a possible area of European legislative intervention. In between is a range of areas in which a European public interest is at stake to a greater or lesser degree, including the achievement of agreed goals of European integration. In these cases, the assumption by private actors of responsibilities within a European framework is seen as inherently positive, whether in terms of effectiveness (incentives to go beyond minimum requirements, flexibility, rapidity, cost-effectiveness) or legitimacy (stakeholder participation and good governance). The authorities are nonetheless expected to monitor these arrangements to ensure that public interests are attained, whether or not these have been formally recognized as agreed targets. If not, there may have to be recourse to European legislation.

The potential impact of enlargement may therefore be assessed in terms of its effect on the following three dimensions of regulatory interaction:

- *The credibility of the threat of legislation.* As at national level, 'voluntary' arrangements almost always require 'the shadow of the law' to be effective.

- *The effectiveness of the private commitment.* Effectiveness requires not only will but representativeness on the part of the European association, and the capability of its members to implement agreements on the ground.
- *Necessary framework conditions.* A self-regulatory arrangement depends also on continuing incentives for the industrial actors involved, including effective public actions in assuring adequate framework conditions – for example, universal enforcement of regulations, or guaranteeing fair competition.

While remaining cautious as to how far one can draw general conclusions from specific cases, this section looks at two sectors in which self- and co-regulation at European level have been prominently explored and in which there has been a change in the pattern of regulatory interaction in recent years. The aim is to assess whether any such enlargement-related factors have played, or may come to play, a significant role in this process. These are the European social dialogue and energy efficiency.

The European Social Dialogue

The 1990s saw a number of legislative acts adopted by the Council on the basis of cross-industry agreements reached between the social partners, which were largely shaped by institutional interests, as well as the prospect of legislation or treaty reform (as had been the case in the initial acceptance by the employers of the whole arrangement in 1991). Following the failure of the first negotiations, on European works councils, an agreement on parental leave led to a directive in 1996. Only minimum standards were being proposed, and again the perspective of treaty change was influential. 'With the 1996–1997 IGC approaching and with the threat of a sceptical, if not hostile Parliament, the social partners feared that another failure might mean the end of their co-legislation powers' (Dølvik and Visser 2001, p. 26). After this came 'atypical work'. With a proposal being repeatedly blocked in the Council, the Commission initiated consultations on 'flexibility in working time and security for employees'. The Union of Industrial and Employers' Confederations of Europe (UNICE) preferred to distinguish between part-time work, fixed-term work and temporary work. The strategy eventually adopted by the European Trade Union Confederation (ETUC) agreed to concentrate the initial negotiations on part-time work. Negotiations started in October 1996, and seemed deadlocked until June 1997 when agreement was suddenly reached within the space of one week. There was strong criticism of the results among trade unions, as well as in the European Parliament. Very modest results had been accepted by ETUC, it seemed, mainly out of institutional self-interest. The decisive factor was again 'the ongoing IGC and the shared interest of protecting the social partners' co-regulatory role in EU social policy' (Dølvik 1997). In the case of fixed-term work, UNICE actually initiated the negotiations in order to pre-empt possible legislation (Branch and Greenwood 2001, pp. 62–3). An agreement was reached and an implementing directive adopted in June 1999.

Well before the 2004 enlargement, pressures for change were felt. In 1999 both sides of the European social partnership were clearly dissatisfied. The results of the cross-industry agreements were considered pretty meagre by many in the trade unions. In 1999 the ETUC therefore agreed to evaluate the experience with the social dialogue, the conditions under which negotiations are to be preferred to legislation, and how they can be improved. It was 'a signal that the ETUC [was] no longer willing to negotiate at any price' (Dølvik and Visser 2001, p. 29).

It was against this background that the first major failure occurred. The Commission had been asking the social partners since 1995 to consider talks on temporary agency work. UNICE agreed in May 2000 to start negotiations, but these broke down in May 2001.

In this context, an interaction took place between the evolution of steering modes in the EU, and developments in the relationship between public and private actors. UNICE, never really convinced of the benefits of binding European agreements of any sort, now discovered OMC. Responding to the Commission's consultation on modernizing and improving employment relations in October 2000, UNICE argued that:

> For European employers, the starting point of any process for modernising employment relations should be based on national evaluations of the rules governing the functioning of labour markets. At European level, UNICE considers that the method which should be retained is that of *open coordination* advocated by the Lisbon European Council.

This approach seemed to be encouraged by the High Level Group on Industrial Relations and Change in the European Union set up by the Prodi Commission, which reported in 2002. The report (CEC 2002) stressed that 'New approaches on regulation also underline the fact that regulation can be based not only on a normative approach leading to binding rules (legal provisions or social agreements), but also on a learning process based on guidelines and benchmarks designed to improve actual behaviour.' It proposed, among other things, 'the development of an open method of co-ordination by the social partners'. Given the observable problems in negotiating agreements which are implemented by law, it was also suggested that social partners should 'fully explore the possibility of entering into voluntary framework agreements to be implemented through their own national procedures'.

The joint contribution by the social partners to the Laeken European Council in December 2001 stated their 'wish to develop a work programme for a more autonomous social dialogue'. Since 2002 there have been various manifestations of this tendency to come out from under the 'shadow of the law'. In some respects, the lead seemed to be taken over by the social partners. In November 2002, the social partners adopted a work programme for 2003–5 in which they indicated a series of autonomous initiatives for the coming years. A second work programme for 2006–8 was signed in March 2006.

In this context, moreover, the social partners started to implement cross-sectoral framework agreements by the non-legislative route. The first case was the 2002 agreement on telework. A second such 'autonomous agreement', on stress at work, was agreed in 2004. A third, on harassment and violence at work, was signed in March 2007. These agreements raise some questions about coverage, implementation and monitoring. Implementation will necessarily take different forms and have different degrees of coverage in different countries. Unless national law is used, it depends on the existence of social partners at national level who are capable of adopting and overseeing collective agreements. While generally supporting these developments as a new phase which strengthens the involvement of national actors, the Commission has insisted on the need to evaluate implementation and to leave open the possibility of legislative action (CEC 2004b).

However, the original 'co-regulatory' dynamics underlying the European social dialogue – whether the threat of 'you negotiate or we legislate' or the hope that 'you negotiate because we can't legislate' – have been superseded by rather different processes. There is no longer much of a legislative agenda anyway in the relevant areas – and it may become even harder in the future to adopt some of the proposals which are on the table. The social partners, and especially UNICE,[4] have opted for purely bilateral negotiations without any pressure from the Commission, and for 'autonomous' forms of implementation, rather than using Community law. The nature of agreements is changing, away from rules towards the idea of common approaches such as a framework of actions ('process-oriented texts', in the terminology of the Commission) which are characterized more by the spirit of exchanges of good practice. Two such frameworks have been signed, on lifelong learning (2002) and gender equality (2005).

Enlargement may affect the credibility of autonomous agreements in terms of implementation. Most new member states have much weaker structures for bipartite social dialogue, as opposed to tripartite structures involving the government, which function relatively well (Vaughan-Whitehead 2005). Although Malta and Cyprus are comparable to many older member states in this respect, the social partners had a weak membership basis in the Central and Eastern European (CEE) eight on the eve of accession. Levels of trade unionization had declined to strikingly low levels (the average density figure in Poland being only 14.1 per cent in 2001) as a result of a trend towards more services, privatization and the growth in small and medium enterprises. Employers' organizations had low affiliation rates and often lacked the authorization of their affiliates to undertake binding commitments. The vast majority of workers in the CEE eight were not covered by collective agreements – whereas in 2000–2002 coverage rates were up to 100 per cent in Belgium and Austria, over 90 per cent in Sweden, Finland and France, and more than two-thirds in Denmark, Spain, the Netherlands and Germany. Except in Slovenia, bargaining was single-level, with no tradition of central bilateral bargaining which might lead to binding agreements. Sectoral bargaining was particularly weak.

Capacity-building may help bring about change. Assistance has been offered by the International Labour Organization, the International Monetary Fund and the World Bank. The European Economic and Social Committee tried to involve economic and social actors in joint consultative committees. The Commission has provided support through the European Social Fund, the PHARE programme, TAIEX and other mechanisms. The social partners implemented joint initiatives and an integrated programme between December 2004 and May 2006, followed by other steps.[5] Yet there may be limits to what can be expected in the short term: 'The social dialogue in the CEE countries has been conducted and rapidly redeveloped through a top-down process, whereas the same development in the West was gradual and dominated by bottom-up processes' (Mailand and Due 2004, p. 195).

It is too early to tell what the longer-term impact may be. On the one hand, the weakness of social dialogue structures in the new member states may help undermine the credibility of autonomous agreements as EU instruments. If there is to be such uneven and varied implementation, then this approach may come to be little more than a loose exchange of practices. On the other hand, the 'shadow of the law' may also become all the less credible. The impact of enlargement in the Council has not been as dramatic as was widely expected, and the new member states have in fact tended to split between camps over social policy, albeit with a slight majority tending towards the UK-led group. Nonetheless, this still does not make it any easier to adopt new measures.

Energy Efficiency

Energy efficiency has been one of the areas in which non-legislative methods have seemed to show greatest potential since the mid-1990s. With household appliances accounting for some 25 per cent of final energy needs in the EU, efforts began in the early 1990s to reduce consumption. On the one hand, the 1992 directive on energy labelling for household appliances[6] and subsequent implementing directives aimed to increase consumer awareness and to influence choice in favour of more efficient products. On the other hand, measures began to be pursued to impose minimum efficiency requirements at European level, partly driven by internal market considerations. Minimum efficiency performance standards (MEPs) were introduced by some member states. Since energy efficiency was not a sufficient reason to justify barriers to trade, the logical outcome was to propose Europe-wide MEPs. The first case concerned refrigerators and freezers. Following the Dutch notification in 1992, the Commission prepared a proposal which was presented to the Parliament and the Council in December 1994 and only adopted in September 1996.[7] This long delay was due both to strong opposition from manufacturers and strong differences between member states. In the course of the negotiations, a variety of pressures and arguments was brought to bear in favour of negotiated agreements rather than regulation: greater flexibility to reach a target average efficiency, or greater speed to adapt than with legislation requiring years of negotiation (Bertoldi 1999).

Four agreements on energy efficiency were endorsed by the Commission in the form of negative clearances/exemptions under competition policy.[8] These first experiences were held to show various positive elements. Yet it also remained clear that, since the Community environmental agreements could only take the form of unilateral non-binding commitments, 'there is a requirement to have a credible threat of legislation and to use these agreements together with other instruments' (Lefèvre 2000). The Commission's 2000 action plan to improve energy efficiency thus argued that, although a large number of appliances could be subject to such agreements, a framework directive was still desirable (CEC 2000). The main result has been the 2005 Eco-design Directive, which lays down generic eco-design requirements. If an energy-using product is sold in large volumes and has a significant environmental impact, the Commission should adopt an implementing measure laying down specific requirements, after the draft is approved by a 'comitology' committee. As an alternative, 'voluntary agreements or other self-regulation measures' should be encouraged 'where such action is likely to deliver the policy objectives faster or in a less costly manner than mandatory requirements'. These are to be assessed by a consultation forum representing 'a balanced participation of Member States' representatives and all interested parties concerned' against a set of indicative criteria, including the need for an industrial association to represent 'a large majority' of the sector.[9]

At the same time, however, the commitments made by CECED have been reconsidered. In March 2007, CECED announced that the association would 'discontinue' its voluntary energy efficiency agreements for large appliances, calling for 'legislative measures to ensure future energy performance standards as an alternative to continued updating of the voluntary agreements'. Too many governments were failing to stop 'careless or unscrupulous' operators from claiming that their products had better energy efficiency than they really delivered.[10] Without proper market surveillance and enforcement, manufacturers which had made the effort to improve products were not receiving their fair rewards in terms of consumer choice. With targets now needing to become even more ambitious, the stakes were even higher: 'To go the extra mile now manufacturers need to be very sure that they will have a return on their investment' (CECED 2007, p. 2).

The key issues involved are not a result of enlargement. On the one hand, the manufacturers' position must be seen in the context of increased competition from cheaper products imported from outside the EU, notably from Asia, independently of the problem of proper labelling. On the other hand, and to the extent that problems within the EU are indeed involved, significant shortcomings in implementation of the EU energy label scheme have been identified across Europe. A 2006 study conducted in nine of the EU15 by the European Association for the Coordination of Consumer Representation in Standardisation (ANEC) also called for strengthened market surveillance through collective European action supervised by the Commission.[11] However, enlargement seems to have exacerbated the situation. '[C]omprehensive compliance problems' were reported in the new member states, owing to a high market share of unlabelled C-class appliances imported from Asia, promotion of unlabelled products made by manufacturers owned by retailers, and use of A-class labels often on products with lower efficiency levels. Moreover, new member states were said to 'lag seriously behind in implementing information campaigns' (ANEC 2007, pp. 16, 20).

Enlargement may thus strengthen pressures to move back, at least temporarily, from the reliance on 'soft' approaches towards mandatory requirements and a concentration on improving the capability of public actors to ensure effective enforcement of the rules.

Some issues result from a capacity gap which can be overcome. Capacity-building initiatives have been pursued. CEECAP (Central and Eastern

European Countries Appliance Policy Project) was launched in 2002 by the International Energy Agency (IEA – created by the OECD in 1974) with the aim of supporting Central and Eastern European countries in creating suitable conditions for implementing appliance labelling and efficiency policies in accordance with EU appliance efficiency legislation and programmes. A new version (Implementing EU Appliance Policy in Central and Eastern Europe) started in 2006 with support from the European Commission's programme Intelligent Energy – Europe. As of 2007, however, there clearly remained much to do.

Some aspects seem to be more structural. The effectiveness of energy labelling also depends on the consumer, not only in terms of general environmental awareness, which is widely seen to be lower in the new member states than in (many of) the older ones (Von Homeyer 2004; Skjaerseth and Wettestad 2007), but also in terms of specific interest regarding energy. There will continue to be objective reasons for this to remain relatively weak in new member states if relative energy prices remain low.[12]

CONCLUSIONS

The adoption of non-binding forms of policy coordination in some new areas in the 1990s was not caused by enlargement. These new approaches were emerging anyway as a result of the evolving policy context and the nature of the issues. Nevertheless, the increase in underlying diversity within the Union as a result of enlargement was a relevant factor in this overall process of change, and enlargement did bring about some changes in the balance of forces within the Union regarding the design of specific forms of cooperation.

By the same token, it is inappropriate to talk of a specific impact of enlargement on the development and perspectives of OMC. The new member states were introduced gradually into the process in advance of accession, while OMC is in part conceived precisely as a means to manage diversity with flexibility. The situation thus seems stable, although this does not exclude the possibility that some actors affected negatively by liberalization of movement *without* greater similarity of conditions may push for a shift towards harder measures concerning minimum standards.

Enlargement has not been a factor in any sense, on the other hand, in the initiation of alternative methods of regulation involving new forms of public–private interaction. It could, however, have an impact on the further evolution of such methods as a result of its impact on the credibility of legislative alternatives, the effectiveness of private commitments or the provision of necessary framework conditions. Two cases were examined in this perspective. In the case of the European social dialogue, the major shifts in the pattern of regulatory interaction in recent years were not caused by enlargement. However, the relative weakness of the social partners in most of the new member states may affect the credibility of Europe-wide autonomous agreements, while enlargement will not increase the prospect of any legislative alternatives. The result may be to weaken all EU-level action in the areas concerned. In the case of energy efficiency, one of the most promising areas for self-regulation within an EU framework, the prospects for further consolidation of this approach were challenged in 2007 as a result of problems in assuring suitable framework conditions. Enlargement was not the cause of these problems, but has exacerbated some aspects. For rather different reasons, in this case, there may be new pressures to move towards legislation. In both cases, the issues largely reflect capacity gaps, which may be overcome. Yet there are also more structural dimensions which will not disappear, at least in the near future.

No simple overall conclusions can therefore be drawn regarding the importance of enlargement for the evolution of non-legislative methods in the EU. First, there are important differences between the two main classes of non-legislative approach identified. Second, even to the extent that enlargement has been relevant, as in the case of the evolution of policy coordination, it is inappropriate to think in terms of an 'impact' of enlargement, given that these new methods were emerging in parallel and in interaction with the process of preparation for the 2004/2007 enlargements. And third, even where one can detect an influence of enlargement on the perspectives for further development of these approaches, the challenge remains of distinguishing between issues resulting from capacity gaps, which may be overcome, and those reflecting underlying structural differences.

NOTES

1. This is partly adapted from a similar matrix in Treib *et al.* (2005).
2. These three dimensions of legalization of international agreements proposed by Abbott *et al.* (2000) remain very useful parameters for disaggregating particular relationships.
3. The bodies which are recognized as having 'cross-industrial' or 'inter-professional' representativeness for the purposes of European Social Dialogue are the Union of Industrial and Employers' Confederations of Europe (UNICE) – renamed BUSINESSEUROPE in January 2007 – which has a cooperation agreement for these purposes with the European Association of Craft, Small and Medium-sized Enterprises (UEAPME); the European Centre of Enterprises with Public Participation (CEEP); and the European Trade Union Confederation (ETUC). Other bodies are recognized as being representative in particular sectors.
4. In January 2007, UNICE was renamed BUSINESSEUROPE.
5. See http://europa.eu.int/comm/employment_social/social_dialogue/enlarge_en.htm.

6. *Council Directive 92/75/EEC of 22 September 1992 on the indication by labelling and standard product information of the consumption of energy and other resources by household appliances*, OJ L 297 of 13 October 1992, pp. 16–19.

7. *Directive 96/57/EC of the European Parliament and of the Council of 3 September 1996 on energy efficiency requirements for household electric refrigerators, freezers and combinations thereof*, OJ L 236 of 18 September 1996, pp. 36–43.

8. Notices pursuant to Article 19(3) of Council Regulation No. 17/62(1) in OJ C 12 of 16 January 1998; OJ C 382 of 9 December 1998; OJ C 250 of 8 September 2001. These were a commitment by the European Association of Consumer Electronics Manufacturers (EACEM) for the reduction of standby losses of TVs and VCRs (1997), and commitments by the European Committee of Domestic Equipment Manufacturers (CECED) on the cessation of production and imports of low-energy efficiency washing machines (1997), household dishwashers (1999) and water heaters (1999). EACEM adopted a further commitment for the reduction of standby losses of audio products in standby mode in 2000. The European Information, Communications and Consumer Electronics Technology Industry Association (EICTA) also adopted a voluntary commitment to improve the energy performance of household consumer electronic products (2003). CECED agreed a second voluntary commitment on reducing energy consumption of domestic washing machines (2002), and a voluntary commitment on reducing energy consumption of household refrigerators, freezers and their combinations (2002). These were cleared by DG Competition in 2003. The Commission seemed to give informal encouragement to CECED's initiatives as a 'campaign associate' in the context of the Sustainable Energy Europe programme (see for example the June 2006 newsletter on http://www.sustenergy.net), as well as suggesting on its website that voluntary agreements can be 'particularly successful' in this area (http://ec.europa.eu/energy/demand/vol_agreements/index_en.htm). The Commission itself proposed codes of conduct for external power supplies, and set-top boxes and digital TVs.

9. *Directive 2006/32/EC of the European Parliament and of the Council of 5 April 2006 on energy end-use efficiency and energy services and repealing Council Directive 93/76/EEC.* OJ L 114 of 27 April 2006.

10. CECED press release, 21 March 2007, 'Top Executives Discontinue Voluntary Energy Efficient Agreements for Large Appliances'.

11 ANEC press release 11 May 2007, 'ANEC Study Reveals Significant Shortcomings in Implementation of EU Energy Label scheme', ANEC-R&T-2007-ENV-003 final.

12. In terms of price level indices (EU average = 100), all 12 new member states were below 90, with six below 60. It should be added that six of the EU15 were below the average, the lowest being Greece at 69 (Leetmaa 2006).

REFERENCES

Abbott, K.W., Keohane, R.O., Moravscik, A., Slaughter, A.-M. and Snidal, D. (2000), 'The Concept of Legalization', *International Organization,* **54** (3), 401–19.

ANEC (European Association for the Coordination of Consumer Representation in Standardisation) (2007), *A Review of the Range of Activity throughout Member States Related to Compliance with the EU Energy Label Regulations in those Countries*, ANEC-R&T-2006-ENV-008 (final), January, Brussels: ANEC.

Arrowsmith, J., Sisson, K. and Marginson, P. (2004), 'What Can "Benchmarking" Offer the Open Method of Co-ordination?', *Journal of European Public Policy*, **11** (2), 311–28.

Bertoldi, P. (1999), 'Energy Efficient Equipment within SAVE: Activities, Strategies, Success and Barriers', SAVE Conference – For an Energy Efficient Millennium, Graz, 8–10 November, http://www.eva.ac.at/publ/pdf/s4_11.pdf.

Branch, A. and Greenwood, J. (2001), 'European Employers: Social Partners?', in H. Compston and J. Greenwood (eds), *Social Partnership in the European Union*, Basingstoke: Palgrave, pp. 41–70.

CECED (European Committee of Domestic Equipment Manufacturers) (2007), Position Paper, 'CECED Vision on Energy Efficiency', GS-07-76, Brussels, 1 July.

Celin, M. (2003), 'European Employment Strategy: The Right Answer for the Candidate Countries?', *TRANSFER*, 2003/1.

Commission of the European Communities (CEC) (1993a), *White Paper on Growth, Competitiveness and Employment*, COM (93) 700 final/A and B, 5 December.

Commission of the European Communities (CEC) (1993b), *Green Paper on European Social Policy – Options for the Union*, COM(93) 551 final, 17 November.

Commission of the European Communities (CEC) (1994), *White Paper: European Social Policy – a Way Forward for the Union*, COM(94) 333 final, 27 July.

Commission of the European Communities (CEC) (1996), Communication, *Benchmarking the Competitiveness of Europe in Industry*, COM(96) 463 final, 9 October.

Commission of the European Communities (CEC) (2000), Communication from the Commission to the Council, the European Parliament, the Economic and Social Committee and the Committee of the Regions, *Action Plan to Improve Energy Efficiency in the European Community*, COM (2000) 247 final, 26 April.

Commission of the European Communities (CEC) (2004a), Directorate-General for Employment and Social Affairs, *Report of the High Level Group on the Future of Social Policy in an Enlarged European Union*.

Commission of the European Communities (CEC) (2004b), *Partnership for Change in an Enlarged Europe – Enhancing the Contribution of European Social Dialogue*, COM(2004) 557 final, 12 August.

De la Rosa, S. (2005), 'The Open Method of Coordination in the New Member States – the Perspectives for its Use as a Tool of Soft Law', *European Law Journal*, **11** (5), 618–40.

Dølvik, J.-E. (1997), *Redrawing Boundaries of Solidarity? ETUC, Social Dialogue and the Europeanisation of Trade Unions in the 1990s*, ARENA report 5/97.

Dølvik, J.-E. and Visser, J. (2001), 'ETUC and European Social Partnership: A Third Turning-Point?', in H. Compston and J. Greenwood (eds), *Social Partnership in the European Union*, Basingstoke: Palgrave, pp. 11–40.

ERT (European Round Table of Industrialists) (1996), *Benchmarking for Policy-Makers: The Way to Competitiveness, Growth and Job Creation*, Brussels: ERT.

Esping-Andersen, G. (1990), *Three Worlds of Welfare Capitalism*, New York: Oxford University Press.

Eurofound (2006), *Employment in Social Care in Europe*, Luxembourg: Office for Official Publications of the European Communities/European Foundation for the Improvement of Living and Working Conditions.

Jenson, J. and Pochet, P. (2003), 'Employment and Social Policy since Maastricht: Standing up to the European Monetary Union', Paper prepared for 'The Year of the Euro', Nanovic Institute for European Studies, University of Notre Dame, 5–8 December 2002, http://eucenter.wisc.edu/Calendar/Spring 03/jensonpochet. pdf.

Johansson, K.-M. (1999), 'Tracing the Employment Title in the Amsterdam Treaty: Uncovering Transnational Coalitions', *Journal of European Public Policy*, **6** (1), 85–101.

Juncker, J.-C. (2002), 'Preface' in E. Best and D. Bossaert (eds), *From Luxembourg to Lisbon and Beyond: Making the Employment Strategy Work*, Maastricht: EIPA, pp. ix–xi.

Koutalakis, C. (2004), ' "Smoothing" Eastern Enlargement through New Modes of Governance? Conceptualising the Role of Independent Regulatory Agencies and Non-Hierarchical Steering in Pre-accession Negotiations', http://www.eu-newgov.org/database/deliv/D14D01_seeira_report.pdf.

Leetmaa, P. (2006), 'Comparative Price Levels for Selected Consumer Services in Europe for 2005', *Statistics in Focus, Economy* EUROSTAT, European Communities, http://epp.eurostat.ec.europa.eu/cache/ity_offpub/ks-nj-06-012/en/ks-nj-06-012-en.pdf.

Lefèvre, P. (2000), 'Voluntary Agreements in EU Environmental Policy – Critical Review and Perspectives', *CAVA Working Paper*, 2000/2, 7 August.

Lightfoot, S. (1997), 'An Employment Union for Europe? The Role of the Swedish Government', *Politics*, **17** (2), 109–15.

Mailand, M. (2005), 'The Revision of the European Employment Strategy and its Further Development at EU Level', Working Paper, University of Copenhagen Employment Relations Research Centre.

Mailand, M. and Due, J. (2004), 'Social Dialogue in Central and Eastern Europe: Present State and Future Development', *European Journal of Industrial Relations*, **10** (2), 179–97.

Pochet, P. (2005), 'The OMC and the Construction of Social Europe', in J. Zeitlin and P. Pochet (eds) with L. Magnusson, *The Open Method of Co-ordination in Action: The European Employment and Social Inclusion Strategies*, Brussels: PIE – Peter Lang, pp. 37–82.

Preston, C. (1995), 'Obstacles to EU Enlargement: The Classical Community Method and the Prospects for a Wider Europe', *Journal of Common Market Studies*, **33** (3), 451–63.

Sapir, A. (2005), 'Globalisation and the Reform of European Social Models', *Bruegel Policy Brief*, 2005/01.

Schaefer, A. (2004), 'Beyond the Community Method: Why the Open Method of Coordination Was Introduced to EU Policy-Making', *European Integration online Papers*, **8**, 13.

Scharpf, F. (2002), 'The European Social Model: Coping with the Challenges of Diversity', *Journal of Common Market Studies*, **40** (4), 645–70.

Skjaerseth, J.B. and Wettestad, J. (2007), 'Is EU Enlargement Bad for Environmental Policy? Confronting Gloomy Expectations with Evidence', *International Environmental Agreements*, Online edition, 2 March.

Treib, O., Bähr, H. and Falkner, G. (2005), 'Modes of Governance: A Note towards Conceptual Clarification', *European Governance Papers* (EUROGOV), No. N-05-02, http://www.connex-network.org/eurogov/pdf/egp-newgov-N-05-02.pdf.

Tulmets, E. (2005), 'The Introduction of the Open Method of Coordination in the European Enlargement Policy: Analysing the Impact of the New PHARE/Twinning Instrument', *European Political Economy Review*, **3** (1), 54–90.

Vaughan-Whitehead, D. (2005), 'The World of Work in the New Member States: Diversity and Convergence', in D. Vaughan-Whitehead (ed.), *Working and Employment Conditions in New Member States: Convergence or Diversity?*, Geneva: International Labour Organization and European Commission, pp. 1–43.

Von Homeyer, I. (2004), 'Differential Effects of Enlargement on EU Environmental Governance', *Environmental Politics*, **13** (1), 52–76.

13. Conclusion

Thomas Christiansen, Edward Best and Pierpaolo Settembri

At the outset of this book we observed that several studies had indicated that the impact of enlargement on the institutions of the EU was more limited than initial expectations had suggested. In the light of the detailed, empirical studies of the key institutions of the European Union we can talk with greater confidence about the remarkable continuity the institutional architecture of the EU has been demonstrating. Indeed, on the basis of the studies of individual institutions and governance mechanisms that this volume brings together, we are able to say that the – sometimes apocalyptic – pronunciations of a 'break-down', '*blocage*' or 'collapse' of the enlarged EU have turned out to be wide of the mark. Instead, the overwhelming evidence that the contributors to this book have brought together points to a conclusion of a Union doing 'business as usual', albeit with some variation across different institutions.

The accession of 12 new member states, even before the EU reformed itself through a revision of the treaties, was not the kind of critical juncture that would have forced difficult decisions about the functioning of its institutions. As Kenneth Dyson points out in Chapter 7, such a crisis may yet occur – and it may or may not be related to the Union's enlarged membership – but at the beginning of 2008 there was no sign of it. Enlargement has done numerous things to the EU – caused certain difficulties in some respects, but also prompted the search for greater efficiency elsewhere – but what it has not done, on the evidence presented here, is to lead to any general malaise in the work of the institutional mechanisms of the EU.

One consideration that we need to address before going into the findings in more detail is the question about the possibility of a *delayed* impact of enlargement. Several of the authors here indicate that it is still early days for the enlarged EU, and that pressure for change may build for quite some time before becoming visible to the eye of the observer. In some cases, authors have indicated the early signs for such future pressures – the language issue in the comitology system being one such example – but on the whole even the sensitivity to future developments does not change the verdict about the way in which EU enlargement has not fundamentally altered the functioning of the EU's institutions.

In the terms of the analytical framework that was developed in the opening chapter of this book, we must therefore conclude that enlargement is best characterized as a combination of assimilation (of the new member states into the EU system) and adaptation (of the EU system for its operation with/for 27 member states). While there is no evidence of any fundamental transformation of the EU's institutions, the EU has adapted many of its working practices, internal rules of procedure and informal arrangements to the presence of new members and a greater number of actors.

In terms of the dichotomy presented in the title of this book (change and continuity), it is therefore evident that there have been certain changes, but that the overall trend has been towards continuity, both with respect to the Union's architecture and with regard to the functioning of individual institutions. Given the considerable shock the system received through the momentous growth to, first, 25 and, now, 27 members, the resilience of the institutional structure is noteworthy. After all, not only has membership nearly doubled over the past few years, but also diversity has increased exponentially – diversity of different political and administrative cultures, of economic and social systems, of languages and world-views, and thus the diversity of the preferences that are being communicated to the European level and need to be integrated in the decision-making processes of the Union.

In the light of this challenge, the ability of the system not only to cope, but to continue to function in a largely unchanged manner, is remarkable. But perhaps it should not come as a surprise – the very purpose of *institutionalizing* cooperation among states in the way practised by the EU is to create a decision-making system that is flexible enough to respond to change, while being stable enough to persist in face of 'external shocks'. By this standard, not only is it evident that enlargement is one of the most successful experiences of the EU, but indeed so is the institutional adaptation that has occurred alongside it.

Institutional inertia is a hallmark of the EU that is often criticized, especially when 'Brussels' is slow to address public concerns that the more volatile world of domestic politics might process more quickly. But the way in which the arrival of a large and diverse number of new members has been digested without major upheaval by the EU is the other side of this coin. Inertia demonstrates its benefits in situations like this by preserving the established patterns of interaction despite significantly higher numbers and a radically changed distribution of interests.

Looking at the long and at times tortuous path of accession negotiations between the EU and its new members, one might therefore be tempted to conclude that 'All is well that ends well.' The long period of preparation – both in the institutions and in the new member states – seems to have contributed to an outcome which meant that, once the date of accession was reached, the system would continue to work. 'Breakdown' has been avoided, the activities of the institutions of the EU continue pretty much as before, and the result is 'business as usual' in the enlarged EU.

Such a conclusion would, however, be both simplistic and premature. The various studies that have been undertaken in order to bring together the contributions to this volume allow us to be more subtle and sophisticated in our analysis of the effect that the arrival of the new member states has had on the EU's key institutions and processes. Across the chapters of this book, four important dynamics have been observed that require a more detailed treatment at this point: first, the way in which the interaction between formal and informal arrangements has been affected by enlargement; second, the impact that enlargement has had on the relative weight of decisions taken in the political and administrative spheres of the EU's institutions; third, a growing trend of 'presidentialization' which sees those chairing meetings and heading institutions assuming greater power; and, fourth, a pattern of enlargement turning out to be the catalyst in the search for greater efficiency. In the following, we will look at each of these points in turn.

We argued in the introductory chapter that an important distinction to be made in the analysis of the institutional politics of the Union is that between their formal and informal aspects. The relevance of this point has been demonstrated in the subsequent empirical analyses of EU institutions – on many occasions it has become clear that this is in fact a crucial dimension when it comes to the study of EU enlargement.

What has happened in the context of EU institutions preparing their operation for the arrival of further member states has been the 'tightening' of internal procedures, involving revisions to rules of procedure. Existing formal arrangements have been made more explicit and specific, and in some cases unwritten rules have become codified. For example, in the Council, the procedures for discussions in the ministerial meetings have become more specific as to who can speak for how long, and there also a detailed interpretation and translation regime has been developed.

Similar processes of increasing formalization have also been reported from the other institutions, though it is not clear whether enlargement has been the only or even the main driver in such internal reforms. The European Court of Justice, the Committee of the Regions and the Economic and Social Committee all have revised their internal procedures, but, as Caroline Naômé points out in Chapter 6, other pressures had been at work for some time prior to the arrival of enlargement. In the case of comitology, greater formalization has meant that the pre-existing rules of procedure are now being applied more frequently.

While EP, CoR and EESC all have had to cope with the additional demands for a much greater number of official languages, neither the Court nor comitology made changes to their, more selective, approach to interpretation and translation. But the overall impact of political life in the enlarged – and multi-lingual – Union has been that institutions have generally become more careful about the extent of their commitment to written (printed) or spoken (interpreted) words. Both the length of official documents and the allocated speaking times are becoming regulated, and additional information is often being presented in the form of annexes or unofficial texts which are not available in all language versions.

This is the tip of the iceberg in terms of the wider phenomenon that has been identified: alongside the greater formalization of procedures, a secular trend towards an increased use of informal practices can be observed. Indeed, informality is probably the only way in which the more formal processes of internal and inter-institutional decision-making processes can be made to work. If, for example, participation in Council debates is to rely on one member state speaking for a group of like-minded countries, then clearly this will need to lead to more intense consultations (and pre-agreements) in advance of the formal meeting.

Indeed, across the board of the institutional politics of the EU we see how the relative weight of formal meetings gives way to informal arrangements, as the constraints of time, space and language increasingly limit opportunities for deliberation and decision-taking in such fora. 'Pre-cooking' of decisions had always been a feature of EU decision-making, but in the enlarged EU it is becoming more commonplace. This is the case not only inside institutions like Council or the European Parliament, but also with regard to the legislative procedure, where there is now a much higher incidence of agreement being reached at first reading. Here the informal tripartite meetings between representatives of the legislative institutions become even more important than they have already been in the past. In the case of the CoR, Simona Piattoni has charted the way in which the powerful players in the institution – the regions with legislative powers – have positioned themselves as an independent actor ('REGLEG') *outside* the formal institutional framework of CoR.

If key decisions are increasingly prepared outside the formal arenas, because these have become too crowded and too formalistic to allow for genuine debate and deliberation, then this has wider repercussions for European governance. There clearly is an issue about transparency that needs to be discussed: while we know ever more, and in all the official languages, about the formal proceedings, relatively less is known about the deliberations, consultations and pre-decisions which take place in the *couloirs*. In other words, the *official* approach to transparency in the EU is progressively being hollowed out as the actual loci of power become less accessible. Clearly we have here a normative challenge for European governance in the years to come: while it might have been possible to preserve the efficiency of the system to take decisions, the legitimacy of such decision-making might be called into question.

Closely related to the issue of greater formalization and rising informality in the EU's institutional politics is the second important conclusion we can draw from the research that the contributors to this volume have presented in the various chapters. This concerns the challenge for *political* decision-making and the greater prominence of *administrative* decision-making. As EU decision-making moves out of formal, political arenas – whether it is the ministerial level in the Council, the College of Commissioners in the European Commission or the plenary in the European Parliament – the administrative domain becomes more influential. This means, for example, that in the Council structure Coreper as well as other committees, working groups and Secretariat officials are even more important than they already were in the past. In the European Commission, there is an increasing trend to delegate detailed decision-making to the administrative levels, and in the EP the aspiration to maintain the efficiency of internal procedures after enlargement has enhanced the responsibilities of the Secretariat staff.

Comitology – like the ECJ and the ECB – is also seen as the realm of technocracy, and here an increasing distance to political levels of decision-making is discernible. With more and more decisions prepared in advance, deliberation in meetings becomes less important, or simply occurs less, which also means that fewer delegations arrive with specific mandates from their domestic hierarchies. The overall result here is a strengthening of the position of the Commission and of the voices of the larger member states that the Commission is more systematically consulting in advance.

There is a pattern here that has been observed, especially but not only in the area of comitology, of the system continuing to function well in part because the new members in committees (or representatives in Council working groups, or ministers, or Commissioners in the College, or judges in the ECJ, or delegates in CoR and EESC) tend, on the whole, not to 'rock the boat'. The overall impression is that, rather than the character of meetings at the EU level changing, the pressures of socialization are fairly strong, and new members are generally compliant with the established practices and 'rules of the game'.[1] Indeed, as many of the new member state representatives first entered the institutions as observers, there may have been a socialization effect of simply sitting quietly in the back, rather than actively participating in deliberations and decision-making.

Beyond the group dynamics in meetings, which are likely to change as time goes by, there seems to be a wider issue here with regard to the (missing) link between EU-level decision-making and national preference formation in the new member states. Owing to a variety of factors – administrative resources, language, the limited domestic adaptation to EU procedures – the administrations in the new member states are often at a much greater distance from their national representatives in Brussels than those of their counterparts of the EU15. This 'distance' between Brussels and domestic administrations may severely limit the ability of the delegations representing the new member states in the institutions of the EU to properly coordinate a national negotiating position, gather the necessary political support for a particular stance or consult the public and interest groups more widely on proposed legislation. As a result, the domestic circuit of interest representation – political class, administrative systems, political parties, organized interests – is progressively disenfranchised with regard to EU decision-making. While this is not a development that would be unique to the new member states, as the EU15 have experienced similar problems, it appears to be much more pronounced there.

Overall we therefore observe the gradual shift of EU decision-making taking place in the more administrative or diplomatic realm, away from the formal sites of political contestation. Increasingly, when elected politicians debate about and decide on matters in the institutions of the EU, this has a more symbolic character, whereas real power is exercised by bureaucrats, technocrats, diplomats, judges and central bankers meeting behind closed doors. And just as the drift towards informal governance has implications for normative values such as openness and transparency, the increasing depoliticization of EU decision-making raises questions about accountability. It simply becomes more and more difficult to identify those involved in taking (or preparing) decisions, and thus to hold them to account. It may not be *impossible* to trace who has done what in the process of EU decision-making, but that in turn means that those with better informational and other resources – lobbyists – have the upper hand when it comes to trying to influence decision-making.

At the same time, there is a parallel process of what could be called increasing 'presidentialization' of the system: in many institutional contexts, we see a stronger role now being assumed by those who chair meetings and/or lead the debates: in the European Commission, the relative power of the Commission President vis-à-vis the Commissioners, and of the cabinets vis-à-vis the services, has increased, while, in the Council, the Presidency and the Secretariat-General are becoming more influential. We already noted above the stronger role of the Commission, as agenda-setter and chair, in the area of comitology. Such developments are a reflection of the greater numbers of participants in meetings, and the perceived need to strengthen the power of the chair in each of these contexts. It ties in with the above-mentioned dynamics of greater informality and technocratiza-tion of EU decision-making, as such 'presidentialization' allows those in the chair to seek solutions and prepare decisions in advance of formal meetings.

To be sure, EU enlargement did not cause these developments, nor is it alone responsible for maintaining them. But while these are long-term trends of European governance, it is evident from the contributions to the present volume that the impact of enlargement has been to interact with these dynamics, reinforcing trends that pre-existed. The same can also be said with respect to the fourth pattern that we have observed – the way in which enlargement has neither caused nor impeded the search for greater efficiency in the running of the EU's institutions, but has in some ways acted as a catalyst or accelerator of internal reforms. The launch of major internal reforms that were undertaken by the Commission and by the Council pre-dates enlargement, but the prospect of enlargement became intertwined with these, as the discussions by Peterson and Birdsall (Chapter 4), and by Best and Settembri (Chapter 3), demonstrate. The same is true for comitology, while in the case of the ECJ it was only after enlargement that – in any case needed – internal reforms were undertaken. Enlargement, in such cases, is probably best seen as the 'last straw that breaks the camel's back': inefficiencies in the running of the institutions, and in their relations with one another, might have been bearable until then, but were not accept-able any more afterwards.

In the same vein, we can see how the arrival of the new member states, rather than being the *cause* of change, has served as the *justification* for change – it was the convincing argument, when previous arguments had failed, in the attempt to address some of the problems that have persisted in the institutional structure of the EU. In that sense, it would be appro-priate to credit the process of EU enlargement with the positive effect of forcing through efficiency reforms that were long overdue but that would not have been undertaken for years to come.

At this point we can summarize the key findings that cut across practi-cally all of the contributions to this volume: first, that the direct impact of enlargement on the institutions of the EU has been limited, and that no transformative changes have been identified; second, that enlargement has interacted with trends already present in the EU, in particular with the gradual drift of important decisions being taken not in the formal arenas, but through informal channels in the administrative and diplomatic domains; and, third, that enlargement increased the pressures for reforms aimed at increasing the efficiency of the EU institutions, acting as a catalyst for quicker change.

Based on these observations, we can also reassess the normative dimension of enlargement. What is surprising in this regard is that the greatest normative concern that had been debated prior to enlargement – the negative impact that this process might have on the efficient functioning of the institutions of the EU and its decision-making procedures – has, by and large, not materialized. Instead, it is in fact possible to argue, based on the evidence presented in this book, that the efficiency of the system has in some ways even increased.

There are, of course, numerous instances in which the taking of specific decisions has become more difficult, and the contributions to this volume provide a number of examples. But the capacity of the Union to function and take decisions remains unchanged, with regard to legislation, implementation or adjudication. Even with respect to the revision of the treaties – a subject not covered in the present volume – the Union has managed to maintain the momentum, with the speedy conclusion of the 2007 IGC and the agreement on the Lisbon Treaty. However, the normative evaluation would be incomplete if it were reduced to just looking at institutional efficiency and decision-making capacity. We have also observed that decision-making increasingly takes place through informal channels and is more and more dominated by administrative elites, at the expense of the formal arenas of political deliberation and public scrutiny. The accountability of EU decision-making is becoming more fragile, and this can be in part related to the impact that enlargement has had on the functioning of the institutions of the Union.

The saga of the Constitutional Treaty, first adopted with great political fanfare, only to be rejected in popular votes (in two of the *oldest* member states) and then resuscitated in only moderately changed form through one of the most secretive IGCs of recent times, perfectly matches this trend we have observed here. While this treaty reform may be justified in terms of maintaining and enhancing the efficiency of the enlarged Union, it is also a prime example of key decisions being taken outside the accountable fora of the EU, with the bulk of the detailed provisions of the Lisbon Treaty negotiated by lawyers, diplomats and administrators.

What appears to be under threat, then, in the institutional life of the enlarged European Union is not so much the efficiency of the system as the ability of citizens in the member states, and in particular in the new member states, to hold decision-makers to account. In this respect, the enlarged European Parliament has not become more 'efficient' as the guardian of accountability, even though its powers have increased with the reform of comitology and would expand further if and when the provisions of the Lisbon Treaty come into force. As Brendan Donnelly and Milena Bigatto observe in Chapter 5, the EP's larger numbers do not make the formation of majorities easier, and enlargement has also contributed to a trend of increasing internal differentiation among the political views in the Parliament.

Thus the normative balance-sheet of the institutional impact of EU enlargement is mixed. The EU has managed to protect the administrative efficiency of the system rather well, but democratic accountability is further challenged by the greater resort to informal arrangements in order to make the Union work post-enlargement. Given that it is still early days for the enlarged Union, much will hinge on future developments before a definite verdict is possible in this regard. Several authors have indicated that, while institutional adaptation to enlargement has been relatively smooth, there are signs that problems may only come to the fore in the future. The difficulty of squaring the increase in the number of official languages with the need for more accountability is one such issue. For the time being, the language issue has been 'managed', but it is likely to come up again to disturb the peace.

The overwhelming sensation when looking across the board of institutional politics in the EU is that enlargement is not the single cause of any change, whether positive or negative, but that it must be seen in the context of existing developments. It is the intertwining between these secular trends and the additional and new demands coming from a greater and more diverse membership of the Union that constitutes the impact of enlargement. Enlargement is an ongoing process, and how these pressures will be managed in the future and to what extent they ultimately change the institutional life of the EU remain uncertain.

Uncertainty is conditioned also by the ongoing reform of the treaties. This major reform exercise, which began in the 1990s, remained incomplete with the Nice Treaty and almost stumbled over the non-ratification of the Constitutional Treaty, now depends on the ratification and implementation of the Lisbon Treaty. Many provisions in that treaty are meant to address the concerns that have arisen over the impact of enlargement, both with respect to efficiency and with respect to democratic accountability. It remains to be seen how well the new treaty, if and when it comes into force, succeeds in doing so.

While it is too early to speculate about the outcome of that process at the time of writing, in late 2007, we can already say now with some confidence that enlargement has not fundamentally altered the functioning and performance of the EU institutions. It has, however, interacted with existing developments and reinforced some of the problems that had already been present in the institutional politics of the EU. What this shows is that 'widening' and 'deepening' are not opposites, but indeed go together: 'widening' (enlargement) has not prevented a 'deepening' of the integration process (be it through legislation or treaty reform), but it has also deepened the normative concerns about accountability and democratic legitimacy that are increasingly associated with European integration.

ACKNOWLEDGEMENT

We are grateful for useful comments received from Sonia Piedrafita on an earlier draft of this chapter. The usual disclaimer applies, of course.

NOTE

1. The case of Poland frequently raising objections in the European Council is not typical of the attitude of representatives of the new member states, but rather the exception to the rule. And even then it only applied to the highest political level, not the administration, and there it changed radically with the election of a new government in the autumn of 2007.

Appendix

The dataset used in Chapters 3 and 10 refers to all acts adopted by the Council (alone or jointly with another institution, usually the EP) during four presidencies: the two held in 2003 by Greece and Italy, respectively, the one held in the second semester of 2005 by the United Kingdom and the one held in the first half of 2006 by Austria.[1]

Three semesters of decision-making are thus deliberately excluded: the whole of 2004 and the first half of 2005. The explanation is that the months immediately surrounding the accession of ten new member states in May 2004 were in many respects a period of extraordinary administration. The European elections of June 2004 caused a suspension of all the codecision files until after the summer. The troublesome appointment of a new Commission meant that the European executive was only ready and operational at the beginning of 2005, and it took a few additional months until proposals introduced by the new Commission were discussed and adopted by the other institutions. Quantitative studies widely and unanimously document two trends. On the one hand, there was a dramatic but unsurprising drop in the amount of legislation adopted in the months after enlargement (Dehousse et al. 2006, p. 26; Hagemann and De Clerck-Sachsse 2007, p. 10).[2] On the other, an extraordinarily high number of acts was passed in the months preceding the entry of the new members.[3] Given the specificity of these three semesters, it was decided to exclude them.

The dataset includes acts adopted on the basis of a proposal put forward by the Commission or by one or more member states,[4] as well as acts having as a legal basis a treaty article or a piece of secondary legislation. It contains information on 934 acts, gathered through combined reliance on two databases: the Commission's Prelex[5] and the Monthly Summary of Council Acts[6] (Annexes I and III). Information concerning the final title and the length of acts is acquired on the basis of the text published in the *Official Journal of the European Communities*.[7]

In particular, the following information has been collected for each act:

- Institutional identification code[8]
- Title of the proposed act
- Type of act
- Paternity of the act[9]

- Procedure pursued
- Act adopted on a proposal from the Commission?
- Council's internal decision mode[10]
- Document adopted
- Annex of the monthly summary of Council acts where the information is reported[11]
- Majority requirements
- Number of delegations against
- Number of delegations abstaining
- Number of statements for each Council decision
- Number of corrigenda to the original document in the Council
- Number of revisions to the original document in the Council
- Number of addenda to the original document in the Council
- Nature of legal basis[12]
- Date of adoption of the Commission proposal
- Commission's internal decision mode
- Number of discussions in the Council as a 'B point' – at first reading
- Has formal adoption by the Council been preceded by a political agreement – at first reading?
- Number of discussions in the Council as a 'B point' – at second reading
- Has formal adoption by the Council been preceded by a political agreement – at second reading?
- Date of final adoption (or signature) of the act
- Number of days between introduction of the proposal and final adoption
- Number of delegations represented by a minister at the moment of reaching political agreement or on the occasion of the last discussion as a 'B point' in the Council – at first reading
- Number of delegations represented by a deputy minister (or equivalent political representative) at the moment of reaching political agreement or on the occasion of the last discussion as a 'B point' in the Council – at first reading
- Number of delegations represented by a diplomat at the moment of reaching political agreement or on the occasion of the last discussion as a 'B point' in the Council – at first reading
- Final title, as published by the *Official Journal*, of the adopted act
- Length of adopted legislation, measured by the number of words
- Does the final act contain 'comitology' provisions?
- Number of 'opinions' delivered by EP committees on the adopted act
- Stage of codecision procedure at which the act has been adopted.

NOTES

1. To determine whether one act 'belongs' to one of the four presidencies, the dataset takes into account the date of formal adoption by the Council (or that of the signature by EP and Council for codecision acts).
2. Please see the bibliographies of Chapters 3 and 10 for additional references.
3. In the first four months of 2004, the EU adopted a number of acts equal to 85 per cent of the acts adopted in the whole of 2003. As practitioners report, this was due to additional legislation adopted in preparation for accession and also to a number of politically sensitive files concluded on purpose before enlargement took place. (Presentation by A. George (Council General Secretariat) to the second EU-CONSENT Plenary Conference, Brussels, 12–13 October 2006; Hagemann and De Clerck-Sachsse 2007, p. 11.)
4. It thus includes also acts adopted in the framework of the II and III pillars.
5. The database on inter-institutional procedures, monitoring the stages of the decision-making process between the Commission and the other EU institutions. Accessible at http://ec.europa.eu/prelex/apcnet.cfm.
6. This is prepared by the General Secretariat of the Council. When necessary, the information of the summaries has been complemented by other sources from Council: these include, in particular, Council minutes, press releases and other documents searched through its Register. All information is accessible at http://www.consilium.europa.eu.
7. Accessible via Eur-lex: http://eur-lex.europa.eu/JOIndex.do.
8. The Commission's code number and the inter-institutional code number for acts adopted on the basis of a Commission proposal or nonetheless included in the Prelex database; the Council's reference document for all other acts.
9. For example: 'Act of the Council', 'Act of the European Parliament and the Council', etc.
10. Written or oral procedure.
11. There is a crucial difference between Annexes I and III. Annex I lists all definitive legislative acts adopted by the Council in the month to which the summary refers. As prescribed by Art. 207(3) of the EC Treaty, the list shows any opposing votes and abstentions, voting explanations and voting rules applicable. The acts considered as 'legislative' are those acts that the Council adopts in its legislative capacity. In its rules of procedure (Art. 7), the Council explains that it acts in its legislative capacity when 'it adopts rules which are legally binding in or for the Member States, by means of regulations, directives, framework decisions or decisions, on the basis of the relevant provisions of the Treaties'. This excludes, for example, budgetary acts, appointments, acts concerning international or inter-institutional relations as well as all non-binding acts. Annex III lists all these other acts and shows voting results, voting explanations and statements only when the Council has decided to make them public.
12. Primary or secondary.

REFERENCES

Dehousse, R., Deloche-Gaudez, F. and Duhamel, O. (2006), *Élargissement: Comment l'Europe s'adapte*, Paris: Presses de Sciences Po.

Hagemann, S. and De Clerck-Sachsse, J. (2007), *Old Rules, New Game: Decision-making in the Council of Ministers after the 2004 Enlargement*, CEPS Special Report, March.

Index